This book offers a readable yet scholarly account of the life of one of the great statesmen of empire, William Pitt the Elder, First Earl of Chatham (1708–78). Chatham is seen as a political outsider who rose to direct British policy in the Seven Years War, the crucial struggle that gave Canada to Britain. A critic of domestic corruption, he was subsequently a champion of American liberties.

Chatham's achievement was all the more remarkable for a politician who was dogged for much of his life by poor physical health and considerable mental stress. His position as an outsider was crucial: it helped to make his reputation, and to make him an unsettling figure. It also caused problems when he gained office, but it ensured that Chatham was, and seemed, 'different'. He was a man with whom the national interest could be associated, not simply because he made the claim himself, but also because he seemed apart from the world of court and connection. Chatham was a Hanoverian hero, tarnished by the exigencies, complexities and compromises of politics, but a hero for a country that wished to hear the bells of victory.

Pitt the Elder

BRITISH LIVES

Edited by Maurice Cowling
Fellow of Peterhouse, Cambridge

and John Vincent
Professor of History, University of Bristol

This is a series of short biographical studies which will address the lives of major figures from the early medieval period to modern times. Each figure will be of political, intellectual or religious significance in British or British imperial history. A major aim of the series is to seek out and scrutinise figures whose current interpretation has become stale or conventional, and to establish a lively interaction between author and subject in an attempt to place each historical figure in a new light.

Pitt the Elder

JEREMY BLACK

University of Durham

CAMBRIDGE
UNIVERSITY PRESS

Published by the Press Syndicate of the University of Cambridge
The Pitt Building, Trumpington Street, Cambridge CB2 1RP
40 West 20th Street, New York, NY10011–4211, USA
10 Stamford Road, Oakleigh, Victoria 3166, Australia

First published 1992

Printed in Great Britain by Redwood Press Limited, Melksham, Wiltshire

A catalogue record for this book is available from the British Library

Library of Congress cataloguing in publication data
Black, Jeremy.
Pitt the Elder/Jeremy Black.
p.   cm. – (British lives)
Includes bibliographical references and index.
ISBN 0 521 39116 4 (hard back). – ISBN 0 521 39806 1 (paperback)
1. Pitt, William, Earl of Chatham, 1708–1778.   2. Great Britain–
Politics and government – 18th century.   3. Statesmen – Great
Britain–Biography.   I. Title.   II. Series
DA483.P6B57   1992
941.07′3′092 – dc20
[B]   91-27059 CIP

ISBN 0 521 39116 4 hardback
ISBN 0 521 39806 1 paperback

To Vivienne

Contents

Preface

Prince or pauper, it is never easy to assess the personality of anyone, rarely simple to discuss his impact on others and on events. Apparent certainties and promising clues dissolve under scrutiny; actions, words and writings turn out to be incomplete, ambiguous and misleading. As detective, the historian is rarely master of his subject, especially when he turns from the arid glibness of models to the problems of recreating the past and deals, as he should, with people, both individually and collectively, in their variety and complexity. There can have been few British statesmen who were as complex as William Pitt the Elder, First Earl of Chatham. Acclaimed, both in his lifetime and subsequently, as a great warleader, in what can be justly claimed as the first global war in which Britain was involved, indeed the great warleader until Churchill's apotheosis in World War Two, a peerless Patriot, the Great Commoner, a man of determination, integrity and vision; Pitt was also castigated by contemporaries and later historians as an arrant hypocrite, a man without balance or moderation, who would say anything to serve his purposes, a politician without honour. These failings have been variously ascribed, but generally blamed on temperamental and psychological faults.

The arrogance, egotism and overweening ambition that

contemporaries denounced have been subsequently portrayed as facets of psychiatric illnesses, notably manic-depression. Pitt's imperiousness and extravagant behaviour and language were unbalanced. His favourite sister Ann died in a home for the mentally disturbed, and another sister, Elizabeth, suffered from mental illness. Pitt's second son, William Pitt the Younger, also suffered from a degree of unevenness of temperament, though not to such an extent. He was described by one ministerial colleague as always being 'up in the garret or down in the cellar'. The sanity of his cousin, Thomas Pitt, Second Lord Camelford (1775–1804) was questioned. The Earl of Shelburne, who knew Pitt the Elder quite well from the 1760s, when he served as Secretary of State in the Chatham ministry, observed that 'there was a great degree of madness in the family'.[1]

It is not only his personality that has been re-examined: Pitt has also been challenged as a politician and a statesman. The problems he encountered in gaining office in the 1740s and a high rank the following decade have been ascribed in part to the difficulties his personality and views presented to other politicians and to the King, George II. Pitt's fall from office in 1761, the subsequent failure of his opposition to the treaty he denounced, the Peace of Paris of 1763, the disharmony and lack of success of his ministry (1766–8) and his limited impact, both in opposition politics in 1769–71 and subsequently, following the outbreak of the War of American Independence, can be explained in large measure by his personal faults, his inability to co-operate with others for long and his failure to appreciate both different views and unwelcome circumstances. Contemporaries queried his views and successes, especially during the Seven Years War

[1] Lord E. Fitzmaurice, *Life of William, Earl of Shelburne* (3 vols., 1875) I, 71.

(1756–63), a process that Victorian apologists tended to overlook or to attribute to malice and self-interestedness. Recent scholarship has lent force to some contemporary charges. The extent of Pitt's popularity has been qualified, as has his responsibilty for conceiving and executing a strategy to win the war. The American Revolution has been distanced from the epic nature of past myths and Pitt's views have been placed in a less heroic context.

Clio rarely sleeps in the same bed for long: all historical writing is a progress report, and the reputations of figures of national greatness are especially prone to revisionist assessment. In Pitt's case this has essentially returned him to the position during his lifetime. Having been abstracted from his political background of bitter controversy, by later apologists who needed a heroic figure to personalise the rise of Britain to imperial greatness, Pitt has been returned by recent scholarship to a context of contention and complexity. This removal from a patriotic pantheon opens up, however, a number of important questions relating to the political ethos and system of eighteenth-century Britain. Pitt's career and contemporary reputation raises the issue of the nature of the constitution. Why did a man with no dependents rise so far? What was the importance of Pitt's connections as a member of the 'Cobham cubs'? What was the importance of 'popularity' and how was it created, composed and understood? How far were issues of importance in the advancement of political careers, and why did certain views count in the professional political world and set off a wider resonance? What was the nature of political achievement and reputation? What was the importance of military success? How far did the political world change during this period? What was the nature of heroism in this period? Repeatedly, ambiguity is revealed: the equivocal nature of political conventions, the confused and confusing behaviour of individuals under stress, the indefinite importance of particular offices, the varying relevance of individual issues and positions.

It is only possible to discuss certain aspects of the enigmatic Pitt and his ambivalent political world. Problems of psychological classification and explanation of motive and action bulk large, and it is impossible to present every judgement with the necessary qualifications. The sources only cover some aspects and episodes of Pitt's life and it is worth noting the comment of the recent biographer of George Grenville, an important ally of his brother-in-law William Pitt who became one of his leading opponents. The biography is subtitled *A Political Life* and Grenville's life is presented essentially as a political narrative, 'The image that remains from the personal papers of the years 1712–60 is of a man whose whole life revolves around sittings of the House of Commons.'[2]

To understand Pitt's convictions, of which a belief in himself was foremost, although not unchallenged by doubt, it is necessary to look critically at the world of contemporary politics and government. A sense of frustration akin to that which anyone of ability would feel in a sphere dominated by timeservers, the petty corruptions of convenience, appointments without merit and promotions gained through longevity and connection, appears to have affected Pitt for much of his career. It is easy to deride his fulminations as egotistical, self-serving and disposable to suit his career, but the ministries he criticised did stumble in the face of adverse circumstances to a degree that suggests today, as it did to contemporaries, incompetence and bankruptcy. The inability of the Walpole ministry to defeat Spain in the War of Jenkins' Ear paled before the domestic and international

---

[2] P. Lawson, *George Grenville* (Oxford, 1984) v.

failures of the Carteret ministry (1742–4), the Jacobite advance to Derby (1745), and the collapse of the Pelhamite political world in 1756. Pitt cannot be denied all the credit for the success of the wartime Pitt–Newcastle ministry (1757–61), which contrasted so markedly with the situation during the years of Anglo-French hostilities in the War of the Austrian Succession (1743–8).

This has been an instructive book for me. Much of my work has been on Walpole. Pitt made his name opposing the great minister, 'the Falstaff of politics' in the words of one newspaper, though he came later to praise him, as did many others, such as Dr Johnson. Walpole's reputation derives from his ministerial longevity and his manipulation of a political world he understood well. He sought peace and was a great finance minister. Pitt, in contrast, made his reputation as a denouncer of government policies and as a warleader. He had little real success as a peacetime politician and, despite his period as Paymaster General, did not seek to make his reputation through financial administration. Comparing the two men throws much light on their political world.

I would like to thank Linda Heitmann and Wendy Duery for their dexterity with the word processor and Stephen Baskerville, Ian Christie, Jonathan Clark, Linda Colley, Eveline Cruickshanks, John Derry, Grayson Ditchfield, Peter Luff, Alastair Massie, Frank O'Gorman, Peter Shilston and Philip Woodfine for commenting on earlier drafts. I am grateful to all the archivists who have provided assistance, especially Marie Devine and Stephen Parks, and the owners of manuscripts who have given me permission to cite their collections, including the Earl of Malmesbury and Olive, Countess Fitzwilliam's Wentworth Settlement Trustees and the Director of Libraries, Sheffield. I would like to thank Eveline Cruickshanks for granting me access to transcripts held by the History of Parliament trust. I am grateful to the

British Academy and the Staff Travel and Research Fund of Durham University for their assistance.

The dedication of this book is to my sister, but I would also like to record my gratitude to Radio 3: I find music invaluable when writing. Though it has no significance I am aware of, the introduction to this work was begun while listening to *Tannhäuser* and the work finished, possibly more appropriately, to the accompaniment of a harpsichord piece by Arne.

Abbreviations

Add.	Additional Manuscripts
AE	Paris Quai d'Orsay, Archives du Ministère des Affaires Etrangères
AST LM Ing.	Turin, Archivio di Stato, Lettere Ministri Inghilterra
Bedford	Bedford Estate Office, Russell Manuscript Letters
Beinecke	New Haven, Beinecke Library
BL	London, British Library
Bod.	Oxford, Bodleian Library
Cawdor	Carmarthen, Dyfed Record Office, Cawdor papers
CP	Correspondance Politique
Eg.	Egerton Manuscripts
Farmington	Farmington, Lewis Walpole Library
Hanover	Hanover, Niedersächsisches Hauptstaatsarchiv
Harris	Papers of James Harris, HP transcripts
HL	San Marino California, Huntington Library
HMC	Historical Manuscripts Commission

List of abbreviations

HP	London, History of Parliament Trust, transcripts
MO	Montagu papers
MS	Mount Stuart, Isle of Bute, papers of Third Earl of Bute
Munich	Munich, Bayerisches Hauptstaatsarchiv
NeC	Nottingham, University Library, Clumber papers
PRO	London, Public Record Office
STG	Stowe papers, general correspondence
Weston-Underwood	Iden Green Kent, papers of Edward Weston in the possession of John Weston-Underwood
WW	Sheffield, Archives, Wentworth Woodhouse muniments, papers of Second Marquis of Rockingham

Chapter 1

A political outsider and his world

Despite appearances to the contrary, Pitt was in part a political outsider, though this was more a matter of temperament than birth. His paternal background offered an instructive example of the flexibility of the English *ancien régime*, its ability to absorb new wealth and rising men. Pitt's paternal background might appear undistinguished, though the Pitt clan contained solid gentry, even eminent local magnates of elite status at Strathfieldsaye in Hampshire and Encombe in Dorset. Pitt's grandfather, the masterful and determined Thomas Pitt of Boconnoc (1653–1726), known as 'Diamond' Pitt because of a famous diamond he brought back from India, was the son of a Reverend John Pitt, a Dorset cleric, whose brother was Mayor of Dorchester, whose uncle was a MP and prominent official under James I and whose grandfather was a wealthy official of Elizabeth I. 'Diamond' Pitt made a famous fortune in India, much of it gained while opposing the interests of the East India Company; this he invested in the purchase of English estates, some of which brought electoral influence. In 1691 he bought Old Sarum, the site of a depopulated medieval borough near Salisbury, from the trustees of the Earl of Salisbury and he sat in Parliament for that seat, Salisbury, or Thirsk in 1689–98, 1710–16 and from 1717 until his death in 1726.

'Diamond' Pitt's wealth launched his children into prominence. His eldest son Robert (c.1680–1727) was William's father. He sat in Parliament for Old Sarum, Salisbury and Okehampton, in which his father had been purchasing property since 1717, from 1705 until 1727. Robert married a member of a leading aristocratic house, Harriet Villiers, daughter of the eldest son of the Fourth Viscount Grandison and Katherine Fitzgerald, an Irish heiress. Thomas' second son, another Thomas (c. 1688–1729), entered the army in 1709 with a troop of dragoons bought for 1,100 guineas, was an MP, mostly for Wilton, from 1713 until his death, a borough he also served as mayor and near which his father had bought an estate, married the daughter and co-heiress of the Irish Earl of Londonderry and became Earl himself, a Colonel and Governor of the Leeward Isles. The third son, John (c. 1698–1754), an Etonian who married the daughter of Viscount Fauconberg, was given a company in the Guards, in which he rose to be a Lieutenant-Colonel, was an MP (1720–2, 1724–34) and an aide-de-camp to George I. One daughter, Essex, married Charles Cholmondeley, himself the son and grandson of MPs, a Tory MP for Cheshire from 1710 until 1715 and 1722 until his death in 1756, while her younger sister Lucy married James Stanhope, one of the leading ministers from 1714 until his death in 1721.

It was due to Stanhope that Robert, although a Tory, was in 1716 appointed Clerk to the household of the Prince of Wales, later George II (1727–60), but he rose no further, thanks to his lack of talent, opposition activities and early death. His son William, born in 1708, went to Eton, which he hated, from 1719 to 1726. The school educated ten of the twenty-six first ministers between 1714 and 1832 (Westminster managed seven), including Walpole and Bute, and 162 of the 519 MPs who served between the elections of 1715 and 1754 and whose schooling is not completely obscure. Pitt, however, was not apparently impressed by the place. He told Shelburne many years later 'that his reason for preferring private to publick education was, that he scarce observed a boy who was not cowed for life at Eton; that a publick school might suit a boy of a turbulent forward disposition, but would not do where there was any gentleness'.[1] The public schools of the period were certainly violent, characterised by bullying, buggery and the bottle. It is unclear whether the strain of life at Eton was responsible for the onset of Pitt's ill-health. He suffered there from gout, but as that illness in his case had definite psychosomatic aspects, it may well have reflected his response to the school.

Gout was not the only problem. A school bill of 1719 included, besides such items as four pence for a pair of garters, bills from what appears to have been some kind of a fit.

	£	s	d
Paid at the house where Mr William was when he fell down	0	13	6
Paid a man and horse to go with me	0	3	0
Paid for a chaize [carriage]	0	5	0
To the Surgeon for attendance, bleeding etc.	2	2	0
To the other Surgeon for going to visit him	1	1	0

The only other medical item in this bill was five shillings 'for curing his chilblanes'.[2] On the other hand he was not ill all the time. A bill of 1723 included no items arising from illness, while William's tutor William Burchett, who found William's elder brother negligent, was impressed by him,

Your younger son has made a great progress since his coming hither, indeed I never was concerned with a young gentleman of so good abilities, and at the same time of so good a disposition, and there is no question to be made but he will answer all your hopes.

William was determined to do well, and wrote to his father in September 1723, 'My time has been pretty much taken up for this three weeks, in my trying for to gett into the fiveth form, and I am now removed into it.'[3]

[1] Lord E. Fitzmaurice, *Life of William, Earl of Shelburne* (3 vols., 1875) I, 72.
[2] BL Add. 69288 no. 1. [3] BL Add. 69288 nos. 2–4.

3

After he went up to Trinity College, Oxford as a gentleman-commoner in 1726, William was forced to explain expenditure, rather than discuss his academic progress. He denied extravagance, but maintaining the Oxonian world of conspicuous consumption among gentlemen scholars was a problem and a source of uncertainty. In one letter he explained his items of expenditure to his father,

Washing £2.1s od., about 3s 6d. per week of which money half a dozen shirts at 4d. each comes to 2s per week . . . one considerable article is a servant, an expence which many are not at, and which I shall be glad to spare, if you shall think it fit, in hopes to convince you I desire nothing superfluous.

In January 1727 William sent his father an account, adding

I have too much reason to fear you may think some of these articles too extravagant, as they really are, but all I have to say for it is humbly to beg you would not attribute it to my extravagance, but to the custom of this place; where we pay for most things too [sic] at a high rate.[4]

William obviously felt under financial pressure, but it is unclear how much significance should be placed on this. Robert Pitt's finances were not sufficiently strong to produce confidence about heavy expenditure, and individual members of the family clearly faced particular problems. Robert's wife, Harriet, was in difficulty after she was widowed in 1727.[5] William suffered from being a second son. Indeed his father appears to have destined him for the church, only changing his mind in 1726.[6] As a landholder Robert would have been able to present his son with a living, and the Church would have been a secure career for a man of talents who lacked considerable wealth. In addition, Wil-

[4] BL Add. 69288 no. 5, 9; Pitt to his mother, 19 March 1727, Farmington, Connecticut, Lewis Walpole Library, Miscellaneous Manuscripts.
[5] BL Add. 69285–6 passim.   [6] BL Add. 69288 no. 6.

liam's poor health and bookish inclinations might have suggested such a future. His account for the first three months of 1727 included

Three months learning french and entrance	2	2	0
For a course of experimental Philosophy	2	2	0
Booksellers bill	5	0	0

although the last was less than the item

For coat and breeches and making . . .	5	18	0.[7]

William was to leave Oxford after only one year without taking his degree for reasons that are unclear. Both gout and the unexpected death of his father in May 1727 have been suggested as reasons. He went next year to Utrecht in the United Provinces (modern Netherlands), a prominent university, where a number of British students, especially Scots and Nonconformists, spent part or all of their studies. There is little information as to how he spent his time in the Netherlands, although not surprisingly, given the ships of the period, his crossing was made with 'much sickness and difficulty'.[8]

By 1730 William was back in England, living on the family estate at Boconnoc in Cornwall. He had inherited little from his father, a rental of about £100 per year, and although his brother had assured him in 1728 that 'nothing that the estate can afford shall be denied me for my advantage and education', relations between the two men were not close. William was soon fed up with his life at Boconnoc, writing in November 1730, 'I grow more and more out of temper with the remoteness of this cursed hiding place.'[9] However, his school-friend George Lyttelton helped to introduce Pitt to his influential uncle, Richard, First Viscount Cobham. In 1731 Cobham offered Pitt a cornetcy in his regiment, the King's Own Regiment of Horse, generally known as Cobham's

---

[7] BL Add. 69288 no. 10.   [8] BL Add. 69288 no. 14.
[9] BL Add. 69288 no. 16, 69289 no. 9.

Own, given the fashion of naming regiments after their colonels. On 5 March 1731 William wrote to his favourite sister Ann, of whom he was extremely fond and with whom he conducted a flirtatious correspondence, 'my commission is signed and I have kissed hands for it, so that my country quarters won't be Cornwall this summer'.[10]

His years as a cornet are obscure, but his biographers have been in no doubt that he spent his time industriously. Lord Rosebery claimed, 'This at least is certain, that he sedulously employed his time, preserved from mess debauches and idle activity by his guardian demon the gout', and referred to his 'unstinted application' in reading military books. A more recent account states that Pitt was free from 'the fashionable vices', possessed 'the lonely ambition that soars above the humdrum preoccupations of the average' and had 'sober' appetites.[11]

William's correspondence with his sister casts some doubt on such portrayals of classical aloofness and heroic virtue. His first letter from Northampton, where his regiment was quartered, to Ann, sent in April 1731, complained,

I am come from an agreeable set of acquaintance in town to a place, where the wings of gallantry must be terribly clip'd, and can hope to soar no higher than to Dolly – who young at the Bar is just learning to score – what must I do? My head is not settled enough to study; nor my heart light enough to find amusement in doing nothing.

As result, Pitt feared that he must 'get drunk with bad port to kill time'. Drinking was clearly an important part in the life of young officers stationed in boring towns and unaware that later scholarship was to present them as the centres of an

[10] BL Add. 69289 no. 5.
[11] Lord Rosebery, *Chatham. His Early Life and Connections* (1910) pp. 46–7; P. D. Brown, *William Pitt Earl of Chatham* (1978) p. 30.

urban renaissance of provincial culture and gentility. Pitt preferred the bottle, writing to Ann as 'her gentle loving shepherd' about

a course of drunken conversation, which I have some days been in. The service would be the most inactive life in the world, if Charles Feilding was out of it; as long as he is with us, we seldom remain long without pretty smart action. I am just releiv'd by one night's rest, from an attaque that lasted sixteen hours but as a heroe should never boast; I have done the state some service and they know't-no more of that.

There is an unexplained reference in a letter to Ann sent from London in March 1731 to two girls banging on the door to get in, William commenting 'every man may have girls worthy his attention', but Northampton seems to have offered drink rather than women, Pitt writing in January 1732 'I come from two hours muzzy conversation to a house full of swearing butchers and drunken butter women, and in short all the blessings of a market day.'[12] William may have been teasing his sister, but Ann was one of the few people to whom he was willing to reveal his thoughts. Heavy drinking was widespread in Britain, Northampton in mid-century having 60 inns and 100 ale-houses for its population of 5,000. Drink was central to conviviality, and an essential antidote to boredom, poor health, miserable accommodation, cold and damp. It was relatively inexpensive and the production, sale and consumption of alcohol was poorly regulated. Much alcohol contained impurities, while many suffered permanent impairment to their health as a result of heavy drinking. William Godolphin MP, the Marquess of Blandford and grandson of Sarah, Duchess of Marlborough, died aged about thirty-two of a 'drinking bout' at Balliol College Oxford in 1731.

[12] BL Add. 69289 nos. 6, 4, 10, 3.

Pitt certainly came to regret the excesses of his youth. He wrote to his nephew Thomas in April 1755,

I am going through a fit of the Gout; with much proper pain and what proper patience I may. Avis au Lecteur, my Sweet Boy: remember thy Creator in the days of thy youth: let no excesses lay the foundations of gout and the rest of Pandora's Box; nor any immoralities, or vicious courses sow the seeds of a too late painful repentance.[13]

It is unclear whether this implies that Pitt suffered from venereal disease, as well as the after-effects of alcoholic excess. This would not have been surprising. The casual sexual opportunities open to young officers in garrison towns often led to lasting and painful after-effects. Pitt may have felt constrained from referring to them openly: he lacked the easy openness of a Charles James Fox, who admitted to the problem. If Pitt did suffer from venereal disease that may have played a role in his late marriage, though other factors, principally his relative poverty, may have been responsible. In May 1731 Pitt referred to 'all the dictates of prudence, all the considerations of interest', when explaining to Ann what appears to have been why he thought he was unlikely to marry. Whereas his elder brother Thomas married at about the age of twenty-six, William did not marry until he was forty-six. In the meantime the sexual customs and social conventions of the upper orders of society ensured that William's opportunities for sexual relations with women of a similar background were extremely remote, and he was probably obliged to resort to casual sex, usually prostitution, with its attendant dangers. It is scarcely surprising that he had a somewhat unstable personality. At this formative stage in his life, Pitt's character was fractured. He found emotional solace in his close relationship with his

---

[13] BL Add. 69288 no. 45.

sister Ann, and physical and mental release in heavy drinking.

In 1733 Pitt took another diversion common then for young men of birth and some estate, the Grand Tour. Combined with his period at Utrecht, this gave him a certain degree of familiarity with the Continent, unlike say a leading political figure in his life the Duke of Newcastle who, though born in 1693, did not go abroad until 1748. However, there is no sign that it led him to appreciate Continental, more especially French, culture and society, let alone her politics or government. Pitt spent much of his time during his 1733–4 trip in Besançon and Luneville, the latter then in the Duchy of Lorraine, an independent principality which was occupied by the French in late 1733 in the opening stages of the War of the Polish Succession. Both towns contained academies where young travellers could learn French and acquire polish and expertise in such attributes of gentility as dancing, fencing and riding, without, it was hoped, being exposed to the vices of Paris. Pitt had gone to the capital first, seeing 'the variety of fine sights' and obtaining letters of introduction from the British Ambassador Earl Waldegrave, but only staying there a few days before pressing on to Besançon where he found his schoolfellow Sir James Gray. Pitt fell in love with a local beauty, the younger daughter of a local squire, and wrote about her to Ann as if he had considered marriage. Pitt regretted that her background was not an exalted one, 'c'est là le diable', and he soon wrote of the relationship as one of the 'flammes passagères', which had left no trace.[14] From Besançon he travelled through Marseilles, Montpellier, Lyons, Geneva and Strasburg to Luneville. He thus did not visit Italy, the crucial destination for most Grand Tourists, such as George Lyttleton in 1729. Pitt's Grand Tour was a limited one as befitted not only a man who

---

[14] BL Add. 69288 nos. 19–20, 69289 nos. 13–16.

already had a position, and could not therefore spend the long period that a lengthy tour entailed, but also someone without great wealth.[15]

William's dependence on the bounty of others was to be demonstrated in 1734–5 at the beginning of his political career. His brother Thomas had inherited his father's political influence in Old Sarum, the quintessential rotten borough. An old but entirely depopulated borough which returned two MPs, the property that carried the right of election had been purchased by 'Diamond' Pitt in 1691. At the general election of 1734, Thomas Pitt had himself returned by the five voters at Old Sarum, but as he chose to sit for Okehampton, where he had a powerful interest and had also been elected, the seat became vacant. Thomas decided to bring William in for it, but changed his mind in October 1734. Thomas then encouraged an offer by Thomas Harrison, who he had brought in for the seat in 1728, and who offered to pay William to give up his claim to it. Given William's subsequent move into opposition to Walpole, it is interesting to note that in late 1734 William criticised the idea of electing Harrison, on the grounds that he was 'a Person declared in Opposition', and again that Thomas should 'chuse a man more agreeable to Sir Robt. than Harrison'.

At the same time, William was 'persecuted with a succession of little impertinent complaints; I have been delivered some time of my broken tooth, by the most dextrous operation, I believe in the World, but am at present in my Room with a sore throat, which is very troublesome to me'.[16] Nevertheless, Harrison's proposal was rejected and William Pitt was launched on his political career, being elected unopposed for Old Sarum on 18 February 1735.

[15] On the Grand Tour in general, J. Black, *The British and the Grand Tour* (1985).
[16] BL Add. 69289 nos. 17–18.

Pitt's election for Old Sarum owed everything to connections, nothing to popularity or power. Much of his career can
be seen as that of an insider. He sat for Old Sarum until 1747
when he was elected for Seaford, a Sussex constituency
substantially influenced by Thomas Pelham-Holles, Duke of
Newcastle, then Secretary of State for the Southern Department. In 1754 he transferred to one seat of the Yorkshire
constituency of Aldborough that was controlled by Newcastle, who had recently been appointed First Lord of the
Treasury. Obliged to seek reelection on being appointed
Secretary of State for the Southern Department in December
1756, Pitt was elected for the Grenville pocket borough of
Buckingham and his own family's seat at Okehampton and
chose to sit for the latter. On being reappointed to office the
following summer he transferred from Okehampton to Bath
which he had been unanimously invited to represent by the
corporation, which enjoyed a monopoly of the franchise. He
represented Bath until he went to the Lords in 1766. Pitt never
sat for a county seat, the common aspiration for those with
social standing. Though he faced a contest at Seaford in 1747,
his elections to Old Sarum in 1735 and 1741, Aldborough in
1754, Buckingham and Okehampton in 1756 and Bath in
1757 and 1761 were uncontested, while the size of the
franchise in these seats was 5, about 50, 13, about 300 and 30
respectively. Pitt also had important connections. In
November 1754 he married Lady Hester Grenville, the
daughter of Richard Grenville MP and niece of Richard
Temple, First Viscount Temple of Stowe. Hester was the sister
of a formidable collection of Grenvilles, all interested in
politics: Richard Grenville, Second Earl Temple, and George,
Henry and James Grenville then respectively an MP and
Treasurer of the Navy, Governor of Barbados, and an MP and
a member of the Board of Trade. Pitt thus strengthened his

position as the member of an important parliamentary group or 'connection'.

And yet in many significant respects Pitt was an outsider. In a number of ways, both subtle and obvious, his position in the 'establishment', however defined, was weak. Every ruling order, though presenting the appearance of a monolith to the unperceptive observer, has in reality many fine distinctions; within the gradations of the English political elite, Pitt's note was not one that would readily be heard naturally, his orbit not the most spectacular. This was most obvious in the matter of his birth. Pitt was not the eldest son and his brother did not die conveniently early. It is instructive to compare William Pitt's early career with that of his elder brother. Thomas Pitt (c.1705–61), another Etonian, succeeded on his father's death in 1727 to estates giving him the nomination of both MPs for Old Sarum, and at Camelford and Okehampton an ability to command one and sometimes both seats. In about 1731 he married Christian, a niece of Cobham's, the eldest daughter of Sir Thomas Lyttelton Bt, who was himself a Lord of the Admiralty and MP for Worcestershire. Active, as a result of Cobham's influence, in opposition circles, Thomas Pitt supported Frederick, Prince of Wales, who went into opposition to his father, George II. As heir, Frederick was Duke of Cornwall and he appointed Thomas to a post there in 1738, promoting him to Lord Warden of the Stannaries in 1742. Thus, when Walpole fell in 1742 Thomas' career was well advanced and he could hope that he would one day rise to further prominence when Frederick succeeded, while William was only Groom of the Bedchamber to Frederick and was dependent on his elder brother for his parliamentary seat. William's military career had been reputably launched by Walpole who had allegedly provided the £1,000 for his commission in Cobham's regiment in order to please Thomas, who could control several seats. Thus when Thomas went into opposition, William's lines of patronage were crossed, and he found himself dismissed in 1736, both for his opposition in Parliament and because the supposed compact of 1731 had been broken. William had little money. The legacies from his grandfather, father and mother, who died in 1736, were each about £100 a year and concern about the costs of an establishment and of children may have played a role in the lateness of his marriage. In 1757 the Second Earl of Egmont noted Pitt's dependence on the patronage of the Pelhams in the 1747 and 1754 elections, and wrote of his 'publicly acting with the Ministers who have brought you into the House for their own boroughs for you had not interest or friends but them in any corner of the kingdom to have found your way to Parliament without them'.

Egmont himself, like many of Pitt's critics, was accomplished in the practices he condemned in others. In 1747, thanks to Pelham's support, he was returned on petition for a seat at Weobley, although he had been defeated at the poll. Egmont at once switched to the Prince of Wales, and attacked the Pelhams. It is probable that politicians like Egmont disliked Pitt particularly strongly because he was more successful than they were at winning public support and more successful in combining it with the pursuit of advancement. Pitt was certainly more successful than Egmont, who, although he sat in the Commons from 1741, did not gain office under the Crown until 1762. It is not surprising that Pitt was more successful in striking popular chords than Egmont, who both spent £3,000 in the 1740s producing a history of his family that give it a spuriously exalted genealogy, and in 1763–5 pressed George III to settle the North American island of St John on a feudal basis with

Egmont as Lord Paramount and 40 capital lords and 400 lords of manors holding land by military tenure.[17]

Pitt was not alone in facing the problems of being a second son, which were especially weighty in a society which drew most of its leaders from a landed order that practised dynastic preservation and aggrandisement through primogeniture. Henry Pelham, First Lord of the Treasury from 1743 until his death in 1754, had an uneasy relationship with his elder brother Newcastle, to whom he owed his election, firstly for Seaford and then for Sussex. Though he was not always compliant, especially when it came to financing Newcastle's diplomatic schemes in the early 1750s or managing the House of Commons, Pelham was in no doubt of his secondary position, which contrasted with the importance of his office. He was an insider, very much part of the establishment, a consequence both of his conciliatory temperament and of his brother's role in the government. George Grenville, Pitt's brother-in-law, was for long over-shadowed by his elder brother Temple, who returned him for Buckingham. Grenville's third son, William Wyndham, later Lord Grenville, had a difficult relationship with his eldest brother, another George, who had succeeded his uncle as Third Earl Temple in 1779. William Wyndham Grenville owed his parliamentary seats to his brother but, in turn, faced considerable difficulties in supporting the latter's interests, such as his demand for a dukedom in 1784.

William Pitt's relationship with Thomas was less close. They both went into opposition with Lord Cobham in the mid-1730s, but, after the fall of Walpole in 1742, Thomas followed the Prince of Wales in his reconciliation with the court and reconstituted ministry, while William, angry with

---

[17] Egmont, BL Add. 47012 B f. 177; R. R. Sedgwick, *The History of Parliament. The House of Commons 1715–54* (2 vols., 1970) II, 339–40; L. B. Namier and J. Brooke, *The History of Parliament. The House of Commons 1754–1790* (3 vols., 1964) III, 266–7.

the failure to create a new political order, remained in opposition until November 1744. Links were attenuated further in 1747 when Thomas followed Frederick into opposition again while William, now an office-holder, was returned to Parliament on Newcastle's interest. However, these weaker fraternal links, weaker certainly compared with the Pelhams and the Grenvilles, or Walpole and his brother Horatio and, to a lesser extent, Henry and Stephen Fox, did not reflect complete independence on William's part, because in his early years he was very much under the influence of Cobham and was indeed known as one of 'Cobham's cubs'. He spent long periods at Cobham's house of Stowe, including several months in 1735, where, besides playing 'very well at cricket', he came to admire Cobham greatly, seeing him in part as a surrogate father. At a highly charged moment during a contentious Cabinet Council meeting on 14 August 1761, Pitt asserted his patriotic and Whig credentials linking both to Cobham, declaring 'that he was a British subject and he knew he stood upon British ground; that he had learnt his maxims and principles under the great Lord Cobham and the disciples of the greatest lawyers, generals and patriots of King William [III]'s days'.[18] The 'cubs', the most talented connection of young politicians in the Commons, were opposed to Walpole and dissatisfied with the reconstitution of the ministry in 1742. Composed also of Cobham's nephews George Lyttelton and the Grenvilles, they provided William with a social role and a political connection greater than that of a dependent brother of the somewhat unimpressive Thomas Pitt. For many years William's career was to be closely linked to the Grenvilles and though his abilities and personality rescued him from a

[18] BL Add. 69289 nos. 20–31; P. D. Brown and K. W. Schweizer (eds.), *The Devonshire Diary. William Cavendish Fourth Duke of Devonshire. Memoranda on State of Affairs 1759–1762* (1982) p. 111.

subordinate position the relationship was not without difficulties.

Politically Pitt had no secure base within a coherent political group. He suffered from his lack of a large and secure parliamentary connection and more particularly from the absence of a peerage or a secure constituency base. The knowledge that one would not succeed to estates or a title made some men strive harder for eminence in politics, and this certainly seems to have affected Pitt. It may be idle to speculate on what the effect of his inheriting the family's parliamentary interest would have been, in terms of personal security, political weight and the assurance of controlling a number of MPs; it is difficult to believe that Pitt did not consider the matter often. In one respect he was dependent on his elder brother in the same way that his sisters were. In 1747 Thomas received a letter making it clear that an offer to marry one of his sisters depended on the size of her fortune and on the suitor being elected for one of Thomas' seats.[19] Only wealth could bring independence. Had William inherited those Marlborough and Sunderland estates to which he was made heir presumptive under the 1744 wills of Sarah, Duchess of Marlborough and her grandson John Spencer, Pitt intended to purchase Old Sarum from his financially embarrassed elder brother. Under these wills he would, in the event of the death of John's infant son, have inherited Sarah's property in Buckinghamshire, Staffordshire and Northamptonshire, formerly the estates of Richard Hampden, Lord Fauconberg and Lord Crewe, and the Sunderland estates. John Spencer died in 1746 but his son, another John, survived and was created Lord Spencer in 1761 and Earl Spencer four years later. Pitt was thus deprived through chance of the opportunity of founding a great

[19] William Crosbie to Pitt, 18 June 1747, BL Add. 69286.

landed dynasty and neither the wealth he was bequeathed nor the income he gained from office provided a substitute sufficient to permit him to be a social equal in the great world of Whig grandees. His dependence on Newcastle for his parliamentary seat was certainly an inconvenience for Pitt in 1754 when he advanced his political claims after the death of Pelham.

For all his political identification with the world of mercantile enterprise, imperial expansion and metropolitan politics, an identification for which chance, his role as warleader, his political value to others and subsequent historical writing was largely responsible, Pitt never sat for a metropolitan seat, or for one of the other great ports, not that representing such a constituency was necessary, and he showed a strong interest in the pleasures of country land ownership. Though he had links with London and Middlesex 'radicals', Pitt never stood for Middlesex, which elected in 1734 and 1741 the prominent opposition Whig William Pulteney, and from 1768 John Wilkes; nor for Westminster which elected another prominent opposition Whig Lord Perceval in 1741 and, in the 1780s, Charles James Fox; nor for London, which returned an opposition outsider, the West Indian planter William Beckford in 1754, 1761 and 1768; nor for Bristol, which returned a number of opposition members, including in 1774 Edmund Burke. Pitt 'abused the City [of London] without measure' on 19 December 1745 for supporting the use of Hessian troops against the Jacobites. He offered a contrast between urban greed and rural virtue that would have been familiar to the Tories of his father's generation. Calling the citizens of London 'shopkeepers', he said

let us show that there are hundreds of gentlemen in this House who have thoughts of deeper policy, more courage, and less mean, less narrow considerations, than men frighten'd for their money out of their senses. We are not to think as they do; rather let us advise the citizen of London, when he is weighing his money with his right hand, with his left at least a little to feel for the Constitution.

In contrast, he was more emollient when in office and defending the expensive strategy being followed in the Seven Years War. In November 1758 he told the Commons that 'so much weight was to be given to everything that fell from a gentleman who represented the greatest city in the world'.

Nevertheless, in April 1760 Pitt supported the Tory bill 'to enforce and render more effectual the laws relating to the Qualifications of Members' of Parliament. The Tories had long argued that the stipulated landownership was not being enforced, a claim also made with regard to the requirements for being a Justice of the Peace, and one that they traced to Whig preference for upstarts lacking a landed position, some of whom were substantial tradesmen. Resistance to new wealth with its corrosive implications was an important theme in Tory thought, one that could take on a pronounced anti-mercantile emphasis. Newcastle was unhappy about the bill and Thomas Townshend attacked it as a Tory measure, but Pitt spoke in its favour, praising the 'landed interest in this House, without which I could never have helped to load the country with fifteen millions of taxation'. He also stated the anti-party philosophy that had so often characterised critics of the Whig establishment, declaring 'I shall always think it better for government to act with a whole nation than with only a party.' The bill became law.

Seven years earlier Pitt had taken a critical stance towards the successful popular agitation for the repeal of the recently passed Jewish Naturalization Act. As a member of a ministry that supported repeal in order not to arouse hostility in the forthcoming general election, Pitt had to accept the new policy, but he told the Commons that he regarded the original act as 'in itself right' and he rejected what he saw as an attempt to revive 'a Church spirit'. He was clearly unhappy with the 'enthusiastic spirit that has taken hold of the people'.[20]

Pitt's preferred world was that of the country estate. He had been very impressed by Cobham's Stowe and he spent much of his time in the 1740s and early 1750s during the lengthy summer parliamentary recess, when not taking the waters for his assorted ailments, in visiting his connections in their country seats, especially the Grenvilles at Wotton, the Lytteltons at Hagley, Sanderson Miller at Radway and his cousin John Pitt at Encombe on the Dorset coast. Summoning John to London in May 1751 for the debates over the Regency Bill, Pitt sent his 'benedictions to the hills, rocks, pines, shores, seas etc. of Encombe'. In July 1753 he wrote to John, 'I long to be with you, kicking my heels upon your cliffs, and looking like a shepherd in Theocritus.' Clearly delighted by the scenery there, he expressed his hope to see Encombe and its 'dashing waves' in 1754. In May 1752 William wrote to his friend Charles Lyttelton, Dean of Exeter Cathedral, from the Duke of Queensberry's seat at Ambresbury, where Pitt was in company with the Cobhams. 'In motion from place to place', he was due to go on with them to Stowe, before returning to London and then going to Boconnoc for the summer. Two months later he wrote to Charles from Stowe, looking forward to visiting him at Exeter and to the 'good things of this world', including 'a bottle of port and madeira'. Two years later Pitt referred to 'the pure air, delightful scenes, and happy society of your Hagley and its inhabitants'.[21]

Pitt's principal hobby was the fashionable and expensive one of landscape gardening, possibly because it was both

[20] W. Cobbett, *Parliamentary History of England from . . . 1066 to . . . 1803* (36 vols., 1806–20) XV, 154.
[21] Georgiana, Lady Chatterton, *Memorials of Admiral Lord Gambier* (2 vols., 1861) I, 53, 61–2; BL Add. 69288 nos. 21–2, 25.

relaxing and gave him a sense of control. He was interested in laying out grounds, not in townscapes, and he played a role in works at Encombe, Hagley, Shenstone, Stowe, West Wickham and Wotton. These created a social ambience of shared pastimes. In his own possessions Pitt's active desire for improvement was voracious. With his income as Paymaster he purchased in 1747 the lease of South Lodge in Enfield Chase with 65 acres attached, and carried out extensive and expensive works on house and grounds. The Great Commoner is not usually associated with temples dedicated to Pan, garden pyramids and billiard tables, but he had one of each added to South Lodge, where he invited his friends to shoot for woodcock and snipe. Pitt found little time to enjoy the house and sold the lease in 1753. In 1756 he purchased Hayes Place in Kent and though he sold it in 1766 he bought it back two years later. Pitt was in an abnormal mental state in 1767–9, which may have had something to do with the obsession to recover Hayes. At Hayes he built a new house in the grounds. It had twenty-four bedrooms, stabling for sixteen horses, a fenced park of about 60 acres and another 110 acres. Pitt considerably expanded the estate by buying up every available adjacent property and ended up with several hundred acres. In 1765 Sir William Pynsent, a Somerset baronet who (according to Horace Walpole, never short of a harsh word) had an incestuous relationship with his daughter, and who did not know Pitt personally but greatly admired him, died leaving him his entire estate near Sedgemoor. Pitt decided to sell Hayes in 1766 in order to concentrate on works on the house and estate at his new seat of Burton Pynsent. He was obviously proud of his gain, because when he was raised to the peerage in 1766 it was as Earl of Chatham and Viscount Burton Pynsent. Far from indifferent to majestic surroundings, Pitt added a new wing to the house, erected a column to the memory of his benefactor, and constructed farm buildings in a classical style.

Pitt devoted most of his attention to these country seats, though he did not lack town houses. He had an official house in Whitehall as Paymaster; paid £1,200 in 1753 for a new house in fashionable Bath at number 7 The Circus, which was built by the two John Woods, completed in 1754 and kept by Pitt until 1770; rented 10 St James Square in 1756–61, a house subsequently occupied by two Prime Ministers, Derby and Gladstone, and still called Chatham House; had a small lodging in Bond Street in 1761–5; and rented a house at North End, Hampstead in 1766–7. With the exception of the house at Bath, which he sold to Clive when short of money, it was the rural seats that Pitt was really interested in. He revealed a wish to keep other people at a distance, to banish the problems of the world beneath the cover of broad acres. At Burton Pynsent, where Pitt personally, but unprofitably, supervised the dairy herd, he had a public way, which crossed the estate, sunk between deep banks in order to hide it from view, while he pressed the owner of North End to add numerous bedrooms and to purchase every building that interfered with the view.

Hayes and Burton Pynsent were impressive gains, certainly contrasted with his parental inheritance, but they did not compare with the great seats of Georgian Britain. They were more like Henry Pelham's Esher Place than Blenheim, Castle Howard or Stowe. Moreover, not only was Pitt far from being a great landowner, he was also unable to finance his lifestyle other than through gifts from others. He received legacies of £10,000, £1,000, and £3,000–4,000 per annum, in 1744, 1764 and 1765 from Sarah Marlborough, Ralph Allen and Pynsent respectively and annuities of £300 and £1,000 in 1745 and 1755 from the Duke of Bedford and Earl Temple. When he resigned in 1761 he was given a government pension of £3,000 per annum for his own life and that of his wife and eldest son. These grants did not amount always to what they seemed. The government pension, secured on West Indian revenues, was reduced by fees and duties to £2,000 and was usually a year in arrears.

Pitt's extravagance, especially his imprudent financial attitude and his expenses as an improver and the large amount he paid to regain Hayes, landed him in serious financial difficulties. In 1772 he tried without success to sell Hayes, while parts of the Burton Pynsent estate were sold. Pitt was reduced to borrowing from friends, including the banker Thomas Coutts, Temple, and Captain Alexander Hood who lent £10,000. A mortgage of £13,175 was raised on Burton Pynsent in 1774, another of £10,000 on Hayes in 1778. Pitt still died £20,000 in debt which Parliament voted to pay. Poor financial management and debt were scarcely unique to Pitt. His second son, William Pitt the younger, another heavy drinker, had substantial debts, but even so wealthy a man as Newcastle was forced to sell lands and to borrow in order to pay off the enormous debts he had incurred through electioneering. The government itself was heavily in debt, not least because of the wars with the Bourbons that Pitt had applauded. It is an interesting comment on his personal finances that Pitt had little sympathy during the Seven Years War for calls for peace based in part on government indebtedness.

Far from sharing the values of prudence and restraint advocated for the urban middling orders and displayed by many of them, Pitt displayed many of the characteristics of landed society. His desire for landed property, concern for display and interest in landscape gardening were shared by many gentlemen, and indeed his father had been criticised for extravagance by his grandfather. Being a second son and inheriting little property, unlike for example Sarah Marlborough's second grandson, John Spencer, or John Pitt who inherited Encombe from his mother, William Pitt was obliged to seek his fortune through his own efforts, an unsettling task in a society and political system dominated by inherited position and wealth. It is hardly surprising that William made more of an impact than John Pitt or John Spencer. Most of Pitt's wealth came from legacies and annuities, a precarious source that emphasised his lack of security, not earnings. In addition, even among prominent second sons he was not particularly fortunate. His great rival Henry Fox inherited a fair sum, though in his early years he dissipated it through gambling and was obliged by his debts to leave the country. Fox, who shared Pitt's interest in building, made his fortune as Paymaster, gaining about £400,000 as a result, but his political reputation suffered and his room for manoeuvre was compromised by his desire to hold onto the office and the balances he retained the use of thereafter. As a result he lost political support in 1763, while George III was opposed to Bute's suggestion that year that Fox succeed him at the Treasury because he claimed he was 'a man void of principles'. Fox never obtained the earldom he sought so avidly.

The extent varied to which the need to establish themselves affected the political careers of men born with abilities, connections and aspirations, but neither wealth nor a secure social and political position. It probably played a role in Pitt's determination to gain office in the mid-1740s and his subsequent decision in 1747 to remain with the Pelhams rather than join the promising opposition around the heir to the throne. It is on this basis that Pitt can be seen as an outsider. He was to rise to positions of great eminence, Secretary of State for the Southern Department (1756–61) and Lord Privy Seal (1766–8), and, like Walpole in 1742, to gain an earldom (1766), but he was never one of the great Whig aristocrats, the men who played such a major role in politics. To describe the Second Earl Waldegrave, the Second Duke of Grafton, Lord Chamberlain from 1724 until his death in 1757, or his successor, the Fourth Duke of Devonshire, as major political figures may appear surprising, even though Devonshire was briefly First Lord of the Treasury. However, office was not necessarily a clue to political importance. It was not only that in some spheres of government lines of authority were far from fixed, especially in such matters as confidential extra-departmental correspondences, disposal of departmental patronage and Cabinet representation. Rather, it was more the case that government and politics were intertwined with a social structure whose concern for hierarchy was lubricated by reciprocal relationships of deference and responsibility.

Political connections were part of this world of obligation. It was not the case that principles and issues played no role, but rather that they could not be readily separated from this web of obligations and the habit of obligation. In this world status was important, and status owed much to birth. Of course much of the aristocracy could not trace noble ancestry for many generations. The size of the peerage stood at 178 in 1718, but there had been 152 creations since the Restoration in 1660, and were to be another 38 between 1719 and 1759. Nor was it the case that aristocratic birth necessarily led to self-assurance. Newcastle was anxious and frenetic, if not paranoid. However, the desire for social advancement displayed by, among others, Fox, Pitt and Temple, testified to the value placed upon rank and status. Aristocrats of high rank devoted much effort to obtaining the Garter, an ostentatious mark of royal favour. Those who held high rank might not be without anxiety and their status might be recent, but that did not detract from the attraction and value of social position.

Pitt was not only an outsider because he was a second son of a commoner and without wealth and a secure parliamentary seat. He was also an outsider because he enjoyed playing the outsider. It made him distinctive and gave him a mystique. Pitt both chose to present himself as an outsider and temperamentally found it difficult to feel completely at home in the established political world, especially the court. Neither explanation, however, should be pushed too far. Pitt was an important parliamentary spokesman for the Pelham ministry during his years as Paymaster (1746–55), while the misanthropic ailing recluse of, for example, 1764 was a far cry from the peripatetic country-house visitor of two decades earlier. Although Pitt suffered politically from being an outsider without the backing of a powerful connection prior to 1756, it was of major benefit to him after that date. He came into high office without major obligations to any patron, and this independence ensured that he was very much his own master when it came to the crucial decisions. The nexus of patronage could constrict as well as help, and it was not essential for a career of Pitt's type, which was based on standing in the House of Commons, not on connections. His ability to take a major role on that stage depended on his pose as the politician of conviction and argument, not the dispenser of loaves and fishes to backbenchers. As a tactic it could work well. Pitt had a pre-eminence that in some respects was greater than that of Walpole, because Walpole could not take advantage of 'Patriot' rhetoric and pose as a man totally and selflessly dedicated to the good of his country. This pose strengthened Pitt's position in the Commons, although it did not automatically command support, as Pitt was to discover after he resigned in October 1761.

Pitt's rigorous criticism of government, whether from outside when in opposition or of ministerial colleagues when in office, was not simply a tactic designed to gain attention and to encourage others, not least the ministry, to woo his support. He was happier criticising than defending and this aggressive position was best presented by attacking government, even from within. Although he advised his nephew in 1754 to 'be full of respect, deference, and modesty' towards superiors, as well as against laughing, allegedly a sure sign of lack of self-control,[22] Pitt pushed his views without moderation. He had a sense of his own ability that seemed most challenged by governmental complacency protecting ministerial mediocrity. There is also little sign that he felt at home in the world of court society. He was not close to George II, to George III, either as heir or as monarch, to Prince Frederick, or to George II's other son, the Duke of Cumberland. It is unclear how far he felt antipathy towards a world he could not dominate and which did not value him as he thought fit. Pitt's inadequacy as a courtier was at least as important in defining his relations with George II as was his hostility to Hanover. Walpole, Carteret and Pulteney all came back into royal favour after earlier affronts to George II, either as King or as Prince of Wales.

Many contemporaries saw him as a megalomaniac determined to bend national politics to his will, and, although that aspiration is common to many politicians and political circumstances, few politicians possessed this aspiration to the same degree as Pitt. Pitt's ability and ambition combined to push him into a central political position under two successive monarchs, an unusual feat made more so by the fact that he returned to high office under George III after a period of opposition to that monarch's chosen men and measures. Walpole had served two rulers as first minister, but without any interruption in opposition. Carteret served as a Secretary of State in 1721–4 and as Lord Lieutenant of Ireland in 1724–30, before going into opposition, whence he

---

[22] BL Add. 69288 no. 40.

returned as a Secretary in 1742–4, but his importance in the 1720s was less than that of Pitt three decades later. The Second Earl of Sunderland was both James II's leading minister and, after a period in exile, one of William III's principal advisers, but he was an unpopular figure, dependent on royal favour. Pitt was wilful but it is unlikely that he would have risen as he did, but for the fruitful, though for others unpleasant, combination of his own determination and the weaknesses of several ministries.

Pitt's political career can be summarised briefly, though such abridgements can be misleading. Initially an opposition Whig and a protégé of Cobham's, his maiden speech of 22 April 1735 was against the Walpole ministry on a bill seeking to debar placemen from sitting in Parliament. The following year Pitt criticised George II in the Commons when the King was congratulated on Prince Frederick's marriage and he was dismissed from the army. Pitt continued to attack the Walpole government until its fall in 1742 and when the ministry was then reconstituted the Cobham group remained in opposition, unlike those Whigs who had looked to Carteret and Pulteney. Pitt's violent attacks in 1742–4 on Carteret's foreign policy and the payment of Hanoverian troops it entailed angered George II, but led the Pelhams to seek his support in their struggle with Carteret. Following an agreement between the Pelhams and a number of opposition leaders, including Cobham, in November 1744, Carteret was obliged to resign, while in January 1745 Pitt spoke in favour of continuing a British army in the Austrian Netherlands (Belgium), a commitment that the Pelhams wished to maintain. King George kept Pitt from the Secretaryship at War, which he sought, an office which entailed personal attendance on the King, but in 1746 he gained the Paymastership. The Secretary at War was very much the

King's *commis* for military affairs; whereas being Paymaster did not entail any such personal contact. Pitt was a leading Commons spokesman for the Pelham ministry but his wish to become Secretary of State when Pelham died in 1754 was thwarted by Newcastle and Hardwicke's reluctance to accept him in the post and thus make a rod for their own backs, and by George II's dislike of him.

In November 1754 he attacked the ministry and the following year he reached an agreement with the Earl of Bute, the adviser of Prince George, as a result of which they joined forces in opposition. As the ministry faced a deteriorating international situation and felt vulnerable in the Commons, Pitt was offered a place in the Cabinet in August 1755, but he demanded the leadership of the Commons and refused to support the Anglo-Russian treaty that was known to be crucial for the security of Hanover. As a result Newcastle turned to Fox, provoking Pitt to go into open opposition in November 1755. The ministry, buffeted by the loss of Minorca and divided, collapsed and in December 1756 Pitt became Secretary of State for the Southern Department, with Devonshire as First Lord of the Treasury. Royal hostility and Newcastle's continued influence in the Commons ensured that the new ministry was weak and in July 1757 another based on Pitt and Newcastle was formed. This government took Britain to victory over France, but George III's accession in October 1760 weakened it. Pitt's willingness from 1757 to support a Continental war had alienated the King when Prince of Wales, and relations deteriorated further as a result of the King's promotion of Bute. Pitt resigned in September 1761 when his demand for war with Spain was rejected by the Cabinet.

This resignation ended what had been fifteen years of office with only two short breaks. For the last seventeen years of his life Pitt was to be without office, with the exception of his period as Lord Privy Seal in 1766–8. He was to be of considerable importance, until effectively incapacitated by ill-health in early 1767, but his role was largely that of a spoiler, unwilling to support ministries or to help create a united opposition, adopting a peremptory tone in negotiations and taking a relatively active role in parliamentary debates. Pitt's experience of the policies of George and Bute in 1760–1 led him to insist that he would not take office again unless assured of royal favour and the absence of a favourite. There was no crisis comparable to that of 1756 that he could exploit but Pitt benefited, as he had a decade earlier, from the weakness of the ministries of the period, and the fall of the Rockingham ministry in 1766 allowed him to form an administration. It was a failure. Pitt's aim of governing without faction proved unrealistic, while his health encouraged him to take the peerage that weakened his hold on the Commons. He was faced, as Newcastle had been in 1754, by the problem of finding a reliable Commons manager, and he did not succeed. This political failure was matched by the disappointment of his hopes for rescuing Britain from isolation by alliances with Prussia and Russia. Relinquishing power as a consequence of poor health, Pitt attempted a return in 1769–71, but his opposition to the Grafton and North ministries had little impact. His last political cause was the conciliation of the American colonists, but he lived long enough to see both hostilities break out and the Americans, whose security from France he had regarded as such an important goal in the Seven Years War, turn to France for support. Pitt collapsed dramatically in the Lords on 7 April 1778 and died on 11 May.

Pitt's career was therefore very varied. It cannot really be understood without a thorough appreciation of changing political circumstances, for it was in that context that his choices were taken and it is only in it that they can be judged.

And yet the scale of investigation necessary is illustrated by the 562 pages of text and notes of a recent authoritative work on 1754–7.[23] The process of judgement is not helped by the surviving nature of the sources. Though his papers were not destroyed, as Pulteney's were, Pitt did not leave a correspondence comparable to that of Newcastle or George III, and many of his letters are attempts to persuade rather than to explain. This study is not a comprehensive account of Pitt's political career but a consideration of its major features, one that casts light on the nature of British politics as the state crushed Jacobitism, the most significant domestic challenge of the century, and became a world empire.

[23] J. C. D. Clark, *The Dynamics of Change* (Cambridge, 1982).

Chapter 2

A very inflammatory politician: the rise to high office, 1735–1756

Foremost in ardent Patriot-Bands you stood,
A firm Opposer for the Public Good.

An Epistle to William Pitt (1746)

CRITIC OF WALPOLE

It is said they don't intend to turn out anybody in the King's service who voted . . . for the Prince in either House. If they don't, I think that shows some fear: for Sir Robert in the House of Commons in the debate where it was taken notice of the shameful things they had done in turning out officers of great merit, said that a minister must be a very pitiful fellow if he did not turn out officers who pretended to meddle with the civil government.

Sarah, Duchess of Marlborough, 3 March 1736[1]

It was largely thanks to Walpole that Pitt was to be a great war minister who never fought in the field, unlike Churchill with whom it has been fashionable to compare him. Pitt was born during one war, that of the Spanish Succession (1702–13), rose to prominence during the next major conflict, that of the Austrian Successsion (1743–8), to fame during the next, the Seven Years War (1756–63) and died during the following conflict, the War of American Independence (1775–83). War provided him with political opportunities and reputation.

---

[1] Beinecke, Osborn Shelves, Stair Letters no. 3.

And yet he never saw combat, while his career in the army ended after five years. Walpole was essentially responsible for the fact that Pitt never fought and for the loss of his military position. He played a major role in keeping Britain out of the War of Polish Succession (1733–5), in defiance both of her treaty obligations to Austria and of domestic political pressure from inside and outside the ministry for resistance to the Bourbon aggressors, France and Spain. Pitt was dismissed from his commission in 1736 for parliamentary attacks on Crown and ministry.

Pitt was subsequently to praise Walpole, but during the last years of Walpole's ministry he was a bitter critic, and it is not surprising that Pitt's praise of the late minister in the Commons on 2 December 1755 was greeted with laughter. Earlier he was by no means alone among the younger generation of parliamentarians in being a savage critic of Walpole. Pitt was one of the five young maiden speakers who the First Earl of Egmont noted distinguished themselves in the debate on the Place Bill on 22 April 1735.[2] Yet Pitt was to rise far further than the others: George Lyttelton, who had been brought into Parliament by his brother-in-law Thomas Pitt, was another of Cobham's cubs and was to hold his highest office as Chancellor of the Exchequer in 1755–6; Lord Polwarth, who was to follow a career in Scottish politics; his twin brother Alexander Hume Campbell, who rose to become Lord Clerk Register in Scotland; and Mr Delmer, presumably Peter Delmé, who had in fact spoken the previous year and who never held office.

The different fate of these young men, all born between 1708 and 1710, indicates the unpredictability of political careers during the period and offers a warning against charging Pitt with inconsistency, as has often been done.

---

[2] HMC, *Diary of the First Earl of Egmont* (3 vols., 1920–3) II, 171.

Delmé was consistent, always voting with the opposition and never holding office. He was also wealthy. Lyttelton, Secretary to Prince Frederick 1737–44, became a Lord of the Treasury in the latter year but exerted pressure to gain Pitt's entry to office. He broke with Pitt in 1755, when he refused to follow him into an opposition which he regarded as purely personal against Newcastle. Promoted to Chancellor of the Exchequer, he was excluded from the Pitt–Newcastle ministry formed in 1757 and held no office thereafter. Hume Campbell, appointed Solicitor-General to Frederick in December 1741, followed the Prince into support for the ministry the following year, but in 1744 he spoke and voted with the opposition, in defiance of Frederick's wishes. Allied with Pitt that year, he fell out with him in 1745, and in 1747 was reconciled with the Pelhams, who wished to weaken the opposition. He supported Newcastle against Pitt in the 1754 Parliament and was a victim of the reconciliation between the two men.

This brief consideration reveals the extent to which ambitious politicians in the 1740s and 1750 altered their connections and positions in order to advance their careers. It is inappropriate to criticise Pitt for inconsistency or hypocrisy, without appreciating that similar charges could be made against many peers and MPs, especially those who were active politically. Rather than regarding most contemporary politicians simply as opportunists, it is important to consider the problems they faced.

This perspective encourages an appreciation of the political scene as volatile, in terms both of the 'structure' of politics and the issues facing politicians. This volatility is difficult to grasp because of both the differences between modern and eighteenth-century British political groupings, and the misleading fashion in which the former are often presented, as coherent groups united in the pursuit of policies that are designed to implement an ideological prospectus, rather than as bodies divided by personality, ambition and faction, as well as over policy and ideology. Historians differ in their assessment of eighteenth-century politics. Sir Lewis Namier's atomisation of the political world in the early 1760s into individual and factional ambition and his debunking of the role of political principles[3] was applied by other scholars to much of the Hanoverian period, but it has been challenged for the reigns of the first two Georges. Politics during the two reigns have been presented either in terms of a clash between 'Court' and 'Country', a division between government and opposition that had ideological and cultural aspects as well as being a struggle for power, or in terms of a party rivalry, essentially between Whigs and Tories, though with Whigs in opposition constituting a third force. The latter analysis is most appropriate for the Walpole years, although less so for the 1750s, a period when party distinctions became less marked. Historians who stress the 'Court'/'Country' approach argue that the Tory exclusion from office after the accession of George I in 1714 destroyed their 'court' wing and turned them into a permanent opposition force, united to the opposition Whigs by their common hostility to the governing or 'Old Corps' Whigs. Other scholars stress the ideological and policy divide between Tories and opposition Whigs, which was certainly apparent in the politics of the period and which affected Pitt's career in opposition. The divide between ministerial and opposition Whigs was a porous one, unlike that between ministerial Whigs and Tories. Sharing in antagonism to Roman Catholicism with the Whigs, Tories were keener to defend the prerogatives and position of the Church of England, especially against Protestant Nonconformists, indeed in many respects they

---

[3] L. B Namier, *The Structure of Politics at the Accession of George III* (2nd edn, 1957).

were the Church party; were more committed to an isolationist foreign policy, stressing the importance to national defence of a strong navy, rather than commitment to interventionist diplomatic and military strategies on the Continent, entailing commitments to other powers; and in many cases regretted the Glorious Revolution of 1688 and sympathised with and, to a lesser extent, supported the cause of the exiled Stuarts.[4]

The extent to which Tories and opposition Whigs could co-operate successfully depended on the issue. They united to bring down Walpole in February 1742, after his indifferent showing in the general election of the previous summer. However, they found it impossible to sustain agreement, and, in the aftermath of Walpole's fall, the coalition opposed to the Old Corps (ministerial Whigs) collapsed. This was to be the basis of the political situation over the next four years and the position that Pitt had to confront. Though Walpole had fallen, it was the opposition, not the government that had split, although the ministry was certainly divided. The government had been reconstituted as an uneasy coalition of the bulk of the Old Corps and a group of former opposition Whigs whose most influential members were John, Lord Carteret and William Pulteney, who in 1742 became Earl of Bath. The situation was not to alter again until Frederick, Prince of Wales went into opposition for a second time in 1746. Until then there seemed little possibility that the Old Corps would ever lose office; a politician who was ambitious for power had to hope that he would be able to repeat the success of Carteret and Pulteney and benefit from government weaknesses in order to persuade the ministry to take him in. This attitude could be described as opportunistic, but

---

[4] Guidance to the controversy can be found in J. Black (ed.), *Britain in the Age of Walpole* (1984), and *British Politics and Society from Walpole to Pitt 1742-1789* (1990); and in J. Black, *Robert Walpole and the Nature of British Politics in the Early Eighteenth Century* (1990).

it is difficult to see what other legal alternatives opposition politicians possessed. Under the Septennial Act of 1716, which stipulated that general elections in Britain (but not Ireland) had to be held at least once every seven years, no election was due until 1748. Since the Act had been passed, Parliaments had always served their full term, the election of 1727 being necessary because of the accession of a new ruler. Although the next election was actually held a year earlier, in 1747, the limited impact made by opponents of the ministry, both then and in the next general election in 1754, underlined what most politicians knew, that the routes to power ran through courts, both that of the King and that of his heir, more than through Parliament.

On 20 May 1736 Lady Irwin wrote to her father the Earl of Carlisle,

The King two days ago turned out Mr Pitt from a cornecy [sic] for having voted and spoke in Parliament contrary to his approbation; he is a young man of no fortune, a very pretty speaker, one the Prince is particular to, and under the tuition of my Lord Cobham.

Five weeks later a French memorandum claimed that Cobham directed George Grenville, Lyttelton and Pitt, but added that without doubt Pitt was superior to the two others, knowledgeable, modest, poor, courageous and firm, and that sooner or later he would play a role in the country.[5] This prospect first required the fall of Walpole, but Sir Robert, born in 1676, was not a young man and a reconstitution of the Whigs seemed probable. In contrast to modern British political parties, there was no agreed leader or leadership, manifesto, policies, membership or organisation. Developments were unpredictable, and it seemed likely that influence among the Whigs would depend on a shifting pattern of

---

[5] HMC, *Manuscripts of the Earl of Carlisle* (1897) p. 172; AE Mémoires et Documents, Angleterre 6 f. 111.

personal relationships and political contingencies, as in the previous period of ministerial volatility: 1714–24. Pitt's chance of office would be improved by the prospect that Frederick, whose relations with his father, George II, and therefore his father's ministers, were poor, would succeed to the throne. George II had been born in 1683. Pitt had offended the King by praising his heir and suggesting that Frederick's marriage was due to the Prince and to public opinion, rather than to George.[6]

After his dismissal from his post in the army in May 1736, Pitt sought to associate himself more clearly with Frederick. That year he was described by Queen Caroline's confidant, the epicene Lord Hervey as 'perpetually with the Prince, and at present in the first rank of his favour', and Hervey suggested that Pitt was responsible for the carefully scripted letter that Frederick sent to Queen Caroline explaining his controversial decision to stay in Kensington Palace. The following February Pitt was one of those who advised Frederick to pursue in Parliament his quarrel with his father about receiving a fixed allowance out of the Civil List, instead of being dependent on George's generosity.[7] Though motions for a fixed allowance of £100,000 were defeated in both houses, Frederick was now clearly associated with opposition to Walpole, who had been obliged to take George's part. The willingness of successive Hanoverian heirs to fall out with their fathers was to provide hope and a measure of legitimacy to a number of eighteenth-century opposition groupings. In the summer of 1737 Pitt was made a Groom of the Bedchamber by Frederick.

Pitt's dismissal from the army led him to speak out on military matters in the Commons. Opposition to a standing army and demands that it be reduced in size were traditional

---

[6] John, Lord Hervey, *Some Materials towards Memoirs of the Reign of King George II*, edited by R. R. Sedgwick (3 vols., 1931) p. 553.   [7] Hervey, *Memoirs* pp. 613, 667.

'Country' measures, that reflected the hostility of many, both Whigs and Tories, both to the executive and to the potential for attacks on the constitution that a large army was believed to provide. Given the close interest taken in military affairs by William III, George I and George II, such attacks also tended to reflect an absence of royal approval and a lack of interest in gaining it. In the debate held on 18 February 1737, Pitt made his second parliamentary speech. Although Basil Williams stated that there is no record of it, there is in fact an account in Somerset Record Office.

Mr Pitt spoke long, and was well heard. Among other things, he took notice, that the privileges of the House of Commons had been notoriously violated; of which he produced his own case, as an instance, whose commission, as cornet of dragoons, had been taken from him for no other reason, that he could guess, but for the liberty of speech he had used in Parliament. Sir Robert took fire at this, and after a long complaint of the ill treatment the ministry had met with from licentious tongues, his passion transported him so far, as to raise his voice with a loftier air, and then, as a True Englishman (he told them) he would now speak his mind, and in that Honourable Assembly of English Gentlemen, he would venture to utter his thoughts freely: That whoever might be his successor in the Administration, he must be a *Pityfull Fellow* if he ever suffered any officers in the army to dictate to him, or censure his actions with an unbecoming freedom, and yet suffer them to continue in their posts. But finding he was not rightly understood by some gentlemen, he explained himself immediately; that it was not his meaning, that any member of that Honourable House, could justly be deprived of any office or employment, for any liberty of speech they should there use; but he thought those officers, who talked with a saucy freedom of the government, out of that House, would not be unjustly used if they lost their places.

Walpole's hostility to Pitt probably arose in part from his likely role in paying for the cost of his commission as cornet, £1,000 according to the official scale. Basil Williams thought that this had probably been waived by Cobham, as Pitt could not have afforded it, but according to the Second Earl of Egmont, writing in 1757, Pitt 'acquired a cornet's commission, not only by the favour of the late Earl of Orford, but by means of his money'. This use of government funds would have been intended to please Thomas Pitt. By 1736, however, Thomas had carried William into opposition and it would have seemed appropriate to Walpole to withdraw favours accordingly, although this was to help make William a political martyr. In the Commons debate on the size of the army on 3 February 1738 Pitt condemned the sacking of officers 'at the arbitrary will and pleasure, perhaps at the whim of a favourite minister', and he pressed for a reduction in the size of the army in order to safeguard the constitution and cut taxation, and thus reduce popular discontent.[8]

In 1738 Pitt also criticised Walpole's alleged failure to defend British trade in the Caribbean from the exacting supervision and depredations of Spanish colonial government in the West Indies. British merchants in turn sought to breach Spanish restrictions on trade with their colonies. Relations with Spain were again the major issue in the session of 1739. The government had negotiated a settlement of the disputes with Spain, the Convention of the Pardo, and this was strongly attacked by opposition politicians. Pitt condemned it as ignominious and a betrayal of national interests and took great 'libertys' in his attack on the ministry, but the government had the Convention accepted by Parliament, only to see it fall victim to Spanish intransigence.[9]

[8] George Harbin to Thomas Carew, 24 February 1737, Taunton, Somerset County Record Office, Trollop-Bellew papers, DD/TB Box 16 FT 18; B. Williams, *Chatham* (2 vols., 1913) I, 67, 41; Egmont, unpublished pamphlet, BL Add. 47012 B f. 177; W. Cobbett, *Parliamentary History of England from . . . 1066 to . . . 1803* (36 vols., 1806–20) XI, 467.

[9] W. Coxe, *Memoirs of the Life and Administration of Sir Robert Walpole* (3 vols., 1798) III, 516; P. L. Woodfine, 'The Anglo-Spanish War of 1739', in J. Black (ed.), *The Origins of War in Early Modern Europe* (Edinburgh, 1987) pp. 185–209.

The subsequent war, which took its name from the loss of Captain Jenkins' ear, allegedly cut off by a Spanish officer in 1731, was not a triumph. Pitt, who had gained further prominence from his call for action against Spain, adding parliamentary polemic to princely favour, had declared then, 'Spain knows the consequence of a war in America; whoever gains, it must prove fatal to her', but this was not the case. Admiral Vernon's early triumph in capturing Porto Bello on the isthmus of Panama in December 1739 was not followed by the collapse of the Spanish empire envisaged by some British commentators, the proponents of the so-called 'Blue Water strategy', who argued that war could be profitably conducted against Spain by mounting attacks on her colonial empire. The difficulty of organising trans-oceanic operations, as well as concern that France would come to the assistance of her ally Spain limited British activity, while local defences and diseases proved sufficient to protect Spanish possessions. The British attack on Cartagena in modern Colombia in 1741 failed, seemingly demonstrating the truth of opposition claims that the war was being conducted badly, a charge made by Pitt on 13 February 1741 when an unsuccessful attack on Walpole's position was mounted in Parliament. He then criticised the minister's 'satiety of power'; the conduct of the war: 'taxes, expenses, misapplications, subsidies, haste'; the failure of the government to support Austria, 'the only power, with which it is our interest to cultivate an inseparable friendship'; and the legacy of the Walpole ministry,

at home debts were increased and taxes multiplied, and the sinking fund alienated; abroad the system of Europe was totally subverted, and at this awful moment, when the greatest scene was opening to Europe that has ever before occurred, he who had lost the confidence of all mankind should not be permitted to continue at the head of the king's government.[10]

Walpole suffered, as Louis XVI was to do with the Dutch crisis of 1787, from the absence of any spectacular success with which he could be associated and through which he could gain the prestige and respect that was so crucial to government. He did badly in the general election of 1741, due less to any groundswell of popular opposition than to the defection of a number of important electoral patrons, including Prince Frederick, who controlled many Cornish boroughs, the Dukes of Argyll and Dorset, and George Dodington. The refusal of Frederick to accept any political settlement with his father unless Walpole fell played a crucial role in the minister's decision, following his loss of an ability to deliver parliamentary majorities, to resign in February 1742. He took shelter in the Lords, accepting the title of Earl of Orford.[11]

The fall of Walpole did not bring Pitt to office and he did not take a major role in the political manoeuvres of early 1742. The Cobham group parted company with Frederick when he settled his differences with his father, and in the Commons Pitt called for an inquiry into Walpole's conduct, a measure that the new ministers were determined to thwart, because they knew that George II and their new allies in the government were opposed to it. The Duke of Newcastle, Secretary of State for the Southern Department, and his brother Henry Pelham were prominent among the Old Corps who remained in office and neither wanted to include Tories in the ministry. Cobham was less ready at first to betray his

---

[10] I. G. Doolittle, 'A First-Hand Account of the Commons Debate on the Removal of Sir Robert Walpole, 13 February 1741', *Bulletin of the Institute of Historical Research*, 53 (1980), pp. 134–5; Cobbett, XI, 1362; Coxe, *Walpole* I, 653.

[11] Black, *Robert Walpole* pp. 40–4.

promises to the Tories than Pulteney. As part of the price of office, Carteret and Pulteney abandoned their former allies and policies, helping to throw out the proposal to repeal the Septennial Act. That had been proposed by those who remained in opposition, on the grounds that by holding more frequent elections it would make the Commons more responsive to the electors and less corruptible. The ability of the executive branch of government, to manipulate Parliament, the legislative branch, would thus be lessened.

However much Pitt and his allies, still in opposition, might blame the failure to create a new political order in 1742 on betrayal and corruption and bitterly condemn both the Old Corps and their new associates, there was also a strong conviction among the Old Corps that the stability and continuity exemplified by Walpole were of value. They were contrasted with disorder and anarchy, a strong temptation in a political culture where the constitutional legitimacy of opposition was in its infancy and the conventions that it should follow unsettled and contentious, as Pitt's contemporary reputation was to demonstrate. John Campbell MP, a supporter of Walpole who lost his Lordship of the Admiralty on the fall of the minister, wrote to his son the following month to criticise the political search for 'Popularity, that is in other words, preferring the false flattery and giddy noisy applause of knaves and fools, to the sober and sincere approbation of men of sense and virtue'. Campbell was very different to Pitt: thirteen years older, related to the Pelhams and wealthy. The views of men like Campbell, suspicious of popular positions and the search for popularity, were to make it difficult for Pitt to gain office, other than as a result of serious governmental problems. Campbell himself became a Lord of the Treasury in June 1746, the month after Pitt became Paymaster, held the post until 1754 and was MP until 1768, with a short interlude in 1761–2. He loathed Pitt, whom he never forgave for his attacks on Walpole, and whom he accused in 1757–8 of 'prevarication, self-contradiction, disregard of truth . . . mad ambition, mean popularity, pride, and the most intemperate passion'.[12]

OPPONENT OF CARTERET, 1742–1746

The focus of opposition attacks in 1738–41 had been first Spanish depredations and then the conduct of the war with Spain. They allegedly demonstrated a governmental failure to understand and defend national interests. In the parliamentary session which opened in November 1742 the focus shifted to the hiring of Hanoverian troops to serve against France in the War of Austrian Succession. In 1740 the Emperor Charles VI, ruler of the Austrian Habsburg dominions, had died leaving his elder daughter, Maria Theresa, as his heir. Although this arrangement, the Pragmatic Sanction, had been guaranteed by most of the European rulers, a number chose to press claims to a portion of the inheritance. Frederick II (the Great) of Prussia invaded the Austrian province of Silesia (modern south-west Poland) in December 1740. In response, his uncle George II, who was one of the guarantors of the Habsburg inheritance, sought to organise opposition to Frederick, while in April 1741 Parliament voted Maria Theresa financial assistance. However, in the summer of 1741 France intervened against her and, in the face of another advancing French army, George II, then in Hanover, was obliged to accept a neutrality convention and to promise to support Charles Albert, Elector of Bavaria, the French candidate, as Emperor. The following spring the fall

---

[12] Cobbett, XII, 526–7; John to Pryse Campbell, 24 March 1742, Cawdor, Box 138; Horace Walpole, *Memoirs of King George II*, edited by J. Brooke (3 vols., New Haven, 1985) II, 218; L. B. Namier and J. Brooke (eds.), *The House of Commons 1754–1790* (3 vols., 1964) II, 187.

of Walpole, the rise of Carteret to become in effect foreign minister and a more belligerent note on the part of George combined to give a pronounced anti-French direction to British policy. British forces under the Earl of Stair were sent to the Austrian Netherlands (modern Belgium and Luxemburg), preparatory to an intended invasion of France that was however postponed due to bad weather, and Carteret sought to create a powerful anti-French league.[13]

The hiring of Hanoverian forces was an important element in Carteret's plans. The British army was not large, Britain's Dutch ally was unhappy about the prospect of war with France, the Austrians were more concerned about the military situation in Bavaria, Bohemia and Italy, and the easiest way to create a large army in the Austrian Netherlands appeared to be to offer subsidy treaties to friendly German rulers. This method had been followed by both William III and Anne: the Duke of Marlborough's victories were very much Anglo-Dutch-German affairs. However, the decision to hire Hanoverians was contentious. Critics could claim that George II was being paid to do what he should do anyway as Elector of Hanover, and was making a handsome profit over it. The payment of Hanoverians became the central issue in attacks on British foreign and military policy, which, it was alleged, was no longer directed to the pursuit of national goals against Spain, but was instead seeking more nebulous ends, and leading to intervention on the Continent, that was likely to be expensive and unsuccessful, when a 'Blue Water' policy, naval war with Spain, supposedly offered victory and profit. This was a theme that Tories and opposition Whigs could share, and one that looked back to a long tradition of debate over British foreign and military policy.

[13] J. Black, 'The Problems of the Small State: Bavaria and Britain in the Second Quarter of the Eighteenth Century', *European History Quarterly*, 19 (1989), pp. 14–18; J. Black, *A System of Ambition? British Foreign Policy 1660–1793* (1991) pp. 164–8.

Pitt was to make his name as a politician as an impassioned critic of Hanoverian commitments. His stand on this issue helped to delay his rise to office, by ensuring that George II, who already disliked Pitt because of his links with the Prince of Wales in the 1730s, was both hostile and determined to keep him away from crucial posts where he could influence policy. Pitt's decision to attack Hanoverian subsidies can therefore be seen as a mistake, but he was not a politician who was likely to rise through royal favour, especially after Frederick's reconciliation with his father in February 1742. His chance of office seemed greatest if he could repeat the tactics of the opposition Whigs who had eventually joined the ministry following Walpole's fall, but their willingness to do a deal with the Old Corps had discredited the opposition arguments employed against Walpole, especially the attack on domestic corruption. The opposition had also been badly divided by the events of 1742. The opposition Whigs had split, more staying in opposition with the Tories than joining the government. To revitalise and reunite opposition to the ministry a new issue had to be found and Hanoverian subsidies provided this, as the very large numbers of MPs who voted in crucial divisions on 10 December 1742 and 18 January 1744 indicate. The issue could be used to press the charge that the new ministers had abandoned their principles and could not be trusted to defend national interests. It could also serve to recruit popular support for the new opposition.

Pitt's claim that ministerial policies were unpopular and his appeal for the backing of the 'political nation', those who were interested in politics whether or not they enjoyed or were able to exercise their votes, were scarcely novel, but such opposition arguments sought not only to bolster the morale of opponents to the ministry but also to focus on a central ambiguity in the Whig inheritance: the desire to use the powers of government to maintain power, while

45

restating a belief in parliamentary sovereignty based on the representation of electoral views, but in fact not enjoying the support of a clear majority of the electorate. On 9 March 1742 Pitt had told the Commons that it ought to express 'the voice of the people' and that this was represented in crowd demonstrations, a crucial departure from the distinction between the people and mobs drawn by ministerial Whigs. Instead, Pitt stated that 'as the mob consists chiefly of children, journeymen and servants, who speak the sentiments of their parents and masters, we may thence judge of the sentiments of the better sort of people'. The accuracy of the parliamentary reports of the period is unclear, though, for want of other sources, they have to be employed and it is probable that major speeches, such as those of Pitt, were those that were reported most accurately, although politicians complained about errors.[14]

On 23 March 1742, during the debate over establishing an inquiry into Walpole's conduct, Pitt presented the Commons as an essential bridge between the popular will and the Crown,

The desire of bringing the people into our sentiments is so natural to mankind ... We meet here to communicate to our sovereign the sentiments of his people: we meet here to redress the grievances of the people. By performing our duty in these two respects we shall always be able to . . . prevent the people's being led into insurrections or rebellions by misrepresentations or false surmises. When the people complain, they must be in the right or in the wrong. If they are in the right, we are in duty bound to enquire into the conduct of the ministers, and punish those who shall appear to have been the most guilty: if the people are in the wrong, we ought to enquire into the conduct of our ministers, in order to be able to convince the people, that they have been misled . . . we must be

---

[14] Cobbett, XII, 485, 491; J. Black, *The English Press in the Eighteenth Century* (1987) pp. 113–31; J. Black, 'Parliamentary Reporting in England in the Early Eighteenth Century', *Parliaments, Estates and Representation*, 7 (1987), pp. 61–9.

governed by the sentiments of our constituents, if we are resolved to perform our duty, either as true representatives of the people, or as faithful messengers to our sovereign.[15]

Pitt therefore proposed to make MPs responsible to their constituents and ministers answerable to and in Parliament when they differed from the views of the electorate. The failure to press home the inquiry into Walpole's conduct was a major blow to this strategy, and John Tucker, an opposition Whig MP, was correct in suggesting that 'the Walpoleian system of government is to be continued'.[16] However, the Hanoverian troops issue offered the possibility of challenging ministerial control of Parliament and therefore of demonstrating that the Commons could fulfil the role of intermediary between Crown and people. The Tories could be expected to co-operate with the opposition Whigs, while the cohesion of the divided ministry might be shaken. The prospect of defining government and opposition in as favourable a light for the latter as possible, in both membership and policy, in the new political world created by the reconstitution of the ministry after Walpole's fall was a welcome one to politicians encouraged by the chance of change and power presented by that fall, but demoralised by their failure to achieve their ends.

The session began on 18 November 1742. In the Commons debate on the Address opposition politicians focused on the Hanoverian issue. John Campbell, sceptical of the loyalty to the Hanoverian dynasty of critics of Hanover, was nevertheless impressed by Pitt, but noted the independence of spirit that made him such a difficult figure for those who proposed or sought to sustain political combinations. 'Mr William Pitt I believe does not intend to be under any one, and he has to be sure a very good way of speaking, and parts very fit to make a

---

[15] Cobbett, XII, 557–62.
[16] John to Richard Tucker, 27 April 1742, Bod. MS Don. c. 105 f. 94.

figure in Parliament.' According to another Walpolean MP, Henry Fox, Pitt gave the only good speech on the opposition side.[17] On 2 December Pitt spoke in a bitter debate over investigating the Walpole ministry, Campbell commenting, 'I think some gentlemen like to display their oratory in public too well to deprive themselves of the opportunity of doing it. Mr William Pitt is indeed an orator and has great talents to rob a people of their liberty under pretence of giving them more.' The ministry took a battering over Hanover, but won the divisions. On 10 December Pitt attacked what he claimed were 'unnecessary alliances' and engaging in Continental quarrels, and criticised George II for being most interested in aggrandising Hanover and for being paid by Britain to do his duty as Elector and support Maria Theresa. His remarks constituted a powerful attack both on the conduct of the King and on the readiness of the ministry to defend national interests,

To dwell upon all the instances of partiality which had been shown, to remark the yearly visits that have been made to that delightful country, to reckon up all the sums that have been spent to aggrandize and enrich it, would be at once invidious and tiresome; tiresome to those who are afraid to hear the truth, and to those who are unwilling to mention facts dishonourable or injurious to their country.

Campbell not surprisingly was unimpressed and his important, pithy comments are worth citing for their evidence of the limited impact that Pitt made on some MPs. On 11 December he wrote to his son, 'Mr Pitt spoke in his oratorical way but I thought had not much argument.' The previous evening the Commons had agreed to hire 16,000 Hanoverian troops by a substantial majority, 260 to 193. Nevertheless, the large opposition vote indicated the import-

---

[17] John to Pryse Campbell, 18 November 1742, Cawdor, Box 138; Earl of Ilchester (ed.), *Henry Fox, First Lord Holland* (2 vols., 1920) I, 93.

ance of the issue as a means of bolstering opposition cohesion.[18]

At a time of rising national feeling, Pitt advanced a definition of loyalty based on the furtherance of national interests, rather than on the defence of the Protestant Succession, and the interests were presented as not arising from royal initiatives. The Protestant Succession had been the keynote of Whig claims for identity and support since the expulsion of James II in 1688, but it had compromised Whig ministries by obliging them to consider the particular interests of foreign monarchs, first William III and then the Hanoverians. This had been less of a problem in the 1730s, as British foreign policy had become less interventionist, in large part thanks to Walpole, but the issue had been brought to the fore again in 1741, as conflict spread in Europe and Britain came to take an increasingly active role. Tucker wrote to his brother on 14 December 1742 that 'all true Englishmen' were opposed to hiring Hanoverian troops, adding, 'Whig and Tory has been laid aside a good while and the distinction of Court and Country is now sunk into that of Englishmen and Hanoverians, which is propagated with great industry by the pamphleteers.'[19] That was certainly the distinction that both Pitt and the opposition pamphleteers were seeking to make, though they were to find that political alignments had not been reworked to this extent.

Pitt was one of the principal opposition speakers in early 1743, even saying 'some handsome things of Lord Orford' as a contrast to the present ministry, and he was prominent in attacks over foreign policy. In February Pitt spoke for

[18] Cobbett, XII, 1036; John to Pryse Campbell, 2, 11 December 1742, Cawdor, Box 138; Philip to Joseph Yorke, 3 December 1742, BL Add. 35363 ff. 15–16; G. C. Gibbs, 'English Attitudes towards Hanover and the Hanoverian Succession in the First Half of the Eighteenth Century', in A. M. Birke and K. Kluxen (eds.), *England und Hannover* (Munich, 1986) p. 33.

[19] John to Richard Tucker, 14 December 1742, Bod. MS Don. c. 105 f. 197.

motions pressing the government to disclose diplomatic correspondence with Vienna, Berlin and The Hague. In the first case he 'made a handsome speech, but went far from the question', a characteristic of his somewhat grandiloquent but often unspecific rhetoric. Pitt was described by Benjamin Keene, a placeman MP, as 'almost the only one in the opposition that is much attended to'.[20] The ministry continued to win the divisions, but after the session was over Pitt was discussed as a possible useful reinforcement for the government. This was increasingly divided between Carteret, who was closest to George II, and the Pelhams, who were advised by Walpole and felt that Carteret was not keeping them informed. After Henry Pelham became First Lord of the Treasury in August 1743, defeating Carteret's choice William Pulteney, now Earl of Bath, Walpole urged him to gain the backing of Pitt who, he noted, was 'thought able and formidable'. He also pressed Pelham to win the support of Fox.[21] Gaining such supporters would facilitate the management of the Commons and thus increase the appeal of the Pelhams to George II. The Pelhams would need support if they were to drive Carteret from his position of power and in the autumn of 1743 they negotiated with the leading opposition Whigs, but their demand that the Hanoverian troops must remain in British pay and their refusal to take in more than a few Tories, and then 'only upon a personal foot', were unacceptable to the opposition, although Fox became a Lord of the Treasury. Pitt did not play a crucial role in the negotiations: that was taken by Cobham and the Earl of Chesterfield, but they were both peers and, as the principal battleground between government and opposition remained

---

[20] John to Pryse Campbell, 15 January, 5 February 1743, Cawdor, Box 138; BL Add. 43441 f. 13.
[21] Orford to Pelham, 25 August 1743, W. Coxe, *Memoirs of the Administration of the Right Honourable Henry Pelham* (2 vols., 1829) I, 91–3.

the Commons, Pitt's importance revived when Parliament resumed in December 1743. However, his relatively minor role in the negotiations revealed the extent to which his oratorical prominence did not carry with it equivalent political consequences. The opposition peers were no more interested than their rivals in the implications of the notion of the Commons as the representatives of the people.

Thwarted in negotiation, Chesterfield argued that the ministry would have to be intimidated into accepting terms and to that end 'the Hanover Flame' would have to be blown 'to the height'. Pitt was clearly the man to do this. Fox predicted accurately that the opposition would 'renew all Pitt's talk of wars of ambition and acquisition, and unattainable ends pursued by mad means'.[22] A member of a new committee of three Whigs and three Tories that planned opposition tactics in the Commons,[23] Pitt proposed the rejection of the Address of Thanks on 1 December 1743, making a stir with a powerful attack on Carteret in which he claimed that the original reasons for British intervention in the war had been distorted and that Parliament was being ignored. The Tory MP Sir Roger Newdigate recorded Pitt as saying,

That it was improper to thank his Majesty for a definitive treaty with the King of Sardinia and Queen of Hungary which we have only a promise to see, but have not seen. That the Parliament never engaged but in a defensive war for the house of Austria not in a war of equivalents, not in a war of indemnification . . . That your promising His Majesty support in these measures, is tying the house down to approve of those measures hereafter, measures which I am concerned to say have very much alienated the hearts of his subjects, of the bravest of his subjects, those execrable measures

[22] Chesterfield to Earl Gower, 2 October 1743, PRO 30/39/1/11 ff. 285–6: Farmington, Hanbury Williams Papers (hereafter HW) 48 f. 76.
[23] J. B. Owen, The Rise of the Pelhams (1957) p. 199.

which it is plain were concerted by one sole minister, by that minister, who seems to have renounced the British nation. I can never approve of a war of which neither the end or the means have yet been ascertained.

The Whig Earl of Bessborough described it as 'a very inflammatory speech exceedingly abusive . . . some very gross things against Lord Carteret, called him an execrable minister, one who had renounced the interest of the British nation by advising that measure of taking the Hanoverians into our pay'. According to another account 'Pitt called him the most enormous minister ever heard of; described him as one who had deserted his native country and turned German.' The Second Earl of Egmont, who was then an MP, argued subsequently that Pitt's 'factious opposition' to the use of Hanoverian troops helped the Jacobite cause,

it can never be forgot how the poison he had infused, and the inflammation he had raised upon this base topic operated to distract the kingdom in the midst of the war . . . it raised the Jacobite interest.[24]

Alongside the counterpointing of Hanover and Britain,[25] that was designed to castigate Carteret without alienating the Pelhams, Pitt had advanced a more reasoned critique of foreign policy that was designed to highlight a switch that had indeed taken place from the defence of the integrity of the Habsburg inheritance to less clear but more aggressive goals. In addition, he placed parliamentary approval at the centre of his picture of a sound foreign policy, implying that only a policy explained in and supported by Parliament could

---

[24] Warwick, County Record Office, CR 136 B2530/22; Bessborough to Duke of Devonshire, 1 December 1743, HP Chatsworth; Richard Woolfe to Simon Yorke, 3 December 1743, Hawarden, Clwyd Record Office D/E/875; John to Richard Tucker, 6 December 1743, Bod. MS Don. c. 106 f. 112; Cobbett XIII, 135, 142, 152–70; Egmont, BL Add. 47097.

[25] Thomas Sherlock, Bishop of Salisbury, to Edward Weston, Under-Secretary, 8 October 1743, Farmington, Weston papers, vol. 3.

be in tune with national interests. However, the bitterness of his criticisms and the extreme proposal to refrain from thanking George II for his speech, was unacceptable to some of the opposition and the government won the division by a large majority on a vote of 278 to 149. Pitt's language was again extreme when the opposition moved on 6 December 1743 to address George II to discontinue the British payment of Hanoverian troops. One Tory noted 'Mr Pitt signalized himself upon this occasion, as a bold champion, as well as an Orator.' Pitt declared that in articulating anti-Hanoverian sentiment he spoke 'to what every man feels', adding 'that it was no ways premature but most parliamentary when his Majesty is on the brink of losing the affections of his People to endeavour to stretch out a friendly arm to deliver him from the grasp of an infamous minister'. The opposition lost the division 181 to 131, but a number of ministerial supporters failed to back the government.[26]

Pitt's criticism of the Hanoverians was an obvious attack on Carteret who told the Lords that the interests of Britain and Hanover were 'inseparable'.[27] However, continued negotiations with the Pelhams and the simultaneous desire to retain Tory support, without which the opposition Whigs were of limited political weight, placed Pitt in a difficult position, one that was to face him for much of his career. The exigencies of political manoeuvre and compromise clashed with the more consistent and partisan attitude of committed opposition. This was to pose a major difficulty for Pitt during the years of the Pitt–Newcastle ministry (1757–61), but by then the intensity of the party struggle had diminished, in part because the Tories were by then less divorced from the world of political compromise, while success in the Seven Years

---

[26] George Harbin to Mrs Bamfyld, 10 December 1743, Taunton, Somerset County Record Office, DD/SAS FA 41/C 795; Warwick CR 136 B2530/2.
[27] Cobbett, XIII, 356.

War helped to bring a greater measure of cohesion in the political system, or at least acceptance of the ministry. This was not the case in the mid-1740s, when, in addition, political animosities were rawer and the Tories were suspicious of being betrayed by Whig allies, as they had been in 1742. Furthermore, the possibility of Jacobite action added a potent note of suspicion and instability, while passions were raised over what seemed to be a blatant diversion of British resources to Hanoverian ends. Pitt and George Lyttelton argued that the Hanoverians should be discarded, but that British troops should continue to be stationed in the Austrian Netherlands, a measure that was designed to appeal to the Pelhams and to encourage them to act against Carteret. This support for the stationing of British troops on the Continent clashed not only with Tory views, but also with those of Cobham, who was supported by the Grenvilles. They favoured an all-out attack on the government, and George Grenville replaced Pitt as the group's leading spokesman in the Commons.

The tension within the opposition was revealed at a meeting held at the Fountain Tavern in London on 10 January 1744 when Pitt pressed the need for supporting the army, a measure that Pelham regarded as vital, but which clashed with traditional Tory notions. Tucker, a participant, recorded,

the only thing recommended was early and constant attendance to hold together and admit of no treaty with the Court but on the Broad Bottom and to continue firm in the opposition on the plan settled the last session, by which was understood the giving the army . . . was to be opposed. After several gentlemen were gone Mr Pitt and Mr Lyttelton gave it as their opinion it were better not to vote against the National Troops, since it must furnish the administration with every reasonable objection that it would be impossible to make an honourable peace but with sword in hand, that the situation of affairs was very different now from the last year, that you were not actually engaged in a war on the Continent and disarming yourselves at this juncture would be most impolitic, they desired to be excused from saying anything tomorrow on the debate since they were convinced of the impropriety of the measure of opposing the national troops, though since it seemed to be the unanimous opinion of the company if the House was divided on the question they would both divide with their friends though it was against their opinion. As to the affair of the Hanoverian troops . . . they would oppose and speak against them with their best abilities, though they could not be brought to think it was proper at this time to refuse the National Troops . . . Many people seemed surprised at this difference of opinion . . . and it will doubtless give great cause of jealousies.[28]

It is easy to appreciate from this account both why Pitt was accused of inconsistency and opportunism, and why he was increasingly unwilling to accept the consequences of being a junior partner in the opposition. To other opposition politicians his willingness to support a large British army, while criticising Carteret's direction of foreign policy, seemed suspicious. To Pitt the Tories and other all-out opponents of the ministry were failing to appreciate the need to abandon rigid views in face of changes in British policy and were unable to distinguish sufficiently between help to Hanover and a national commitment to the anti-French cause on the Continent. This distinction was to be vital when Pitt defended the dispatch of British forces to Germany during the Seven Years War, but it already in the mid-1740s served to pose a question mark against his continued acceptance of the views of other opponents of the government. Willing to ally with the Tories for tactical reasons, Pitt nevertheless saw himself as a Whig partisan. He might seek a reconstitution of

[28] John to Richard Tucker, 10 January 1744, Bod. MS Don. c. 106 f. 128; R. Glover, *Memoirs by a Celebrated Literary and Political Character from . . . 1742 to . . . 1757* (1814) pp. 17–20; P. Lawson, *George Grenville* (Oxford, 1984) pp. 18–22.

the ministry to create a 'Broad Bottom' that would encompass the Tories, but he was unenthusiastic about their views on the army and on foreign policy, and this was noted, Tucker writing on 12 January 1744, 'Pitt and Lyttelton were as good as their words to vote with the minority but people are still in great doubt about the extraordinary declarations they made at the Fountain.'[29] In the debates later in the month on the Hanoverians Pitt attacked their employment 'as a job to continue the ministry in power and put money into the pockets of . . . [sic]', but did not condemn the idea of having an army on the Continent, as other opposition speakers did. He was clearly seeking to appeal to those supporters of the ministry who were opposed to Carteret.[30] Pitt argued that the purpose of keeping British troops on the Continent had altered, that in place of a 'war of acquisition' the government was now seeking peace.[31] This shift of emphasis was to be vindicated when the French demonstrated the seriousness of the situation by sending their Brest fleet into the Channel in order to cover a planned invasion from Dunkirk on behalf of the Pretender, 'James III'. When on 15 February Parliament was informed by a royal message of this danger, Pitt protested his loyalty. Nine days later he 'spoke handsomely' in support of a government motion promising parliamentary funds for an increase in the army and the navy in the face of possible invasion.[32]

Though increasingly distancing himself both from the Tories and from the Grenvilles, whose criticism of the ministry continued to be consistently harsh, Pitt had not

[29] John to Richard Tucker, 12 January 1744, Bod. MS Don. c. 106 f. 131.
[30] John to Richard Tucker, 19, 23 January 1744, Bod. MS Don. c. 106 f. 142, 155; Cobbett XIII, 469–71, 473; Owen, Pelhams p. 207.
[31] Newdigate notes, 23 January 1744, Warwick CR 136 B2532.
[32] Black, Culloden and the '45 (Stroud, 1990) pp. 56–7; John to Pryse Campbell, 25 February 1744, Cawdor, Box 138; Lord Hartington to Duke of Devonshire, 16 February 1744, HP Chatsworth; Cobbett, XIII, 647–8, 666–7.

become a simple supporter of governmental policy. In the eyes of pro-government MPs he remained a strident critic. Campbell, observing a debate on 9 February about a disputed election return, reported 'Pitt without any provocation used Mr Pelham with the utmost brutality, it seems to me to be the measure of the opposition to bear down the friends of the Government by rage, fury, noise and insolence.' A week later he referred to 'his usual insulting and menacing stile'. Hartington wrote of Pitt's support on 15 February for an inquiry into naval mismanagement, 'Pitt was very hot.'[33] The difficulty of his position and the apparent ambiguity of his attitude was revealed when on 1 March during a debate on a government motion for the temporary suspension of habeas corpus in order to proceed against Jacobites in Britain Pitt and Lyttelton left before the division. While prepared to ally with the Tories, Pitt did not wish to associate himself with Jacobite positions. Pitt's vigour and intensity in these years probably owed much to the central role that politics played in his life. He was an intensely political person, with little other emotional life before his marriage in 1754.

Despite the strains in opposition ranks, the ministry was still bitterly divided and it had not been united by the Jacobite threat. Bad weather and British naval movements had thwarted French plans in February 1744 and the political agenda was soon dominated again by the struggle between Carteret and the Pelhams. In order to isolate Carteret and to put pressure on George to dismiss him, the Pelhams agreed with Chesterfield in the autumn of 1744 to form a 'broad bottom' ministry. Carteret was forced to resign on 24 November and many of the former opposition Whigs who had gained office in 1742 were dismissed, to make way for a

[33] John to Pryse Campbell, 9, 16 February 1744, Cawdor, Box 138; Hartington to Devonshire, 16 February 1744, HP Chatsworth; John to Richard Tucker, 26 January 1744, Bod. MS Don. c. 106 f. 160.

group of their former colleagues – Chesterfield, Dodington, George Grenville, Lyttelton, the Duke of Bedford and the Earl of Sandwich – and a number of Tories. Pitt was the sole leading opposition Whig who did not gain office, as George refused to grant him the post of Secretary at War that he sought. However, Pitt accepted the Pelhams' assurance that they would do their best to persuade the King to change his mind. Horace Walpole, claiming that Pitt wished 'to preserve his character and authority in the parliament', suggested that he pressed for the post because he knew he would not be appointed. This is not impossible, though it is difficult to see how Pitt could have hoped to benefit from the good opinion of those excluded from the new settlement: Carteret's supporters and the large number of Tories who rejected compromise. It is more probable that Pitt misjudged his position and was a victim of George II's firmness and resentment of Pitt's attacks on the use of Hanoverian troops. By the death of Sarah, Duchess of Marlborough, a crusty critic of Old Corps corruption, on 14 October 1744 Pitt had inherited £10,000 'upon account of his merit in the noble defence he had made for the support of the laws of England, and to prevent the ruin of his country', and this may have reduced the pressure on him to accept whatever he was offered, but Pitt was also both seriously ill of the gout and not close to the aristocrats who laid the basis for the new ministry. However satisfied he might have been with the exclusion of Carteret (now Earl Granville), Pitt was still a marginal political figure and the reconstitution of the ministry left him in an anomalous position,

Pitt has nothing. Says in his infirm state of health he has more money than he wants so did not desire a lucrative employment without business. Should have liked to be Secretary at War, but could not desire or expect His Majesty to part with so old and useful a servant as Sir William Yonge [who held the post], but he hoped to behave so as to deserve His Majesty's favour when an opportunity should offer, these are fine words but I fear they will butter no parsnips.[34]

Pitt was thirty-six. Walpole had been thirty-one when he became Secretary at War in 1708, William Pulteney thirty (1714), Henry Pelham twenty-nine (1724). When Parliament met in January 1745 Pitt was not 'well enough to attend the House', being met by Campbell on the 19th 'airing in his chariot wrapt up in a cloak'.[35] Politically, his presence or absence was of little consequence. On 23 January Pitt appeared in the Commons, speaking in support of Pelham's proposal to increase the British force in the Austrian Netherlands. Campbell recorded,

Pitt rose and though he looked thin and weak and doubtless is so, yet his voice was strong and he indeed spoke as finely in support of the Question as ever he did in Opposition, he expressed his good opinion and confidence in Mr Pelham, in as high and strong terms as was possible, and said if ever any Minister deserved well of his Country he certainly did in the highest degree, meaning for delivering it from Lord Granville who he lashed in a masterly way with the general applause of the House, and without the abusive language that used to be thrown out against Ministers contrary to all decency and good manners. He exhorted strongly to unanimity in this question, and insinuated for one strong reason that it would effectually secure us against the return of Lord Granville. He expressed a warm zeal for the King who he always mentioned in a becoming manner. His speech was a very great and fine performance.

Distancing himself from the Tory position, Pitt rejected Newdigate's claim that the new ministry was pursuing Carteret's policies, and therefore that the new ministers had

---

[34] John to Pryse Campbell, 18, 22 (quote) December 1744, Cawdor, Box 138.
[35] John to Richard Tucker, 18 January 1745, Bod. MS Don. c. 107 f. 75; John to Pryse Campbell, 19 January 1745, Cawdor, Box 138.

betrayed their principles, and offered both a reasoned contrast of the respective foreign policies and a characteristic hyperbole, 'I believe a dawn of salvation has broken forth: I shall follow it as far as it will lead me.' Such dramatic grandiloquence is more often cited than, for example, the argument in the same speech that Dutch policy was becoming more favourable, but to recall the one without the other is inappropriate. Pitt's 'fulminating eloquence', his platitudinous rhetoric, was made credible by his knowledge, the fact that he had something more to offer the house than the repetition of stale formulae. Sir Henry Liddell MP, who heard the speech on the 23rd and thought that Pitt carried his criticism of Carteret as far as was possible, reported that he spoke for forty-five minutes. Fulmination alone could not fill such periods. A French memorandum of the previous February stated that Pitt lacked the sang-froid of a party head but that 'son éloquence est mâle et rapide. Il parle avec feu et precision, et met surtout une grande force dans ses raisons'.[36]

Only one MP voted against the motion on the 23rd. On 18 February Pitt again supported the ministry on a contentious motion that conflicted with what had been consistently held opposition views. In a debate in the Committee of Supply over the proposal to increase Maria Theresa's subsidy, in order, as was generally understood, to enable her to take over the financing of the Hanoverians from the British Treasury, the Tories and four New Whigs (as those opposition Whigs who joined the ministry in 1742 were thereafter called) attacked the ministry for inconsistency. Pitt did not criticise the government on a number of controversial measures that arose between 22 February and 21 March, including a

---

[36] John to Pryse Campbell, 24 January 1745, Cawdor, Box 138; Liddell to Henry Ellison, 24 January 1745, Gateshead, Public Library, Ellison MS A31 no. 39; AE Mémoires et Documents Ang. 8 f. 267; Cobbett, XIII, 1054–6.

subsidy for Augustus III of Saxony-Poland and a vote of credit for extraordinary expenses. It was not surprising that Pelham was prepared to discuss matters with Pitt.[37] However, his restraint did not bring Pitt office. Instead, George II was continuing to listen to Granville, thus making the Pelham ministry appear precarious, while its position was further placed under strain by the opposition of most of the Tories to 'broad bottom'.

The political situation was made more volatile by the landing of Charles Edward Stuart (Bonnie Prince Charlie), the eldest son of the Jacobite claimant of the throne, on the west coast of Scotland on 25 July 1745, his successful march to Edinburgh and his defeat of Sir John Cope at nearby Prestonpans on 21 September. Granville's supporters in the ministry, especially the Marquess of Tweeddale, the Secretary of State for Scotland, had underrated the danger and in the eyes of the Pelhams it appeared both necessary and possible to force George to break with Granville, who the King wanted to restore to office. Pitt also saw the new session as an opportunity to put pressure on George, in his case to force his way into office. On 17 October, when the new session of Parliament opened, Pitt spoke against the attempt by Sir Francis Dashwood, an opposition Whig, to move an amendment to the Address pressing for shorter parliaments and free elections, arguing that the moment was not appropriate. Six days later, however, he moved a motion that was designed to embarrass the ministry, an address to George to recall all British troops still remaining in the Austrian Netherlands.[38] All the infantry had, in fact, already been

---

[37] Cobbett, XIII, 1175–8; Andrew Stone, Under-Secretary, to Newcastle, 16 February 1745, BL Add. 32704 f. 72.

[38] Notes of Sir Dudley Ryder, Attorney General, 23 October, Hartington to Devonshire, 24 October 1745, HP; John to Richard Tucker, 24 October 1745, Bod. MS Don. c. 107 f. 151, Cobbett, XIII, 1348–51.

recalled to confront the likely Jacobite invasion of England, and cavalry were difficult to transport, but Pitt's motion offered an opportunity to press the ministers on a sensitive subject and to demonstrate the problems he could create. Pelham defeated the motion by a majority of only eight (148 to 136), an extremely low figure by the standards of an age when the absence of marked party discipline lent an air of instability to ministries that could not command substantial majorities.

Pitt's tactics worked up to a point. The Pelhams decided to win Pitt over and pressed George II on the need for this. On 25 October 1745 Pelham saw Pitt in order to hear his conditions. They were both populist and could be presented as issues of principle. Pitt demanded a Place Bill to exclude from the Commons junior officers, who were assumed to be easily influenced or intimidated, a measure that would have kept him from Parliament in 1735–6; the removal from office of Granville's remaining followers; and a redirection of British policy, restricting assistance to the Dutch to 10,000 troops and concentrating on a naval war with the Bourbons.[39] The first was acceptable to the Pelhams; the second posed serious problems, as George could not be expected to accept dictation about the membership of his household; the third was impossible if Britain's alliances were to be maintained. The issues that arose in the interview were to recur again in Pitt's career and played a central role in his departure from office in 1761. Then he was unwilling to accept the implications of George III's favour for the Earl of Bute, though as Bute was already a Secretary of State Pitt could not be accused of seeking to interfere in the royal household, while his stand over foreign policy in 1761, although

[39] Newcastle to Chesterfield, 20 November 1745, BL Add. 32705 ff. 319–20.

designed to ensure action against Spain, was set within the context of a firm conviction of the importance of maintaining Britain's Prussian alliance.

Pitt was at the time, and has subsequently been, accused of being egocentric, of an unwillingness and inability to restrain his demands and his language, that reflected a lack of understanding and acceptance of political conventions. The disquiet among former allies of Pitt in opposition who were now in office was expressed by Chesterfield, who wrote to Gower,

I am very much surprised at Pitt's not informing you beforehand of his motion, which in my opinion was an improper one, for though I am as much for a peace as any man in England, and as much against sending back our troops to Flanders; yet I see no necessity of declaring it already both to the Dutch, and to the French.

This criticism, however, should not be pushed too far. If in 1745 Pitt wanted George II to part with certain favourites and adopt particular policies, the same was true of the Pelhams. In 1717–20 Walpole had opposed the Whig Stanhope–Sunderland ministry in order to demonstrate his indispensability. In the winter of 1745–6 Pitt sought entry into the ministry, not its overthrow. His motives were no longer as opaque as they had been in 1742, when, to a certain extent, he had hidden behind somewhat meaningless statements about being true to his principles and connections without making it clear what he really wanted. In 1745 Pitt clearly wanted office. On 28 October 1745 he seconded Hume Campbell's motion for a Select Committee to inquire into the causes of the rebellion, but this was a measure aimed against Granville's Scottish allies, not the Pelhams, and it had been discussed with Pelham in advance. The Bishop of Llandaff certainly did not see the motion as excessively contentious, 'the debate was a good one: all agreed an inquiry into the causes and progress of the rebellion would in its time be very proper but not now. This was all the difference of opinion'.[40] The motion was defeated 194 to 112.

George II argued that the defeat of opposition motions revealed that Pitt's support was unnecessary, but the Pelhams were unconvinced and wished to strengthen their hand against Granville. Negotiations between Pitt and the ministry continued. On 16 November, the day that the keys of surrendered Carlisle were presented to Bonnie Prince Charlie, Pitt and Cobham met Hardwicke, Harrington, Bedford, Gower and the Pelhams at a meeting at Gower's. Pitt was now taking part in conferences over the reconstruction of the government, as he had not done in 1744. His prominent role in the Commons was paying dividends, as was the uncertain position of the Pelhams. Newcastle's account of the conference on the 16th revealed that foreign policy was at the heart of continuing differences,

Everything passed very civilly, but Lord Cobham and Mr Pitt were strongly of opinion, against the other six. That we ought to declare to the Dutch that we could not assist them with more than 12,000 men . . . We insisted that such an abrupt declaration would force them into a separate peace with France, which we thought ought to be prevented if possible, and that therefore we should acquaint the Dutch that we would assist them as far as was consistent with our present circumstances . . . They insisted that they could not bring their friends to place that confidence, which they had done last year . . . I am afraid this difference will prevent our coming to such an agreement with Mr Pitt, as seems absolutely necessary in our present circumstances.

Pitt therefore resolved to see what the impact of a more hostile attitude in the Commons would be. On 21 November

---

[40] PRO 30/29/1/11 ff. 294–5; Bishop of Llandaff to John or Pryse Campbell, 29 October 1745, Cawdor, Box 138; Farmington, HW 71 f. 112; G. H. Rose (ed.), *A Selection from the Papers of the Earls of Marchmont* (3 vols., 1851), I, 143–7.

1745 'in consequence of his favourite notion of a maritime war', he proposed augmenting the navy and criticised Pelham, but, in a thin house, lost the division by 81 to 36. Pelham's argument that the middle of a rebellion was not the best moment to discuss the future of the navy won support. It was, anyway, not possible to put more ships to sea.[41] Although, despite Horace Walpole's opinion, Pitt had more than simply 'his words, and his haughtiness, and his Lytteltons, and his Grenvilles' to support him, he was in a difficult position if the ministry stayed firm. Henry Fox, still a Lord of the Treasury, did not see how Pitt's pride would allow him to manoeuvre himself into a better situation,

Pitt seems to have made it hardly reputable for Pelham to act with him on any terms, at the same time that it is I think become as little possible for him *sans de dedire* (which so great a man won't to be sure submit to) to concur in any other measures than such as are thought impracticable and improper by everybody but 5 or 6 family friends of his. And to think that all the Royal Family, all the Cabinet Council, except Cobham only, and both Houses of Parliament should submit is surely beyond his pride to imagine.

Another MP, Charles Wyndham, reflected,

As to the motion in the house though a very strange one I am not at all surprised at anything that comes from the mover, the only reflection I make upon it is that since he is so solicitious about increasing the forces by sea, I imagine him not likely to have any immediate connection with the forces by land.

On 19 December 1745 Pitt moved onto another popular topic, opposition to the use of foreign troops, but, as with the navy on 21 November, his timing was poor. Bonnie Prince Charlie had only turned back from Derby on 6 December and the Hessians, whose use Pitt castigated, were widely seen as

---

[41] Newcastle to Devonshire, 21 November 1745, HP Chatsworth; Newcastle to Chesterfield, 20 November 1745, BL Add. 32705 ff. 322–9.

necessary for planned operations against the Jacobites. On 10 December Pitt had sought to cast doubt on ministerial assurances that the British cavalry had been recalled from the Austrian Netherlands, 'a most unreasonable and I think indecent debate', according to Pelham, in which Pitt was defeated 138 to 44 with the Tories acting very coldly towards him.[42] On the 19th the margin was even larger, 190 to 44, and Pitt's conduct appeared extraordinary, for the use of the Hessians was supported in the Cabinet by the members whose views were closest to him, Cobham, Bedford and Gower. Pitt was increasingly split from the New Allies, those who had joined the Pelhams in 1744. His abuse on the 19th of the City of London, whose representatives supported the ministry over the issue, was singular for an opposition politician. Pitt's criticism of the citizens as 'shopkeepers' who cared more for money than the constitution was regarded as abusive. The views of London were commonly presented as indicative of the voice of the incorruptible part of the nation, as well as being important in their own right, although during the '45 Common Council was muzzled for fear that it would attack the ministry. Chesterfield, now Lord Lieutenant of Ireland, wrote to Gower on 30 December 1745,

I cannot decypher Pitt's behaviour; His open opposition, not only to the bent of the house, but also to that of the whole nation; his abuse of the City, his personal reflections upon Pelham, and all this at the head of thirty or forty people only, astonishes me. And I do not know what to ascribe it to, unless to an unreasonable peevishness, that he had not his place, before the time that he pretended to desire it; or to an intention of setting himself at the head of a party, however small, independent of us . . . if he goes on

[42] Lord Dover (ed.), *Letters of Horace Walpole to Sir Horace Mann* (3 vols., 1833) II, 161; Henry to Stephen Fox, 26 November 1745, BL Add. 51417 f. 175; Wyndham to Hanbury Williams, 24 November 1745, Farmington, HW 68; Pelham to Hartington, 10 December, Welbore Ellis MP to Hartington, 12 December 1745, HP Chatsworth.

at this rate, and divides at the head of thirtys and fortys, he will soon fight his sword down to a dagger.[43]

Pitt did not wish to lead a small, independent and impotent party, but rather to negotiate himself into office. This was in accordance with the political practice of the age, of politicians obstructing business in order to elicit offers from the ministry rather than to change the government. This characterised opposition Whig politicians such as Pitt in 1745–6, and Robert Walpole in 1717–20 when in opposition during the Whig Split, and distinguished them from Tories. This difference had been the root cause of the division in opposition ranks in 1742. The events of December 1745 made Pitt's position weaker, for not only had the ministry won substantial majorities in Parliament, but Charles Edward had retreated back to Scotland, Carlisle falling to the Duke of Cumberland on 30 December. As the Pelhams increasingly handled the rebellion fairly efficiently, Pitt's opposition became more obviously ineffective.

However, George II's continued favour for Granville made the Pelhams keen to maximise their support. Pitt's position had deteriorated since November: now in early January 1746 he made the initial approach and abandoned the conditions he had earlier advanced. Instead, he sought the Secretaryship at War and more minor appointments for two more of Cobham's supporters. These more limited requirements seemed acceptable to the Pelhams and they agreed to propose them to the King. Pitt's new attitude led to his adopting a less aggressive role in the Commons. When Parliament reassembled on 14 January 1746 he opposed the amendment to the Address moved by Hume Campbell and seconded by the Tory Watkin Williams Wynn, and told the Commons 'he was not

[43] Ilchester, Fox I, 121; Chesterfield to Gower, 30 December 1745, PRO 30/29/1/11 ff. 297–301; A. W. Massie, 'Great Britain and the Defence of the Low Countries, 1744–1748' (unpublished D.Phil. Oxford, 1988).

for abandoning our allys', a statement that left unclear the terms on which he would support help to them. On the 17th Pitt was absent when the Tory Lord Cornbury moved a motion about Anglo-Dutch relations.[44] Pitt's motives can be glanced at in the explanation Edward Southwell, MP for Bristol, offered for his vote against Hume Campbell's motion. Southwell had acted as an opposition Whig until 1744. He argued that in the winter of 1745–6 it was not in Britain's interest to drive her Dutch ally into neutrality or a separate treaty with France, and claimed more generally,

In time of peace every check upon ministers is parliamentary and constitutional. In time of war and public danger some degree of credit and confidence must be allowed them, or else we must become a prey to foreign enemies, by our delays and our distrusts and our preventing ministers from acting with any vigour.[45]

The overwhelming majority for the ministry on the division indicated the extent to which the opposition had been weakened by the war. A failure to defeat Spain and pro-Hanoverian policies had successively provided attractive themes for their attacks, but by late 1745 the situation had altered and become more immediately one of national interests, survival and cohesion. Pitt moved with this shift and characteristically sought to profit from it, yet because his terms were high he had felt obliged in late 1745 to be difficult. That had not brought him success, in terms of either office or government policy changes, and thus in January 1746 he became more conciliatory.

Pitt's willingness to break with his former allies and his new-found moderation encouraged the Pelhams to press

[44] John Maule MP to Andrew Fletcher, 14 January 1746, Edinburgh, National Library of Scotland (hereafter NLS), MS 16630 f. 14.
[45] Southwell to John Brickdale, 14 January 1746, Bristol, Public Library, Southwell papers vol. 9.

George II to appoint him as Secretary at War. Newcastle argued that the Pelhams could not continue in office without Pitt and his allies. The King refused, treating the demand as an insult. He could not abide Pitt, not only because of his bitter attack on the use of Hanoverian troops, but also due to his personal attack on George's conduct at Dettingen. Pitt offered to desist, 'saying he would not go into the closet against the King's will', a statement that probably did not represent his final view on the matter, but rather a response to an impasse that might lead to his being offered another post. However, George's willingness to ignore the views of his ministers and his preference for the advice of Bath and Granville led the bulk of the ministry to resign on 10 and 11 February 1746, a dramatic means of putting pressure on the King. Fox had not thought they could resign over Pitt 'this single and indefensible and surely not national point'. Nevertheless, Earl Stanhope was not alone in seeing Pitt's ambition as the cause of the political crisis, 'the immediate occasion of all this political hurly burly was the peremptory negative, which our cousin William Pitt's demand of the Secretaryship at War met with in the Closet'. A more balanced account was offered the same day, 11 February, by politicians closer to the centre of government. Lord Chancellor Hardwicke, who was getting ready to resign the following day, on the conclusion of the legal term, wrote to his son Joseph that the resignations did not proceed 'as some will perhaps tell you, from the King's having refused to make a certain gentleman Secretary at War. That is a trifle in comparison of other things and was quite over and the King's pleasure entirely submitted to.' Newcastle stated that the claim that the resignations proceeded from a determination to force George II to take Pitt in as Secretary at War was inaccurate and spread by the Pelhams' enemies, presumably in order to present them as disloyal and aggressive. Instead, he saw it as arising from a determination not to continue in office if they lacked royal support. Tucker, who had accepted office in 1744, claimed,

The generality of mankind who see only the outside of things ascribe all this to the refusal of Mr Pitt to be Secretary at War but that point has been given up these 10 days. The true source is the countenance given to Granville and Bath, who have generally opposed whatever has been proposed by the other party and obstructed all their measures but the affair which immediately concluded towards this resolution was a proposition in Council to carry on the war with the utmost vigour on the Continent even though the Dutch should not declare war, which was opposed with one vote by all the Pelhamites.[46]

The resignations were of short duration. Granville and Bath failed to form a new administration, and within forty-eight hours they had abandoned the attempt, forcing George II to turn again to his former ministers. Granville and Bath had not appreciated how many politicians would resign with the Pelhams and found themselves unable to recruit a sufficient number of supporters, a situation that was exacerbated by the unpropitious circumstances. The midst of a session was not the time for ministers unsure of their majority to form a new government and the middle of a war, when a substantial loan was being negotiated, was not the occasion to dispense with Henry Pelham's goodwill in the City. In turning to the Pelhams again, George had to give posts to Cobham's supporters. The memorandum drawn up by the Pelhams on 13 February that summarised their expectations of the King included, 'That he will be graciously pleased to perfect the

---

[46] Henry to Stephen Fox, 6 February 1746, BL Add. 51417 f. 209; Earl Stanhope to George Stanhope, 11 February 1746, Maidstone, Kent Archive Office, U1590 C708/1; P. Yorke, *Life and Correspondence of Philip Yorke, Earl of Hardwicke* (3 vols., Cambridge, 1913) I, 499; Newcastle to Duke of Richmond, 10 February 1746, Goodwood, MS 104 f. 297; John to Richard Tucker, 11 February 1746, Bod. MS Don. c. 107 ff. 226–7.

scheme lately humbly proposed to him for bringing Mr Pitt into some honourable employment.'[47] As George was firmly opposed to his being Secretary-at-War, Pitt on 22 February 1746 was appointed joint Vice-Treasurer of Ireland, a lucrative sinecure that did not oblige him to go to Ireland and that did not require contact with the King.

Taken into office, Pitt found himself expected not only to dine with former opponents, but also to defend government policy. George had not been completely defeated, as had seemed the case in mid-February. The Pelhams felt it necessary to seek to improve relations with him, and to that end agreed to re-employ the Hanoverian troops. In comparison, the consistency of Pitt's conduct was of no consequence. On 11 April 1746 the Commons, sitting as a Committee of Supply, agreed to pay £300,000 towards the support of 18,000 Hanoverians who were to serve in the Austrian Netherlands. Pitt spoke in favour of the motion and was condemned for inconsistency by the opposers, who drew attention to his previous hostility to paying for the Hanoverians. The Tory Edward Harley, Third Earl of Oxford, noted, 'Mr Pitt who had been so warm against the Hanoverian troops before spoke as warm now for this measure.' It was generally felt that Pitt got the worse of the exchange, but the ministry's majority was substantial: 255 to 122. On the 14th Pitt spoke again and more vigorously, when the report of the Committee of Supply was approved by 199 to 83. He made his new allegiance clear, to the great pleasure of Newcastle. One MP recorded, 'Pitt thrashed about him, abused the opposition, and Lord Granville's party, and said he was glad to be separated from a set of men that were the refuse of all political connections.' The opposition's speeches 'were mostly levelled at their late consort Mr Pitt. Pitt spoke

[47] BL Add. 35870 f. 117; Woolfe to Yorke, 13 February 1746, Hawarden D/E/875.

exceeding well and treated them with the utmost contempt; called them a stubborn blind faction, and compared them to flies who buzzed and tickled, but which with the waft of a hand were dispersed.' It is no surprise that some people hated Pitt after listening to abuse of this kind, and little wonder that a man so sensitive as to his reputation should have spent so much of his political career countering charges of hypocrisy and self-interest. When accused by Horatio Walpole in the Commons in January 1741 of 'excursions of fancy and flights of oratory', Pitt had replied that 'the heat that offended them is the ardour of conviction and that zeal for the service of my country, which neither hope nor fear shall influence me to suppress'.[48] Five years later the hope of preferment appeared more apparent. The basic themes of Pitt's career in later and more famous years were already present in the 1740s, and study of the earlier period throws light on the complex mixture of high-minded sentiment and more mundane political calculation that characterised his later years and so confused and exasperated contemporaries.

PAYMASTER GENERAL AND GOVERNMENT SPOKESMAN, 1746–1754

Pitt's new position brought promotion in the government and obloquy from opposition circles. The death on 23 April 1746 of Thomas Winnington, the Paymaster General, who foolishly departed from his maxim of not trusting doctors, created an important vacancy. Pelham suggested that Sir William Yonge, the sickly Secretary at War, take the post and thus make way for Pitt, but George declared that 'that fellow

---

[48] Maule to Fletcher, 16 April 1746, NLS MS 16630 f. 116; Woolfe to Yorke, 12 April, 1 May 1746, Hawarden D/E/875; Newcastle to Cumberland, 17 April 1746, BL Add. 32707 ff. 67–8; Harley, parliamentary diary, Cambridge University Library, Add. MS 6851 II f. 107; Cobbett XII, 115–16; Ilchester, Fox I, 134–5.

should never come into his closet',[49] and as a result Pitt became Paymaster on 6 May and a Privy Councillor on 28 May, while Yonge was given Pitt's sinecure and Henry Fox became Secretary at War. Pitt would therefore handle army finances while Fox dealt with George and his second son the Duke of Cumberland, the Captain General, on military matters. Recognising that the unpalatable fact of Pitt's promotion had to be presented as an unfortunate necessity, Pelham on 1 May wrote to Henry Fox's elder brother Stephen,

it is determined, since the King will not hear of Pitt's being Secretary at War, that he shall be Paymaster. I don't doubt but you will be surprised that Mr Pitt should be thought on for so high and lucrative an employment; but he must be had and kept. This will do it, and as it will give an opportunity to dispose of many other considerable employments all in favour of old friends, I hope they will see it is a purchase for their sakes . . . this expedient will establish the old Corps, for as long time as Court favours are to be depended on.[50]

Winnington's death, at the age of fifty, also helped Pitt because it removed one of the experienced parliamentarians on the government side. In Walpole's last session in the Commons, Pelham, Winnington and Yonge had been his principal lieutenants. All born in the mid-1690s, the last of them, the sickly Yonge died in 1755. By the standards of their generation of ministerial Whigs, Pitt was a maverick, a politician who had made his name by attacking the Old Corps and the Hanoverian dynasty at a time when they were faced by domestic and foreign enemies. The passing of this generation created opportunities for Pitt and his contempor-

---

[49] Marchmont I, 176.
[50] Earl of Ilchester (ed.), Letters to Henry Fox . . . With a Few Addressed to his Brother Stephen (Roxburghe Club, 1915) pp. 12–13.

aries, principally Fox and William Murray, but there was to be no clear break between political generations when Pelham died in 1754. Older men survived, some, such as Granville (1690–1763), Dodington (c.1691–1762) and Chesterfield (1694–1773), with limited influence, but there were others, Newcastle (1693–1768) and, in particular, George II (1683–1760), who were still powerful and found it difficult to change their perception of Pitt.

If Pitt's new position in the ministry was uneasy, his acceptance of office led to a torrent of abuse from opposition writers. Given the eighteenth-century structure of politics, any man or group pushing his or their way into office always faced the same problem, that of espousing the policies he or they had formerly denounced. Attacks on turncoats were common. A caricature, depicting Sarah, Duchess of Marlborough's ghost, drew attention to the substantial bequest Pitt had received for his independence, as did a number of ballads, including the 'Unembarrassed Countenance' by Sir Charles Hanbury Williams, a government MP with strong satirical inclinations. This described the rise of an MP 'who could talk and could prate', who 'bellowed and roared at the troops of Hanover', until 'by flaming so loudly he got him a name', won Sarah Marlborough's favour and then turned to Pelham.[51] Pitt was now clearly associated with the ministry, though he was not one of its leading members. The critical Egmont wrote subsequently of Pitt in this period,

From this time forward subservient to the two brothers to whom solely you owed your advancement . . . how you acted or rather sat supremely contented without acting at all, but concurring in every measure, and some very far from popular.[52]

---

[51] National Journal 29 May 1746; see also A Duchess's Ghost to Orator Hanover Pitt (1746) and Short Verses in Imitation of Long Verses in an Epistle to William Pitt (1746).
[52] Egmont, BL Add. 47012 B f. 177.

The differing explanations that contemporaries offered for the Pelhams' resignations on 11 February 1746 were symptomatic of the contrasting assessments of Pitt's political importance. To insiders his position had not been the crucial issue, though it had been an important irritant in relations between George and the Pelhams. To those less familiar with the crisis, including many parliamentarians and much of the political nation, Pitt's position had been the central problem. The importance that most contemporaries attached to his fate helped to ensure that his acceptance of office was both controversial and apparently one of the leading consequences of the crisis in February 1746. This contrast between 'insider' and other views of Pitt was to be a major feature of his career. His importance in high political circles did not measure up to the general view held of it and this helped to place Pitt in a difficult position, as it was easy to assume that he had more freedom, and was therefore better placed to avoid measures that might lead to charges of inconsistency, than was in fact the case.

As Paymaster General, Pitt was responsible for army pay. Following Pelham's example, Pitt did not make the customary private profit from the post, not using the balances for his own benefit, as Henry Fox was to do, nor taking the usual commission on subsidies paid to foreign rulers. Pitt's action in this respect was a major factor in the revival of a reputation for disinterested patriotism that had been shattered when he joined the government. In another respect his task as Paymaster directly contradicted his stand against foreign troops earlier in the decade, for he now found himself responsible for the payment of the forces in the Austrian Netherlands, including items such as winter forage for the Hessians in November 1746 and an account for extraordinary expenses for the Hanoverians for the 1746 campaign that even Cumberland found questionable.[53] In addition, Pitt was now playing a role in a ministry that was not only concentrating on Continental engagements, rather than the conquest of Bourbon colonies, but was also failing to defend the Low Countries successfully. In April 1746 Pitt had pressed the case for a strong navy, declaring in the Committee of Supply on the 11th 'I hope I shall never so far differ from myself, as not to say that our naval power is what we must expect peace with France from', adding in the Commons three days later that he had 'always thought it the policy of this nation to be as strong at sea as possible . . . I wish the navy was greater.'[54] In the summer of 1747 Pitt visited Portsmouth, the leading base of the Royal Navy, and toured the dockyard and the ships.

And yet the ministry did not pursue the plan of colonial conquest that its naval superiority appeared to make possible. Louisbourg, on Cape Breton Island, the major maritime base in French Canada, was seized in 1745, in large part due to the efforts of Britain's New England colonists, but plans to follow this up by an attack up the St Lawrence to seize Quebec led nowhere. In part this reflected the degree to which clear naval superiority was not achieved until the two victories off Cape Finisterre in May and October 1747. Without such successes, it was dangerous for a state that was vulnerable to invasion, as the anxious response to threatened French attacks in February 1744, December 1745–January 1746 and October 1747 demonstrated, to run the risk of losing naval superiority in home waters. In large part, however, the military position in the Low Countries appeared too dire to permit the dispatch of large forces elsewhere. In 1745 the possible invasion base of

---

[53] Thomas Orby Hunter, Deputy Paymaster of the Forces in Flanders, to Pelham, 11, 22 November 1746, 28 February 1747, Beinecke, Osborn Shelves, Pelham Box; *Correspondence of William Pitt, Earl of Chatham* (hereafter *Chatham Corresp.*) (4 vols., 1838–40) I, 5–20; Williams, *Chatham* I, 151–7.

[54] Newdigate papers, Warwick CR 136 B2539/17, 2522/4.

Ostend had fallen to the French, in 1746 Brussels and Antwerp; in 1747 Britain's Dutch ally was invaded and the major Dutch fortress of Bergen-op-Zoom stormed. Cumberland was out-generalled by Marshal Saxe. Nevertheless, the political danger of concentrating on the war in the Low Countries was recognised. Newcastle, who believed that Britain could not afford to abandon the Dutch, also argued that if Canada was not attacked 'all the zeal and warmth for the war will . . . cool, if not vanish quite',[55] an interesting claim that looks forward to the popularity of the campaigns in North America during the Pitt–Newcastle ministry of 1757–61.

In May 1746, after being appointed Paymaster, Pitt expressed his concern about the state of public affairs, and he returned to the theme that October, writing from Bath of 'the gloomy scene which I fear is opening in public affairs for this disgraced country'. In September 1747 Pelham recorded that he had 'had a very long conversation with him, upon the state of public affairs, we seem entirely to agree in opinion, which is a melancholy truth, because we both see our condition so bad, that nothing can be thought of, but to take the lesser evil' of a bad peace.[56] Yet Pitt was to play no important role in the formulation of policy, and only a minor one in ministerial correspondence. Bedford, Chesterfield, Cumberland, Hardwicke, Newcastle and Pelham dominated the discussions over strategy, peace with France and relations with other powers in 1746–8. When Chesterfield's unexpected resignation in February 1748 left a Secretaryship of State vacant, Pitt, along with Bedford, Sandwich, Gower and Fox, was mentioned by political commentators as a candidate. He was

[55] Newcastle to Richmond, 4 December 1746, Goodwood MS 104f. 299; Newcastle to Earl of Sandwich, 23 December 1746, BL Add. 32806 ff. 298–9.
[56] Pitt to Robert Trevor, 17 May 1746, Aylesbury, Buckinghamshire County Record Office, Trevor MSS vol. 58; Pelham to George Lyttelton, 24 September 1747, Sotheby's Catalogue, 12 December 1978, *Catalogue of the Lyttelton Papers of Hagley Hall*.

not, however, seriously considered. The Duke of Bedford, who was younger than Pitt, and, like him, lacked diplomatic experience, obtained the post.[57]

Pitt's major contribution was indirect, the firm ministerial control over the Commons that followed his recruitment by the government. The army estimates were accepted in December 1746 without a division, Philip Yorke MP commenting 'the present minority you know make a very contemptible figure both for speakers and numbers'. In March 1748 Newcastle

had a very long conversation with Mr Pitt. I found him entirely possessed with Mr Walpole's opinions, and with great civility and personal professions to me, plainly charging me with having singly obstructed the making the peace this winter, contrary to the declared opinion of every member of the Cabinet Council and that personal regard to me, had been the single occasion, that no notice had been taken of it, in the House of Commons.[58]

Nevertheless, Pitt's contribution to the ministry's position in the Commons should not be overrated. Pelhamite success in the general election of 1747 was far more important, while Pitt's dependent position was underlined when he was returned on Newcastle's interest at Seaford, Old Sarum no longer being available as Thomas Pitt was in opposition with the Prince of Wales. The Duke's estate of Bishopstone adjoined Seaford, he controlled the local Treasury patronage, and in 1747 canvassed the voters for his candidates and sat next to the returning officer during the poll. Pitt and Newcastle's other candidate each received 49 votes, their opponents 23 and 19. When the defeated candidates

[57] Newcastle to Sandwich, 17 November 1747, 9 February 1748, BL Add. 32810 f. 286, 32811 f. 197.
[58] Philip to Joseph Yorke, 23 December 1746, BL Add. 35363 f. 142; John to Richard Tucker, 6 December 1746, Bod. MS Don. c. 109 f. 43; Newcastle to Duke of Cumberland, 4 March 1748, Windsor Castle, Royal Archives, Cumberland Papers 32/182.

petitioned the House of Commons on 20 November 1747, alleging intervention by Newcastle in the election, Pitt ridiculed the petition, hardly an attractive action on the part of a politician who had made his name by condemning misuse of power, and was upbraided for so doing by Thomas Potter, a dissipated son of the Archbishop of Canterbury and a supporter of the Prince of Wales. Potter stressed the need to defend the freedom of Parliament from dependence on Crown and ministry, a theme Pitt himself was to employ against Newcastle in 1754. In 1747 moreover Pitt joined Pelham and Fox in arguing successfully that Luke Robinson was entitled to sit for Hedon despite having been convicted of electoral bribery in 1743. This speech was not recorded by Williams, and there are no details of what Pitt said, although it was clearly not measured. Alexander Hume Campbell recorded 'Mr Pitt spoke to inflame as usual a bill of pains and penalties', while Joseph Danvers, an independently minded supporter of the ministry, 'called Pitt's speech the Lamentation of Jeremiah'. The Hessian envoy Alt wrote that Pitt had become a royalist and a friend of the ministry as a result of his post.[59]

If Pitt was having to execute policies that he had earlier criticised and was playing little role in the formulation of policy, it might be suggested that he had gained little from joining the ministry beyond experience in defending policies he did not believe in, always useful to a politician, but had instead foolishly broken his links with the opposition at an important moment. George II had been born in 1683; if he was to live as long as his father had done he would die in 1750, and the volatile Frederick, Prince of Wales was unlikely to retain his father's ministers; indeed his move towards

[59] Newcastle to Richmond, 21 November 1747, Goodwood, MS 104 f. 313; Williams, *Chatham* I, 159–62; HMC, *Polwarth* V p. 202; Alt to William of Hesse-Cassel, 5 December 1747, Marburg, Staatsarchiv, Bestand 4, England 245.

opposition played a major role in leading the Pelhams to hold the general election in 1747, a year earlier than was necessary, because they hoped that this would deny the Prince sufficient time in which to organise support. Pitt was obliged by his position in the government to take a public role against the new opposition, speaking on 22 January 1747 in a debate not recorded in Williams' list of his speeches. This arose from the proposal for an inquiry into the naval debt and led to a clear difference between the ministry and Frederick's supporters. On behalf of the government 'William Pitt exposed himself and was chiefly answered by Thomas Pitt who spoke well.' William Pitt could therefore be seen as a minor part of a political system that was in danger of being swept aside, a politician recruited to help in the management of the Commons at a difficult juncture, but one whose influence was limited.[60]

There is a measure of truth in this analysis, but it suffers from adopting too static an assessment of Pitt's views and from exaggerating his potential room for manoeuvre. Pitt understood the degree to which the focus of British efforts in the War of the Austrian Succession had changed. In place of Carteret's desire to redraw boundaries and George's wish to act against Prussia, the ministry was now concentrating on a traditional theme, the defence of the Low Countries. Subsidised foreign troops were clearly designed to protect them and thereby British security, rather than to further secret goals. Policy was no longer as concealed as it had been in 1742–4. Criticism of Britain's commitments appeared pointless by 1746. The Low Countries in French hands was unwelcome to all bar Jacobites. If Britain abandoned her allies, the French might negotiate peace with them, make unacceptable gains and help the Stuart cause. Following

---

[60] HMC, Polwarth V p. 194. The Williams' list is in his Chatham II, 338–51.

Granville's failure to form a ministry in February 1746, the public debate over foreign and military policy became less highly charged, as the traditional non-interventionist agenda seemed less relevant and Pitt's move into government can be related to this shift. By December 1747 he was pressing Newcastle to consider a Prussian alliance in order to improve Britain's continental position, 'to see Europe pacified and France contained within some bound'.[61] The same policy was being advocated by Horatio Walpole, who had advised his elder brother Sir Robert on foreign policy and been a former sparring partner of Pitt's in the Commons.

If Pitt responded to a widespread feeling that Pelhamite policies were acceptable, or at least necessary, he could be criticised for failing to appreciate that a new political agenda was emerging. This was to be dominated by the reversionary question, the intentions of the heir to the throne, until the unexpected death of Frederick on 20 March 1751 suspended it; while in strategic terms the issue of Europe versus America arose, both over military planning in 1746–7 and over the peace of 1748. However, Pitt's relations with Frederick were poor, while in early 1746 there was no indication that the opposition would regroup round the Prince, and in the aftermath of Bonnie Prince Charlie's retreat from England and Granville's failure, the favour of the Pelhams was worth having. The importance of Pitt's poor health is unclear, but it may well have reinforced his sense of the fruitlessness of continued opposition.

Walpole, like Pitt, had benefited from a major political crisis, but in 1720 the entire ministry was discredited by the government's role in the South Sea Bubble and Walpole's financial and parliamentary skills were regarded as crucial to any successful solution to the crisis. In 1746, although

---

[61] Pitt to Newcastle, 17 December 1747, BL Add. 32713 f. 517.

George II's lack of confidence in the ministry, and the Jacobite rebellion constituted a serious crisis, the Pelhams were not discredited, while Pitt's appointment was not seen as a crucial solution, however useful it might be in terms of parliamentary management. In 1721–2 Walpole also benefited from the deaths of the senior ministers who were not close to him, Stanhope and Craggs in 1721, Sunderland in 1722, but Pitt was not to be offered an opportunity to become a leading figure until Pelham's unexpected death in 1754, while Newcastle did not die until 1768.

His years as Paymaster were Pitt's longest period in office, but they have never received much attention, in contrast to his more spectacular bouts of opposition and his years as Secretary of State during the Seven Years War. This is understandable as he played a less significant role in politics as Paymaster and was less the centre of comment and speculation, while his position as defender of government policy makes it difficult to ascertain what his real views were. However, these years repay examination because of their possible influence on Pitt's subsequent career. As Paymaster Pitt was an important spokesman for the Pelhams in the Commons, gaining experience as a defender of ministerial policy, experience that was to be useful to him later. Under the Pelhams, Pitt played an active role in defending the government's foreign policy in the face of opposition criticisms that national interests were being ignored and the Bourbons allowed to defy Britain. The charges that had been brought against Walpole were repeated. In February 1750, twenty years after Walpole had been criticised on the same head, the opposition complained that France, with whom peace had been negotiated by the Treaty of Aix-la-Chapelle of 1748, had failed to fulfil her undertaking to destroy the defences of Dunkirk. Pitt replied that the sole alternative to negotiation was war, that Britain was in no state for conflict, that the motion was dangerous as it would incite popular pressure, and, in reply to Egmont's claim that Pitt had formerly adopted the same position, added,

upon some former occasions I have been hurried by the heat of youth, and the warmth of debate, into expressions which, upon cool recollection, I have deeply regretted . . . Nations, as well as individuals, must sometimes forbear from the rigorous exaction of what is due to them. Prudence may require them to tolerate a delay, or even a refusal of justice, especially when their right can no way suffer by such acquiescence.[62]

The ministry won the division by 242 to 115. The following January the opposition attacked the Anglo-Spanish commercial treaty of October 1750, in which the Spanish claim to a right to search British merchantmen had not been explicitly denied. Pitt defended the treaty arguing that he had been wrong to criticise Walpole in 1739 for failing to secure the same repudiation,

I have considered public affairs more coolly and am convinced that the claim of *no search* respecting British vessels near the coast of Spanish America can never be obtained, unless Spain were so reduced as to consent to any terms her conqueror might think proper to impose.

'Pitt, the Thunderer, drove them finely',[63] recorded Henry Harris, Commissioner of Wine Licences and a friend of Fox. Pitt defended the treaty because of the favourable terms obtained for British trade and because it would serve as a basis for better Anglo-Spanish relations. This again represented a departure from standard opposition views on foreign policy. It had been a commonplace of opposition arguments that good relations with either France or Spain were impossible and that instead they had to be regarded as enemies. In contrast, for many decades, ministers had argued not only

[62] Cobbett, XIV, 694.   [63] Farmington, HW 52f. 161; Cobbett, XIV, 801.

that good relations, however difficult to obtain, were possible, but also that they were essential to prevent the development of a hostile Bourbon pact. Whig ministries had been allied to France in 1716–31 and Spain in 1729–33, had sought to bring an end to the War of the Polish Succession, and thus remove the chance of war with the Bourbons, by negotiations with France in 1734–5, had benefited from the French refusal to join Spain in the War of Jenkins' Ear and had sought to detach Spain from France in the last years of the War of Austrian Succession. These alliances and policies had been presented by opposition politicians as a craven failure to defend national interests supposedly linked to a foolish refusal to accept the degree of Bourbon co-operation, but in 1751 Pitt rejected this legacy of polemical analysis. Sir Robert Walpole's younger son Horace, a writer always happy to put the pen in, commented in January 1751 that Pitt 'declared for a peace on any terms . . . recanted his having seconded the famous question for the no search . . . said it was a mad and foolish motion, and that he was since grown ten years older and wiser'.[64]

A man who enjoyed grudges, Horace Walpole was understandably sarcastic about Pitt's change of heart, though it was unfair to single him out. Other members of the ministry, including Earl Gower, Lord Privy Seal, the Duke of Bedford, Secretary of State for the Southern Department and therefore minister responsible for Anglo-Spanish relations, and the Earl of Sandwich, First Lord of the Admiralty, had all opposed Sir Robert Walpole. Pitt's admission that he had changed his mind was honest and disarming, without being politically damaging, and, by drawing attention to the transience of opposition sentiments, possibly implied that the views of the critics of the recent treaty were only adopted

[64] Walpole, Memoirs . . . George II 1, 4–5.

for the occasion. Unlike some of his later changes of position, Pitt was able in 1750–1 to present different views from those with which he was associated without provoking a serious level of criticism, a consequence of the widespread disenchantment with bold views on foreign policy produced by the experience of recent setbacks.

Pitt's view of Anglo-Spanish relations was also important as he was to be responsible, while Secretary of State for the Southern Department, for trying to prevent Spain from joining France in the Seven Years War and as his unsuccessful demand for an attack on Spain was to be the occasion of his resignation in 1761. A consideration of the changes in his attitude towards Anglo-Spanish relations between 1738 and 1761 suggests that, although it is easy to appreciate why charges of hypocrisy and pressing unreasonable claims were advanced, there was also a measure of flexibility that reflected Pitt's response to domestic and foreign circumstances, and that contrasted with his increasing inflexibility in the 1760s and 1770s. His pressure for war in 1761 will be addressed later; his speech a decade earlier appears an intelligent reaction to the events of the 1740s. In Walpole's last years as minister Pitt may have foolishly underestimated the difficulties of defeating Spain, but he was not alone in that and in 1751, as over Dunkirk the previous year, he did not shirk the unpleasant task of explaining the limits of national power, even if he knew he could rely on a solid parliamentary majority.

Pitt had a harder task in defending the Continental subsidies that Newcastle, since 1748 Secretary of State for the Northern Department, was negotiating in order to lend substance to his Imperial Election Scheme: the plan for the election of Maria Theresa's eldest son Joseph, later the Emperor Joseph II, as King of the Romans, and thus next Emperor, which Newcastle hoped would preserve the

European balance of power from possible aggression by Louis XV and his ally Frederick the Great. The ministry was divided over the wisdom of paying large peacetime subsidies, Pelham urging restraint while Newcastle, in return, threatened resignation. The effect of this division was a self-justifying search for reassurance on Newcastle's part that led him in 1750 to defend his policy to Pitt, sending him copies of the diplomatic correspondence. The unsympathetic Horace Walpole presented Pitt as an enthusiast for Newcastle's schemes, recording of his speech on 17 January 1751 that he 'made a great panegyric on the Duke of Newcastle's German negotiations of this summer'. On 22 February 1751 Pitt defended the subsidy to the Elector of Bavaria as necessary for the preservation of the peace. Andrew Stone, who wrote a report on the debate for his patron Newcastle, thought the defence a good one. In the debate Pitt carried his defence of the policies of the Walpole government so far as to say that if the contentious Excise Bill of 1733 was reintroduced he would support it, because he had 'of late seen so much of the deceit of popular clamours, and of the artful surmises upon which they are generally founded'. Horace Walpole criticised Pitt for praising Newcastle's interventionism in German politics and pro-Hanoverian foreign policy, when he had earlier condemned Carteret for the same policies. Pitt's position on foreign policy in this period was to be subsequently castigated by Egmont,

How thus having thrown off all regard to former character or professions he remained an advocate for that lamentable Peace of Aix la Chapelle. How strenuous an advocate to subsidies to Saxony and to Bavaria in lieu of professed peace, covering and concealing and justifying and concurring in all the votes and addresses and questions proposed in Parliament to open the eyes of the people to the growing outrages of the French in America, concurring to throw dust in the eyes of the people, and to prevent those early animadversions upon these depredations, violences, breach of faith, and even open hostilities committed upon this country from the conclusion of that Peace till the breaking out of the present war [1756].[65]

It was easy during wars to condemn the earlier compromises of peacetime, a political device that Pitt himself employed, but Egmont also exaggerated Pitt's influence and misunderstood his position. It was subsequently alleged in John Almon's laudatory and unreliable *Anecdotes of the Life of William Pitt, Earl of Chatham* (1795) that Pitt had told Newcastle in connection with the Bavarian subsidy treaty that the Duke 'engaged for subsidies without knowing the extent of the sums, and for alliances without knowing the terms'. Pitt certainly wrote to Horatio Walpole (Horace's uncle) praising him for his Commons speech criticising the Saxon subsidy treaty, which, Pitt claimed,

breathes the spirit of a man who loves his country. If your endeavours contribute to the honest end you aim at, namely, to check foreign expenses, and prevent entanglements abroad, under a situation burdened and exhausted at present, and liable to many alarming apprehensions in futurity, you deserve the thanks of this generation, and will have those of the next.[66]

Pitt was not alone within the ministry in his doubts over Newcastle's expensive interventions in Continental politics: Pelham also had serious doubts and sought to limit British commitments, while Fox criticised the Saxon treaty. Pitt's opposition to Newcastle's policy was certainly not a major theme in British politics or his career in the early 1750s. It would not have been advisable to take a prominent role and

[65] Walpole, *Memoirs . . . George II*, I, 5–6, 34; Cobbett, XIV, 963–70; Stone, BL Add. 32724 f. 133; Egmont, BL Add. 47012 B f. 177; R. Browning, 'The Duke of Newcastle and the Imperial Election Plan, 1749–1754', *Journal of British Studies*, 7 (1967), pp. 28–47.
[66] J. Almon, *Anecdotes* (3 vols., 1797) I, 254; *Chatham Corresp.* I, 64.

Pitt did not do so. This suggests a measure of calculation on his part in his outbursts of zealous activity. However, Pitt was really, not just conveniently, ill in January 1752 and that was why he did not attend the debate on the Saxon subsidy treaty.

On other points Pitt displayed independence. On 25 January 1751 he attacked Pelham's attempt to reduce the naval establishment from 10 to 8,000; voting with the opposition, only to lose by 167 to 107. The political context of Pitt's move is obscure. Horace Walpole saw it as a bid for power.

Pitt, who, with his faction, was renewing his connections with the Prince of Wales, as it was afterwards discovered, and impatient to be Secretary of State, which he expected to carry, as he had his other preferments, by storm; and the competition between him and Fox, the principal favourite of the Duke [of Cumberland], breaking out more and more.[67]

The account in the papers of Frederick's adviser, John Perceval, Second Earl of Egmont, of a division in the Cabinet two months earlier suggests that Pitt's motivation was primarily defensive, resisting Cumberland's rising influence with the king, and that he was co-operating with Newcastle to woo the Prince. The Tory MP Edward Bayntum Rolt recorded on 7 April 1751, 'Two negotiations were carrying on with the Prince when he died. One by Dodington on the part of the Tories – the other by Lord Cobham on the part of Pitt etc.' On 6 May he suggested that the approach to Frederick 'by Pitt and the Pelhams' arose from their quarrel with Cumberland.[68] Cumberland, a patron of Fox, was no supporter of Pitt, and Pitt attacked him on 16 May 1751 when

---

[67] Walpole, Memoirs . . . George II i, 8–9.
[68] A. N. Newman (ed.), 'Leicester House Politics, 1750–60, from the papers of John, Second Earl of Egmont', Royal Historical Society, Camden 4th series 7 (1969), Camden Miscellany 23 p. 193; Bristol, University Library, Bayntum Rolt diary.

the Commons was debating the Regency Bill. He suggested that Cumberland was less interested in 'protecting the Crown than' in 'wearing it'.[69] It was characteristic of Pitt that he should make his point in a fashion calculated to give offence. His suspicion of Cumberland helped to keep Pitt loyal to the Pelhams. Pitt's speech on 17 January 1751 in the debate on the Address certainly did not suggest a minister ready to break with Newcastle, while Newcastle instructed his dependants in the Commons not to create difficulties for Pitt over his different views about the best number of seamen. It is striking that there is no reference to Pitt as being motivated by specific evidence of Bourbon actions, although the previous summer he had pressed on Newcastle his concern about French threats to the British colony of Nova Scotia, whose frontier with French Canada was disputed. In addition, in September 1753 when Pitt pressed for 'some savings in the army in Scotland, and Gibraltar, in order to provide for the expense of' a projected subsidy to Russia, he also urged Newcastle 'to adhere to our points with France, as to Dunkirk and the West Indies', arguing that a Russian army able to intimidate France's ally Prussia would help achieve this aim.[70]

The Cabinet was certainly divided in the winter of 1750–1, Newcastle opposed to Bedford and Sandwich. Pitt's role in the ministerial struggle is obscure, as is the significance of his stand over the naval estimates, but it is clear that Pitt's position had become more important, both because the ministry was divided and because there was the prospect of a reconstitution of the government that would possibly involve Frederick. In 1751 Pitt demonstrated his independence by calling, against Pelham's wishes, for a parliamentary inquiry into the conduct of General Anstruther as

---

[69] Walpole, *Memoirs . . . George II* I, 91.
[70] Newcastle to Colonel James Pelham, 30 January 1751, BL Add. 32724 f. 105; Williams, *Chatham* I, 182–3; BL Add. 32995 ff. 29–30.

Governor of Minorca. Anstruther, an MP, had apparently used his sweeping powers to deny justice to those he disliked, but the issue also enabled Pitt to criticise the Secretary at War, Fox, who was fast becoming his leading rival among the ministerial spokesmen in the Commons. Pitt's 'warmth' and anger in the matter laid him open to criticism and 'extremely offended both the King and the Whigs', according to Horace Walpole. Walpole's distrust of Pitt was strengthened by the latter having 'at this time had the chief influence with the Duke of Newcastle', another wielder of power who Horace disliked for his supposed role in his father's fall, and because the Duke possessed the authority of office that Horace both considered him unsuited for, and envied without seeking. Whatever the impact on 'the Whigs', there is little doubt that George II would not have welcomed parliamentary attacks on an officer and Pitt's zeal in the matter was politically inopportune. George asked Fox 'with whom it was that Pitt meant to ingratiate himself? Was it with Lord Egmont?', a clear reference to the King's lack of confidence in him and his suspicion that Pitt was indeed trying to align himself with Frederick. Pitt also clashed with Fox in 1751 over the bill to offer naturalisation to foreign Protestants, and thus improve the economy. Pitt supported that measure, Fox supposedly saying 'He is a better speaker than I am, but thank God! I have more judgment.'[71]

The possibility of a major political realignment that would join Newcastle, Pitt and the reversionary interest around Frederick, prefigured the definite attempt to create a similar alliance between Newcastle, Pitt and George III as Prince of Wales in the late 1750s. In 1751, however, soundings were still tentative. Hopes of a government change were dashed when Frederick died unexpectedly on 20 March 1751, his

[71] Walpole, Memoirs . . . George II 1, 42–3; Williams, Chatham 1, 174.

death a striking reminder of the unpredictability of high politics in a system still dominated by the attitudes and affairs of the ruling dynasty. After a post-mortem, Frederick's death was attributed to a blow from a tennis ball three years earlier. In June 1751 there were more changes, a 'quiet ... revolution at court'. Bedford and Sandwich were replaced by the Earl of Holdernesse and Lord Anson, both more pliable from the Pelhams' point of view. Pitt's brother Thomas had told Egmont on 4 April 1751 that Pitt was 'pushing for' the Secretaryship,[72] but Newcastle, and crucially George II, preferred Holdernesse. It would not have been unprecedented to have two Secretaries without diplomatic experience: that had been the case since February 1748; and Pitt was not excluded for that reason. Holdernesse, aside from experience as an envoy, was unlikely to thwart Newcastle's views or those of the King, and Newcastle was disenchanted with having Secretarial colleagues who thought for themselves. He had broken successively with Townshend, Carteret, Harrington, Chesterfield and Bedford, and being Newcastle's Secretarial colleague had become a route to the political graveyard. Holdernesse was a peer without political weight.

After the changes of June 1751, which also saw a more quiescent Granville brought back into the government as Lord President of the Council, the ministry remained substantially unchanged until the death of Pelham on 6 March 1754. The years between constitute the most obscure period of Pitt's political career. Ill-health appears to have been his major preoccupation and hindrance. In late 1751 Pitt was at Bath, and unable to go to Encombe as a result; in May 1753 he went to the fashionable spa of Tunbridge Wells, staying there until September, when he set off to visit the

---

[72] Farmington, HW 54 f. 11; 'Leicester House Politics' p. 208.

country seats of his friends, especially Stowe and Hagley. However, for much of the winter from October 1753 onwards he was seriously ill at Bath. He left it for London in June 1754, though he had to spend another three weeks that summer at the spa at Astrop Wells. Horace Walpole, noting Pitt's presence in the Commons on 27 November 1753, his first speech in the house since 1751, wrote that he 'was just come abroad again after a year of sullen illness'.[73] His return was to be a brief one only.

There is little doubt that Pitt was seriously ill for much of the period: his enforced stay at Bath during the political crisis following Pelham's death moved him to despair. The nature of Pitt's medical problems is, however, somewhat obscure, for medical terms generally lacked the precision of modern clinical descriptions and were employed in a more sweeping fashion. This was certainly true of gout, which had the specific meaning used today, as well as a more general application to pains in much of the body. 'Gout' was often an extremely painful illness, rather than a simple splenetic complaint. In 1742 Sarah, Duchess of Marlborough referred to being executed, 'which as I am past fourscore, won't give me so much pain as one night having the gout'.[74] The relationship between Pitt's 'gout' and his bouts of nervous illness is unclear, though they were generally associated. Pitt suffered badly from gout at both Eton and Oxford, and it played a major role in his early departure from the latter, but thereafter his first serious attack occurred in 1744 at the age of thirty-five. He was then described as suffering from 'gout in his bowels', an attack that had lasted for several months, been unaffected by taking the Bath waters, and 'if it does not affect

---

[73] Georgiana, Lady Chatterton, *Memorials of Admiral Lord Gambier* (2 vols., 1861) I, 54; Walpole, *Memoirs . . . George II* I, 243.

[74] Duchess of Marlborough to John Spencer, 20 January 1742, BL Althorp MS M15 (4).

his life, it may perhaps disable him, and make a cripple of him for ever'. After 1744 Pitt visited Bath most years, though other spas were also favoured, including Tunbridge Wells in 1748. January 1747 found him at Bath, writing to John Pitt that he was 'far from well, and unless I find infinitely more amendment the next week than I have hitherto done since I came hither, I fear I am not able to get through one day's attendance in the House'. Spas were often visited for social as well as medical reasons. It was fashionable and good for the health to leave London during the summer and, for those who did not have country seats, spas provided a genteel and sociable way to pass the time, a pleasant alternative to visiting the houses of friends. They were also places of political intrigue. However, Pitt appears to have visited them primarily for his health.[75]

After 1744 the next bout of protracted serious ill-health that Pitt suffered was in 1752. The extent to which this was related to depression is unclear. Pitt's behaviour at Tunbridge Wells in 1753 was not that of a cripple. Though he spent much of the time drinking the waters, he also went to the assembly-room balls and to lectures on philosophy and on trips into the surrounding countryside, writing to John Pitt in July, 'I find a very great amendment in my health. I have recovered much of my strength, and appetite enough for a Dorsetshire shepherd.' However, he added, 'My stay must still be pretty long here, as my sleep continues very broken, and the irritation not yet off my nerves and out of my blood.'[76] It would be unwise to stress the social aspect of his visits to spas. In August 1752 he wrote to John Pitt from Bath of 'a very considerable load, that of myself, much disordered in my spirits, and otherwise a good deal out of order', adding that he was sorry John was absent, 'especially now that the

---

[75] W. J. Smith (ed.), *The Grenville Papers* (4 vols., 1852–3) I, 32; Chatterton, *Gambier* I, 9.
[76] Chatterton, *Gambier* I, 61–2.

place is quite destitute of amusement or resource, and that solitude is every way contrary to my cure'. In October he was still at Bath, 'well, or very near it, by Bath waters, Raleigh's Cordial, etc.', but regretting that he would be unable to get to Hagley or Exeter that year, for, as he informed Charles Lyttelton, 'I am much better; or rather recovered from my disorder; but advised to continue the waters for some weeks, in order to fortify myself against winter.' The following month he was hindered from drinking the waters by a 'bad cold', and his plan to return to London in mid-December was thwarted by bad health. Pitt described himself then as 'an old piece of Bath lumber', adding, however, that he hoped 'to make a shift to keep upon my legs this winter'.[77] By February 1753 Pitt could write to his sister Ann from his office in the Pay Office in London, although his tone was stoical, 'I continue an invalid, and wait for better weather with as much patience as I can.' On 27 February he added, 'I continue still a good deal out of order, but begin to get ground', and on 5 April he struck a more optimistic note,

I have been ill all the winter with disorders in my bowels, which have kept me very low, and reduced me to a weak state of health. I am now, in many respects better, and seem getting ground, by riding and taking better nourishment. Warmer weather, I am to hope, will be of much service to me, I propose using some mineral waters: Tunbridge, or Sunning Hill or Bath, at their proper seasons. As the main of my complaint is much abated and almost removed, I hope my horse, warm weather and proper nourishment will give me health again.

On 16 April Sir William Lee noted, 'I hear Mr Pitt the Paymaster is advised to travel into a warm country for health, he has been so much out of order that he has hardly appeared this winter and is so weary of his habitation on the Chase

[77] Chatterton, Gambier I, 54–5, 58–9; BL Add. 69288 no. 23.

[Enfield] that he has sold it for a song to the son of Mr Sharp.'
The following month Pitt informed Ann, 'I am much mended
in several respects, and have the greatest hopes given me of
removing my remaining disorder by the help of warmer
weather and Tunbridge waters.'[78] These hopes were to be
illusory. That October Pitt wrote from Bath to Ann, 'I propose
being in town by the meeting of the Parliament, if I am able',
and, although he did speak in the Commons the following
month, by January 1754 he had to describe himself as 'an
invalid'.[79]

It is unclear how far Pitt's poor health was related to
dissatisfaction with his situation. Like most political figures
of the age he was a 'pre-historic figure', his personal life
obscure. The evidence, for example, does not allow any
judgement as to whether he was regularly drinking heavily or
not. In addition, men bred on the classics were accustomed to
the stoical model of a virtuous statesman whose personal life
was one of self-sacrifice and who had no doubts. The high
standard Pitt set is suggested by a letter to his nephew of July
1755,

I ever intend learning as the weapon and instrument only of manly,
honourable, and virtuous action, upon the stage of the world, both
in private and public life; as a gentleman, and as a member of the
Commonwealth, who is to answer all he does, to the laws of his
country, to his own breast and conscience, and at the tribunal of
honour and good fame.[80]

In addition, Pitt was an intensely private man, ready to reveal
his hopes and fears for the country, but reluctant to reveal
those he had for himself.

---

[78] BL Add. 69289 nos. 32–4, 37; Beinecke Library, New Haven, Connecticut,
Osborn Shelves, Lee Family Papers, Box 3.
[79] BL Add. 69289 no. 35, 69288 no. 24.
[80] BL Add. 69288 no. 48.

In the early 1750s Pitt had little reason to be satisfied with his political position. He was not promoted in 1751, nor thereafter, and the nature of his position was indicated by the fact that he was not mentioned as one of the leading ministers in the memorandum on British politics written by the French envoy Mirepoix in October 1751.[81] On 27 November 1752 the Earl of Hillsborough, an Irish peer who was an active spokesman for the ministry in the House of Commons in the early 1750s, playing a greater role than the older Pitt, told George Dodington that he thought Pitt wanted to change the ministry,

He thought there must be some disturbance arise from the Pitt party: that though they were so well placed they were uneasy: that they neither were liked nor liked. – I said I could not conceive that they would stir. – He said yes; for that Pitt's passion was ambition, not avarice. That he was at a full stop as things were, and could have no hopes of going farther: he was once popular: if he could again make a disturbance, and get the country of his side, he might have hopes: now, and on this system, he could have none . . . I said . . . that it was impossible for them to attempt it without holding out a hand to people to extend and fortify their own connections, etc. . . . As to Pitt, the King himself would be against him.

The following March Pelham explained a cause of Pitt's dissatisfaction when he warned Dodington that his offer of support for the ministry might not lead to royal favour, 'that should it be practicable, and I were in any station, and the King should not be brought to behave to me as I might justly expect, I should grow uneasy, and be dissatisfied, as in the case of Pitt, to whom they could never prevail on him to be commonly civil'.[82] George II took no pains to avoid snubbing

---

[81] 'Mémoire de M. le Duc. de Mirepoix sur la Cour d'Angleterre', 18 October 1751, AE CP Angleterre 432 ff. 252–66.

[82] J. Carswell and L. A. Dralle (eds.), *The Political Journal of George Bubb Dodington* (Oxford, 1965) pp. 184–5, 211.

Pitt in public, Henry Harris writing in December 1750, 'Saturday was a devilish dull day at Court . . . Not seven persons in the circle . . . The Paymaster General not spoke to, scarce looked at, upon this thin occasion.' Pitt was not without consequence: the decision in November 1751 to ask for 10,000 seamen for 1752 was attributed to the Pelhams' wish to 'cajole' him;[83] but he appeared to have no prospect of promotion while George II reigned and the political situation remained stable. Hillsborough might regard opposition in these circumstances as logical, but there is no sign that Pitt shared his opinion. Circumstances were no longer as apparently volatile as they had been in the winter of 1750–1, and it is probable that Pelham was correct to see Pitt as dissatisfied, without presenting him as an intriguer. Possibly a measure of despair played a role in Pitt's ill-health in the early 1750s. He was by some standards a political failure. It was unclear that he would defeat Fox in any struggle to succeed Pelham, while younger men, such as Hillsborough, were rising in prominence in the Commons, and a new generation of English aristocrats, Halifax, Hartington, Holdernesse and Waldegrave, were becoming more important in government circles. A general election was due in 1754, one that was likely to present another solid majority for the ministry and in which Pitt would play little role, other than as a dependant of the Pelhams.

At the start of 1754 Pitt was forty-six. He was still Paymaster, the post to which he had been appointed in 1746, and the most fruitful period of his life seemed to be ebbing away with little to show for it. Without a powerful connection and still outside the circles of decision making, Pitt could not afford to stand still. At the same age Walpole had been First Lord of the Treasury and Chancellor of the

[83] Ilchester (ed.), *Letters to Henry Fox* p. 53; Walpole, *Memoirs . . . George II* I, 142.

Exchequer, Stanhope and Newcastle Secretaries of State. Advising his nephew Thomas, then among 'the wits and rakes of Cambridge', on his conduct, Pitt pressed him in January 1754 to 'hold fast by this sheet-anchor of happiness, religion'; a conventional sentiment, but one that appears to have meant something to a depressed and increasingly inconsequential invalid.[84]

THE STRUGGLE TO SUCCEED PELHAM, 1754–1756

He is not out yet, and has declared, he cares not whether he is out or in, for a cow will keep him. He can dine upon milk pottage, as he told Sarah Duchess of Marlborough when she threatened him. (Richard Blacow of Pitt, 6 December 1754)[85]

The cause of all this disorder is that the Duke of Newcastle had the weakness to take in Fox. From which very first moment Fox has been working to traverse the Duke of Newcastle in every measure. Fox dropped his friend Pitt before, to come in himself. Pitt has let Fox go on, and now has made him fall into his own trap. What will be the end of all this, God alone knows. Here nobody will be in haste to embark in this new launched vessel, without having first due and clear proofs of the skill of the commander or pilot. They have hitherto given proofs of eloquence, wit, and shining parts. But those qualities are not what is requisite to save a state. (William Bentinck, The Hague, 22 November 1756)[86]

Pelham's unexpected death on 6 March 1754 touched off a major political crisis that led to Pitt's break from the ministry. It was understandable that Newcastle passed over Pitt for the leadership of the Commons after Pelham died. Pitt was unwell, had played little part in the Commons recently, and was not obviously suited to the Secretaryship of State made

---

[84] BL Add. 69288 no. 39.   [85] Exeter College Oxford, Bray papers.
[86] Bentinck to Robert Keith, 22 November 1756, BL Add. 35481 ff. 155–6.

vacant by Newcastle's move to succeed Pelham at the Treasury. On 9 March Pitt wrote to Ann, 'I am still suffering much pain with gout in both feet, and utterly unable to be carry'd to London. I may hope to be the better for it hereafter but am at present rather worn down than reliev'd by it.' On 4 April he noted signs of recovery,

though I am still at Bath, don't think the worse of my health; but be assured that I am in a fairer way of recovering a tolerable degree of it, than I have been in for a long time past. My gout has been most regular and severe, as well as of a proper continuance to relieve, and perhaps quite remove, the general disorder which had brought me so low. I am recovering my feet, and drinking the waters with more apparent good effects than I ever experienced from them. I have been out of all the bustle of the present conjuncture.

Health was not the sole problem preventing Pitt's promotion. He was not only without diplomatic experience, but he also lacked royal favour and the Secretaryships were posts that required it, for the monarch played a crucial role in the conduct of foreign policy. George II did not want to deal with Pitt personally in the Closet in any circumstances, while Newcastle and Hardwicke's reluctance to see Pitt Secretary and thus make a rod for their own backs was at least as important as George II's dislike of him in explaining why Pitt stayed where he was. The hostile Egmont, in the draft of an unpublished pamphlet, claimed, 'Your known ambition, and your insolence, and a knowledge of your superficial parts determined the matter against you', and certainly from Newcastle's point of view Pitt was a potentially unmanageable dependant.[87]

Newcastle explained to Pitt in April 1754 that George had decided on the promotion of Sir Thomas Robinson, a veteran

---

[87] BL Add. 69289 nos. 36, 38, 47097; Perron, Sardinian envoy, to Charles Emmanuel III of Sardinia, 14 March 1754, Turin, Archivio di Stato, Lettere Ministri Inghilterra 58.

diplomat Newcastle could rely on, to the vacant Secretaryship and the leadership of the Commons and he claimed that the posts given to Pitt's friends, George Grenville and Lyttelton, indicated his own personal regard for him.[88] The successive promotions of Holdernesse and Robinson to Secretaryships indicated George II's determination to have ministers whom he could deal with easily and a preference for men with diplomatic experience over managers of the Commons. Both men had been courtiers. Holdernesse had been one of the Lords of the King's Bedchamber in 1741–4 before beginning his diplomatic career. After his lengthy embassy at Vienna and a brief spell as a member of the Board of Trade, Robinson had been appointed Master of the Great Wardrobe in 1749, a post he held until he became Secretary of State in 1754. Newcastle had attributed Holdernesse's appointment as Secretary directly to the decision of the King and had claimed that he would cabal 'with neither Prince nor subject'.[89]

Pitt could not hope for senior positions on these criteria. For temperamental reasons and because of the political course he had chosen to follow, he was not a man who would be appointed to a great office of state as a result of support at court. In so far as the stability of the political system called for the harmonious co-operation of, indeed the fusion of, legislature and executive, in other words Parliament and government, with the monarch and his court playing a prominent role in the latter, then Pitt was an outsider and the appointments of Holdernesse and Robinson understandable. The experience of 1746–54 suggested that Parliament could be managed under this system with scant difficulty. The system was, however, to be unable to cope with the consequences of the international crisis of the mid-1750s.

[88] *Chatham Corresp.* I, 96–8.
[89] Newcastle to Pelham, 26 September 1750, BL Add. 35411 f. 139.

The military and diplomatic failures of others was to help take Pitt to high office.

Pitt played no significant role in the months after Robinson's appointment. On 17 April 1754 Pitt was returned in the general election for Aldborough in his absence and without contest. Newcastle owned most of the houses in the constituency. Pitt was still at Bath in early May 'lame in my hand', writing only with difficulty and 'tender and weak' in his feet.[90] He was unwell again during the summer seeking 'repairs' by drinking the waters again for several weeks at Astrop, and claiming by September to be 'perfectly well, that is well cobbled up by Astrop waters and the life of a post-boy, always in the saddle'. The following month he was in Bath.[91] However, in late September he had stayed with the Grenvilles at Wotton and fallen in love with Lady Hester Grenville. Thirteen years Pitt's junior, Lady Hester had known Pitt for many years, but it was only that autumn that their romance flourished. There is little doubt from their correspondence of the period, that theirs was a marriage of love not of social convenience, dynastic need or aristocratic economy. Rosebery found the love letters 'stilted, pompous, artificial', but Pitt's language of kissing words, folding Hester's charms with transport in his heart, Hester as his adored life, and the sweet and inexpressible bliss that inhabits her lips was both ardent and demonstrative.[92] Announcing the forthcoming marriage to Ann, he stressed the little of conventional value that he could offer Hester,

She has generosity and goodness enough to join part of her best days to a very shattered part of mine; neither has my fortune

---

[90] BL Add. 69288 no. 43.
[91] Chatterton, *Gambier* I, 72–3; Pitt to William Lyttelton, 12 October 1754, HL HM 22350.
[92] Lord Rosebery, *Chatham. His Early Life and Connections* (1910) p. 355; Williams, *Chatham* I, 242–6.

anything more tempting. I know no motif she can have but wishing to replace to me many things I have not. I can only add, that I have the honour and satisfaction of receiving the most meritorious and amicable of women from the hands of a family already my brothers in harmony and affection . . . to a goodness like Lady Hester Grenville's, perhaps, my infirmities and my poverty are my best titles.[93]

They were married in London on 16 November 1754, but their honeymoon at West Wickham in Kent, the home of Gilbert West, a cousin of the Grenvilles, was brief. The parliamentary session had begun on 14 November and Pitt was keen to attack Newcastle. Although he had initially accepted the failure to promote him with resignation, a consequence probably of his ill-health, by the summer he was convinced that Newcastle and Hardwicke had failed to exert themselves on his behalf. Newcastle himself told the Sardinian envoy on 20 November that only Pitt was capable of managing affairs for the government, but said that he had failed, despite very great efforts, to persuade George II to talk to Pitt, because George detested him. Pitt's position was not propitious. Opposition to Newcastle was weak and fragmented and Pitt himself sat for one of the Duke's boroughs. It is not surprising that in his marriage settlement, Pitt made provision for the purchase, if possible, of the borough of Old Sarum, which had been mortgaged to the Pelhams by the indebted Thomas Pitt after the death of Frederick, Prince of Wales. This clearly expressed Pitt's desire for independence and his awareness that his personal position denied him that. His hope of gaining the borough depended on his interest as heir-presumptive to estates of the Duchess of Marlborough. That was to prove an empty hope and beside that he had little to settle.

On 25 November 1754 Hester wrote to her sister-in-law

[93] BL Add. 69289 no. 39.

Ann that Pitt was well but busy with 'court, committees and the business of this hurrying town'.[94] That day he had attacked Newcastle in the Commons. The occasion, petitions over electoral corruption at Berwick and Reading, led Pitt to present Newcastle's position as a threat to the Commons, which he claimed might 'degenerate into a little assembly, serving no other purpose than to register the arbitrary edicts of one too powerful subject'. Initially provoked by the casual, humorous response to a petition brought by his friend John Wilkes about the Berwick result, Pitt 'was very violent in his professions of Whiggism' and 'his speech both by his friends and enemys is reckoned the finest he ever made'. Henry Harris recorded,

The Paymaster General took this unexpected occasion, and, descending from the Gallery, like the Hebrew lawgiver from Mount Horeb, thundered out such an alarm, as made these merry senators quake, and all the curtains of corruption tremble! . . . A fine performance . . . a greater, instant piece of oratory, never was heard – the drift of it was to abuse the whole frame of power; to raise a spirit; and to waken that House into a sense of its own freedom and dignity.

Pitt was not distracted from his target by the fact that he sat for a Newcastle pocket borough and that his return for Seaford in 1747 had given rise to a petition. Newcastle's lieutenants in the Commons were unable to mount an adequate defence. Earl Waldegrave noted of Robinson,

Sir Thomas, tho' a good Secretary of State, as far as the Business of his Office, and that which related to foreign affairs, was ignorant even of [the] Language of an House of Commons Controversy, and when he play'd the Orator, which he too frequently attempted it was so exceeding ridiculous, that those who loved and esteem'd

[94] Perron to Charles Emmanuel, 21 November 1754, AST LM Ing. 58; BL Add. 69289.

him could not always preserve a friendly composure of Countenance.[95]

Robinson was a minister well suited to a political system of courts and cabinets, but not to one in which Parliament played a major role and parliamentary management could be very difficult. Pitt could be ridiculous in the Commons and outvoted in the divisions, but he was a parliamentarian of note, which was certainly not true of Robinson. On 25 November 1754 Pitt savaged Robinson when he referred to the Reading election, in which an opposition Whig had defeated a court Whig by only one vote, as 'a poor cause'. He said he was surprised and scandalised to hear such a remark on an election coming from a minister, that doubtless that represented the views of all the ministry, that the Commons needed to consider the situation as the freedom of elections was the basis of national freedom, and that to attack the former was to endanger the latter, and that he, Pitt, was too good a patriot not to be outraged by Robinson's remark.[96]

Having bitterly attacked Robinson, who was no orator, on 25 November 1754, Pitt two days later criticised complacency over Jacobitism, an implied stroke against one of Newcastle's leading supporters, William Murray, who had a Jacobite past. His denunciation of Oxford, the ideological centre of Toryism, as a 'seminary' of disaffection where he had lately heard treasonable views expressed,[97] was a new departure, although he had broken with the Tories in 1746. It did, however, accord with Pitt's opposition to those who did not teach Whig principles. In July 1755 he sent his nephew Thomas advice on a course of 'reading. Begin with the revolutions of the Houses of York and Lancaster in Father

---

[95] Farmington, HW 66 f. 146, 60 f. 8, 55–6; J. Clark (ed.), *The Memoirs and Speeches of James, 2nd Earl Waldegrave 1742–1763* (Cambridge, 1988) pp. 160–1.

[96] Précis of Commons debate, AE CP Angleterre 437 ff. 381–3.

[97] Walpole, *Memoirs . . . George II* II, 27–8; P. Palmer to —, 27 November 1754, Bod. MS Top. Oxon. C 209 ff. 25–6.

Orleans, but read no more of him if you mean to read the history of England. The Father contains nothing more than a system of slavery, body and soul; supported by the sincerity and veracity of a Jesuit.' Pitt also advised reading 'the great state pieces' of the mid-seventeenth century and Bolingbroke's *Remarks on the History of England*, a work that, though written by a Tory 'of impious memory', presented politics in terms of a clash between Court and Country, in which the Country exemplified traditional Whig principles. In February 1755, during a debate over Scottish Justice, Pitt gave 'one of his best worded and most spirited declamations for liberty', presented justice as an eternal right and declared that 'Whig and minister were conjuncts he always wished to see'.[98] In other words Tories could not be trusted to preserve liberty, while government, unless motivated by Whig principles, could become simply arbitrary power.

Fox and Pitt had united to attack Robinson, but Newcastle was able to detach Fox in December 1754 with a place in the Cabinet, and Parliament was managed with reasonable success in early 1755. Pitt was not in a strong position and Egmont, writing in 1757, contrasted his current reputation with the situation three years earlier,

Your past conduct was become so detestable and your character so low by your last 10 years' servility, your ambition so glaring, your ingratitude to the Duke [of Newcastle] who had raised you and brought you into Parliament immediately before in his own borough, the indecency so great of holding the great office of Paymaster and acting this part in government, your profligate disregard to a dangerous conjuncture of the public, your mean employs to gain the Whigs, contrasted by the vilest abuse of the Tories, rendered you at that time as every man in Parliament can remember the greatest object of public aversion known in our age,

[98] Williams to Thomas Pitt, 15 April, 23 July 1755, BL Add. 69288 no. 46, PRO 30/ 8/6 ff. 84–5; Walpole, *Memoirs . . . George II* II, 39–40.

and all denominations of men did then ardently concur in wishing you turned out with ignominy and disgrace. Incredible as this may be to be told in 1757, it was undeniably true in 1754.

Pitt was still Paymaster, Hardwicke having convinced George that it would be inopportune to dismiss him. After his attack on Newcastle, Pitt 'was threatened for it, and did not truckle at all, but is to remain'.[99] He had, nevertheless, little prospect of more senior office. In the summer of 1755 Newcastle felt it necessary, however, to strengthen his position. Hostilities with France had broken out in North America in 1754 over the unsettled border between the British and French colonies. A Virginian force under George Washington had been forced to surrender to the French. The decision of the British ministry to send reinforcements and to intercept those that France was sending made war between the two powers likely. Admiral Boscawen, who had sailed on 21 April 1755, attacked the French ships sailing to Canada on 10 June and the French envoy Mirepoix left London on 22 July. Louis XV was allied to Frederick the Great and the danger of a Franco-Prussian attack on Hanover agitated George II and worried his ministers, who were also concerned about the possibility of a French invasion of the vulnerable Austrian Netherlands. Neither the Austrians nor the Dutch, Britain's two leading allies, were willing to offer assistance to Hanover in the event of attack and, as a result, George sought assistance elsewhere, first from Hesse-Cassel and Russia. Treaties with these powers would involve subsidies and Newcastle faced the prospect of having to get these through the Commons. A strong ministerial position in the House also appeared to be necessary in an unstable international situation, but the sensitive nature of foreign policy made the position of the Secretary of State who defended government policy in the

---

[99] Egmont, BL Add. 47102 B f. 178; Farmington, HW 60 f. 59; BL Add. 32996 f. 63.

Commons a difficult one. Writing about colonial disputes with Spain, Benjamin Keene referred in March 1755 to the desirability of preventing 'the noise and malice, of the Pitts in Europe, and the Pitts in America'.

It was therefore necessary to think of Pitt. Hartington, now Lord Lieutenant of Ireland and soon to become Fourth Duke of Devonshire, recommended good relations with Pitt to Fox in May 1755, adding 'though he has ambition and warmth of temper, yet I believe him to be a man of honour, and his abilities are such as will make his friendship useful to anybody'. Two months later Frederick, Prince of Wales' widow Princess Augusta, a figure of increasing importance as George II aged and the succession of her son Prince George (born in 1738) to the throne appeared more imminent, admitted to Newcastle that 'we never could or can do now without either Pitt, or Fox; she was much inclined, as we all are, for the former; but that she knew the King would not make him Secretary of State . . . she at last agreed that we should endeavour to keep Pitt in good humour'.[100]

The subject of this discussion had had 'a fit of the gout' in the spring and spent much of the summer at the spa at Sunninghill in Windsor Forest. He urged his nephew Thomas to join him there, promising him 'we will ride, read, walk, and philosophise, extremely at our ease'.[101] Pitt was, however, ambitious for power and responsibility and Princess Augusta's hope that 'his vanity might be satisfied with regard and confidence'[102] was misplaced. On 11 July 1755, Newcastle wrote that he and Holdernesse

have constantly in our thoughts, the necessity of forming some system in the House of Commons, for the support of such

[100] T. R. Clayton, 'The Duke of Newcastle, the Earl of Halifax, and the American Origins of the Seven Years' War', *Historical Journal*, 24 (1981), pp. 571–603; Black, *System of Ambition?* pp. 190–1; Keene to Robinson, 3 March 1755, Leeds Archive Office Vyner MSS 11850; Ilchester (ed.), *Letters to Henry Fox* p. 64; NeC 3169.
[101] BL Add. 69288 nos. 45, 47, 26.   [102] NeC 3169.

measures, as His Majesty shall, in the present difficult situation of affairs think proper to take . . . whatever party His Majesty shall think proper to take, with regard to the Continent, such opposition may arise to it, in the House of Commons, as may give great disturbance, and obstruction to public business; if that opposition should be headed by persons of weight and ability there. His Majesty has certainly as great a majority in the present House of Commons, as ever was known. But the misfortune is, that persons in the first stations there, in His Majesty's service, have not supported the King's measures, in the manner, they ought to have done; and, if they were to be removed, none could be found, whose talents and parliamentary abilities would enable them, to carry on the King's business, with ease and success, against such an opposition . . . we cannot find any way, so likely to obviate all difficulties as the engaging Mr Pitt, upon reasonable terms, to support His Majesty's measures, with clearness, firmness, and cordiality.

Newcastle hoped that George would be willing to add Pitt to the Cabinet. On 6 July Pitt, however, had seen Hardwicke and asked for 'a pledge of security, which might be the beginning of confidence' and responsibility for the presentation of the ministerial case in the Commons. Newcastle obtained George's consent that month, but Pitt became less accommodating as his relations with the court of George II's grandson and heir, Prince George, improved and as he realised the implications of the government's response to the developing international crisis. On 9 August Pitt told Hardwicke that he would require prior consultation about the policies he was to defend in the Commons and made his views on foreign policy clear,

'twas all open and above board, the support of the maritime and American war, in which we were going to be engaged, and the defence of the King's German dominions, if attacked on account of that English cause. The maritime and American war he came roundly into, though very onerous, and allowed the principle, and the obligation of honour and justice as to the other, but argued strongly against the practicability of it; that subsidiary treaties would not go down, the nation would not bear them; that they were a chain and connection, and would end in a general plan for the Continent, which this country could not possibly support.[103]

On 2 September 1755 Newcastle sought to win Pitt round. Pitt told him that he would only be able to support measures if he had 'an *office of advice* as well as of *execution*', making it clear that he wanted a Secretaryship of State, and declared that he could not back a subsidy treaty with Russia as it would limit the country's ability to fight France. As George did not want Pitt as Secretary, while the treaty with Russia was seen as essential to prevent Prussia from attacking Hanover, there was no possibility of an agreement on these terms,[104] while Hardwicke claimed that Pitt was in no position to insist on them as 'he has no party of his own' in the Commons, 'no support at Court; and the personal disinclination of the King'. The Earl of Marchmont argued that 'Pitt has undone himself' by neglecting to 'always keep with attention to the publick point with softness to every one on the other side'. Newcastle turned to Fox, agreeing on 25 September that he was to succeed Robinson as Secretary of State.[105]

The disappointed Pitt attacked the ministry when the session opened on 13 November 1755. The debate over the Address centred on the issue of subsidy treaties and Gilbert Elliot recorded, 'Mr Pitt and George Grenville . . . spoke the longest and with great ability, Mr Pitt declaring that he would never cease to oppose a minister who made this measure the basis for administration. This matter went very high and will

---

[103] BL Add. 32857 ff. 37–8; Yorke, *Hardwicke* II, 231; Rigby to Gower, 1 October 1755, PRO 30/29/1/14; Clark, *Dynamics of Change* pp. 173–8.

[104] BL Add. 32858 ff. 414–15; Yorke, *Hardwicke* II, 237–44; HMC, *Polwarth V* p. 301.

[105] Yorke, *Hardwicke* II, 248; HMC, *Polwarth V* p. 302; P. A. Luff, 'Henry Fox and the "Lead" in the House of Commons 1754–1755', *Parliamentary History*, 6 (1987), p. 42.

probably furnish matter for the whole session.' Pitt spoke for over ninety minutes and Horace Walpole captured the manner in which his long-suppressed anger exploded,

How his eloquence, like a torrent long obstructed, burst forth, with more commanding impetuosity! . . . haughty, defiant, and conscious of injury and supreme abilities.

Pitt condemned the Hanoverian focus of British foreign policy and the past failure to take sufficient note of the defence of North America, stressed the importance of the navy and offered a very Whiggish account of the royal position: 'the King owes a supreme service to his people'; the people had no such obligation to Hanover. Attacking the subsidy treaties 'he said that measure would hang like a millstone about the neck of the minister who supported it and sink him into disrepute amongst the people'.[106] And yet the government won a clear majority, 311 to 105, Newcastle commenting 'we have nothing to fear'. As there were 76 Tories in the minority, 'the Pitts Grenvilles and their party are confined to a small party'.[107] On 20 November 1755 Pitt was dismissed as Paymaster, his allies Henry Legge and George Grenville also losing their posts. Pitt's brother-in-law Earl Temple helped to compensate for the loss by providing Pitt with £1,000 per annum "till better times',[108] and on 21 November Pitt attacked the ministry for being more concerned about the defence of Hanover than that of America and Britain. He also drew attention to his own call for more seamen in 1751. John Campbell recorded,

Mr Pitt got up, begun with wishing for 50,000 seamen beside the Marines, but desired unanimity and therefore would make no

---

[106] Elliot to his father Lord Minto, 15 November 1755, NLS 11001 f. 15; Walpole, Memoirs . . . George II II, 69–72; Farmington, HW 63 f. 22.

[107] Newcastle to Hartington, 15 November 1755, BL Add. 32860 f. 480; Farmington, HW 63 f. 22.   [108] Grenville Papers I, 149–52.

motion; he soon left the question and went into a long declamation against the Ministers and the Administration for several years past, with very strong things personal to Mr Fox on his ambition, struggle for power, and complying with anything ever so bad to get into the office he now had . . . I do not think P. hurt F. at all last time, though it is true P. was fine and entertaining. I suppose P. intends to give F. little rest.

Fox and Murray accused Pitt of hypocrisy in criticising governmental policy in the early 1750s when he had been a member of the ministry.[109] On 2 December 1755 Pitt criticised the failure to act more forcefully against the French, but the ministry won the division by 211 to 81. On the 10th the subsidy treaties were debated. Pitt lashed Hume Campbell for calling on the Commons to 'punish the eternal invectives' of the opposition and stressed that a Cabinet would have to answer if they concluded 'subsidiary treaties without consent of Parliament'. However, there was little danger of it failing to obtain such consent. The ministry's majority was 318 to 126; on the 12th, when the subject was resumed and Pitt spoke for one and a half hours in the early hours of the morning, 289 to 121; and on the 15th, when Pitt again spoke for one and a half hours, the treaties were approved by 263 to 69 and 259 to 72. Fox complained about 'the excess of business' and 'the very long sittings Mr Pitt's very great ability's occasion'. Henry Digby commented that Pitt had 'made many fine abusive declamations', but that the opposition he headed 'consists of little more than his own family, the Grenvilles, 2 Townshends, and the Tories'.[110]

The failure of the opposition to make any real impact

---

[109] Campbell to his wife, 22 November 1755, Cawdor, Box 138; Walpole, *Memoirs . . . George II* II, 76–80.

[110] Walpole, *Memoirs . . . George II* II, 94–113; Fox to Hanbury Williams, 25 December, 25 December 1755, Farmington, HW 63 f. 1; Digby to Sir Charles Hanbury-Williams, 23 December 1755, BL Add. 69093; Fox to Devonshire, 11, 13 December 1755, HP; Farmington, HW 63 f. 261.

reflected a sense that ministerial measures were necessary. Attacks on Hanover were always problematic because of the issue of loyalty to the dynasty; but at a time when, unlike 1742–4, forces were being sent to America, they also appeared inopportune, especially as the payment of subsidies was less of a commitment than the dispatch of troops to the Continent, which in 1755 these subsidies were designed to render unnecessary. Furthermore, relations between the Tories and Pitt, who had recently attacked them, were not close, while the aggressive and abusive nature of Pitt's rhetoric appears to have had little appeal. The power of his speeches is frequently cited, without adequate consideration being devoted to the extent to which they were judged offensive and extravagant. On 2 December 1755 Murray distinguished between Pitt's 'florid eloquence' and 'the talent of a solid judgment'. On 15 December, when Pitt and Murray were the major speakers, Campbell wrote 'Pitt was indeed the most entertaining. I think he outdid his usual outdoings'. Pitt's style was vulnerable to mockery, as had happened on 25 January 1751 when in the debate over the number of seamen, John Hampden had 'brought him lower than the most able and serious disputants with all their power could ever effect.'[111] Interesting evidence is provided by an unpublished draft pamphlet written by Egmont that is worth citing at length as it is an obscure yet important piece and because the support of politicians such as Egmont was important if Pitt was to succeed in creating a powerful opposition grouping.

He was now returned into the only situation in which he was able to act, for when formerly in employment, neither in ability or speech was he in any degree eminent. His rhetoric and power of speech was in abuse only, and his project and ideas were such as

[111] Cobbett, xv, 606; Campbell to his wife, 16 December 1755, Cawdor, Box 138; Bristol, University Library, Bayntum Rolt diary, 4 February 1754.

suited only with the superficial ideas of the lowest understanding and were strangely defective to a degree of contempt, with men of judgement and experience in business. For these reasons, he was ever obliged to call in to his aid the multitude without doors, which he ever bought at the price of conscience, modesty and honour . . . Nor does history produce in the corruptest times of Athens, Rome or Carthage an incendiary more accomplished than himself.

A self-conceit and an arrogance of nature beyond all parallel bore him up under the marks of displeasure and contempt for his opinions and his conduct which he often encountered in his way . . . to his very defects he owed the success of his wild and dangerous conduct. Had he been less void of judgement, he could never have suited his politics and principles to the genius of the vulgar, and his understanding in spite of his turbulent ambition would have stopped him in his course . . . even his fame as an orator depended upon his total defect as to an argumentative understanding. Incapable of induction or ratiocination, to deduce a long chain of consequences, or to survey with accuracy all the parts of a question so as to draw a just conclusion . . . But possessed of a wonderful power of words, and a pompous diction, improved by the study of the poets, of rhetoric, the speeches of old orators . . . he not only cast alternately a cloud or a glare about his absurd propositions which deceived the lowest, and consequently the most numerous of his audience, but even triumphed over common sense within himself . . . hated by the superior orders of the kingdom, and contemned by the most knowing and desperate therefore of a reconciliation or of acquiring a lead of them, even a kind of necessity obliged him, if his natural genius had not inclined him, to form his system of politics, and to found his projects as he did.

Enough has been said to discover why he has ever been so inconsiderable in times of quiet, and his being so important in times of public distress.[112]

The bitterness of his speeches of late 1755 was only of limited appeal in political circles and the sense of Pitt as spectacle was captured by Horace Walpole who wrote that his speech of 15

[112] BL Add. 47012 B ff. 182–4.

December was 'accompanied with action that would have added reputation to Garrick', a reference to the leading actor of the period. Walpole claimed that Pitt was one of the few speakers to study eloquence, but that set speeches were no longer in vogue. He also claimed that invective in debate was a necessary way to achieve attention. Pitt certainly excelled in this field, but he also employed verbal devices that Walpole argued had fallen into disuse. Nevertheless, as Walpole pointed out, 'the grace and force of words were . . . natural to him'. Henry Harris wrote of Pitt's performance in the subsidy treaty debates that he would

keep any administration in fine breath – he was born for opposition – more excelling in his manner, in his language, and in high invective, than all the public speakers I ever heard of . . . Mr Fox behaved just as a great man, and a minister, I think, should always behave: with the utmost spirit, but with no loss of temper – setting plain facts, and fair argument against all this imposing eloquence – he did not affect, nor would it become his station to imitate the splendid verbiage of his rival.

Harris later referred to Pitt's 'vast tribe of epithets'. Pitt's hyperbole was satirised, as in a ballad of 1756:

> Hark! Hark! I hear a midnight roar!
> St Stephen shakes his strong-bas'd floor:
> Sure there's some Irish Bully!
> No – 'tis two Rivers from the South,
> Now disemboguing at the Mouth,
> Of our unpension'd Tully.
>
> 'Tis fine! 'tis full! the period's round!
> How clear! how musical the Sound!
> The Gesture – oh! – quite striking!
> What Flows! what Flowers of Eloquence!
> I grant it – Yet, a little Sense
> Were much more to my Liking.

I'll teach a Magpye out of Power,
To chatter to ye, by the hour,
Full as good Puerilities.
Then snarl no more: you'll ne'er get in:
Statesmen paid off, must well careen
Ere fit again for Duty.

Pitt, however, was not alone in his methods, nor was he the only MP compared with London actors. James Harris, who sat in the Commons from 1761 to 1780, noted in 1779,

I have seen Fox and Burke (the last in particular) so vociferate and so gesticulate in the House of Commons, that had a Weston or a Shuter done so at Covent Garden or Drury Lane, they had been hissed off the stage for most unnatural extravagance.[113]

Pitt had no success when Parliament resumed after the Christmas recess. The most contentious ministerial policy, the subsidy treaties, had been passed and they appeared vindicated anyway by Frederick II's response to the Anglo-Russian alignment: agreement with George II in the Convention of Westminster of 16 January 1756. This appeared to guarantee Hanover from attack and to oblige France to confine the war to the sea and the colonies, where Britain enjoyed the advantage of superior strength. Newcastle attributed this in large part 'to our Treaty with Russia'. Ministerial control of Parliament impressed foreign observers, Charles Emmanuel III of Sardinia noting on 1 January 'with what vigorous measures the Parliament was determined to support His Majesty'.[114] That month Pitt attacked Fox for allegedly covering up maladministration in

---

[113] Walpole, *Memoirs . . . George II* II, 111, 116-17; Farmington, HW 63 f. 271, 61, f. 20; *The State Farce. A Lyrick* Bod. Firth c. 18 (65); HP Harris memoranda, 20 March 1779. Copies are currently in the Hampshire County Record Office in Winchester.

[114] Newcastle to Devonshire, 2 January 1756, BL Add. 32862 f. 7; Earl of Bristol, envoy in Turin, to Fox, 3 January 1756, PRO SP 92/64.

Jamaica and screening the guilty, and for planning to use for corrupt purposes money that had been voted for America. He also attacked Sir George Lyttelton, now Chancellor of the Exchequer, for his budget, and claimed that there was 'a disjointed ministry, who united only in corrupt and arbitrary measures'. However, Pitt made little impact and on 31 January Fox wrote with some justice of 'Pitt, who has the four last times he has spoke, made such violent speeches (not good ones in their kind) upon such trifling matter, which I have been obliged to take such advantage of, that he is lowered and I am raised by it, beyond what his enemies or my warmest friends could have wished . . . the Speaker says I had a complete conquest'.[115]

The following month Pitt charged the government with failing to take adequate care against hostile French designs ever since 1748, thus condemning the ministry of which he had been a part, and criticised the terms of a bill to allow foreign Protestants to serve in America, on the grounds that it was a breach of the Act of Settlement of 1701 which had forbidden foreigners, even if naturalised, from holding a military commission. He told the Commons 'that it was poison to the constitution'. Pitt's argument was an echo both of traditional suspicion of the political consequences of a standing army, especially if the officers were unreliable, and of hostility towards the House of Hanover and the consequences of having foreign rulers on the throne. Pitt had returned to the ideas and language of his earlier hostility to Walpole and Carteret: the ministry could be trusted neither with the constitution nor the country. They had betrayed the Whig legacy for the sake of power and royal favour and their personal weaknesses and limitations led them to indulge their authoritarian tendencies. Pitt was prepared to imply

---

[115] Fox to Devonshire, 31 January 1756, HP.

duplicity as well as incompetence. He 'said in the House the other day, that he should not be surprised to hear of the French being landed at Torbay, and added, that things were in a worse state than those who had the direction of our affairs and were in the secrets durst acknowledge'.[116]

His analysis was both coherent and extravagant. The various aspects of Pitt's analysis of politics and society and his attack on the ministry were mutually supporting, but they entailed an overcharged assessment of the contemporary situation and his intemperate language carried him even further in that direction. In February 1756 the vigour and zeal of his attacks did not win him support in the Commons: the ministry won the divisions by 165 to 57, 213 to 82 and 198 to 64. Thereafter Pitt played little role in the Commons, presumably due to the poor health that affected him from late February, which he described a month later as a troublesome 'pain in my face and ear'. Nevertheless, pressed by his patron Temple, Pitt left his bed on 29 March 1756 to oppose an address to George to send for Hanoverian troops to prevent a threatened French invasion of England. Pitt argued that the danger should be met by raising new units in Britain, but Lord George Sackville replied 'with great spirit and sense', the Tories gave Pitt only limited support, and the ministry won divisions that day by 259 to 92 and 187 to 88.[117]

Pitt continued his attacks, repeating some of the themes of opposition polemic in the 1740s. On 30 April 1756 he claimed that the cost of using Hessian troops was substantially more than that of employing British forces. On 7 May he attacked the use of Hessians again, arguing implausibly that 'this waste on Hessians would have conquered America or saved Minorca', whilst alleging that the ministry wished to

---

[116] Farmington, HW 61 ff. 11–12, 19; Richard Blacow to Thomas Bray, 11 February 1755, Exeter College Oxford, Bray papers.
[117] Walpole, Memoirs . . . George II II, 140; Farmington, HW 61 f. 27.

lose Minorca to the French in order to increase pressure for, and provide a means of negotiating, a disgraceful peace. Aside from suggesting a possible treasonable design, Pitt made the more reasonable claim that the government was disorganised, without 'system' and indecisive, thus implying that defeat in war would be the responsibility of the ministry, an accusation that it would be difficult to rebut.[118] He returned to the charge on 12 May, comparing 'the Duke of Newcastle to a child in a go-cart upon the brink of a precipice' and arguing 'that it was but common humanity to stop it, or to admonish the child's nurse [Fox] of its danger', but the ministry won the last major division of the session two days later by 210 to 55. Pitt's arguments had not been reflected in rising opposition votes in the Commons, and Holdernesse was not particularly concerned when he wrote on 11 May 1756, 'the torrent of abusive oratory flows as readily as ever from the mouth of Demosthenes P—t Esq; the session now drawing to an end that dangerous weapon his tongue must lie still a little'.[119]

The government's failure in the first major challenge of the war was to alter the political situation in Britain. The Balearic island of Minorca, smaller neighbour of Majorca, had been captured by the British in 1708 during the War of the Spanish Succession, ceded to them by the Peace of Utrecht of 1713, and developed as a Mediterranean naval base. In 1756, by appearing to threaten an invasion of England, the French ensured that British naval forces were concentrated in home waters and that an insufficient force was sent under Admiral Byng to support the British garrison on Minorca. The island was invaded on 18 April, the hesitant Byng avoided pressing home the attack on the French fleet off Minorca on 20 May,

---

[118] Walpole, *Memoirs . . . George II* II, 142.
[119] Yorke, *Hardwicke* II, 290; Holdernesse to Andrew Mitchell, envoy in Berlin, 11 May 1756, BL Add. 6832 f. 64.

and the British garrison surrendered on 29 June. The fate of Minorca had been followed closely in Britain, agitation being raised by conflicting rumours about Byng's success. On 23 June reports reached London that Byng had beaten the French and relieved Minorca. Pitt was delighted by the news, pleased for 'an undone Country, and a gallant worthy friend persecuted and superseded upon the relation of the beaten enemy'. However, the news was speedily contradicted, the Earl of Bath commenting,

one moment all the world is calling our admirals rascals and cowards, and then we are elated to the skies with a little false news, and our fleet it is said did their duty as they ought. Every thing seems to me to be in a state of uncertainty, our news, our counsells, our measures, our intelligence and our ministers themselves, change as they please, I fear nothing can come that is good.[120]

The phoney war was over. Negotiations had continued after the outbreak of hostilities in North America in 1754 and the Atlantic in 1755, but the French attack on a British possession in Europe ended all hope of peace. The British declared war on 17 May 1756.[121] The news from the Mediterranean depressed Pitt, who was also worried, as he wrote to George Grenville, that developments in America and Asia might furnish their 'portion of ignominy and calamity to this degenerate helpless country'. His hyperbolic manner was thus not limited to his speeches, but also characterised his correspondence, though the belief that Britain's position was very serious was widespread during the summer of 1756, when the government appeared indecisive in the face of a threatened invasion. Pitt argued, and not just for public consumption, that national difficulties were the result of

---

[120] BL Add. 69288 no. 27; Bath to Sir John Rushout, 24 June 1756, Worcester County Record Office 705: 66 BA 4221/26.
[121] Black, 'Anglo-French Relations in the Mid-Eighteenth Century', Francia, 17/2 (1990).

mismanagement, writing to Grenville, 'It is an inadequate
and a selfish consolation, but it is a sensible one, to think that
we share only in the common ruin, and not in the guilt of
having left us exposed to the natural and necessary consequences of administration without ability or virtue.' He
returned to the charge later in the month, 'Distress, infinite
Distress, seems to hem us in on all quarters. The same weak
infatuated conduct that begat this distress seems determined
to increase and multiply it upon our heads.'[122] This was
clearly an argument that Pitt accepted, and it helped to bolster
his sense that his rise to power was required if the nation was
to be saved.

Pitt enjoyed himself that summer, predicting doom as a
consequence of the policies of those whose merits he
despised and positions envied, visiting the country houses of
friends at Stowe, Ealing, Pinner and Wickham, and staying at
his own at Hayes, where in the 'pure air' he was 'utterly
unable to move' for ten days in mid-August as a result of 'a
very awkward, uneasy, but not hurtful malady'.[123] At the
same time, Newcastle manoeuvred in order to strengthen his
position in the Commons. Byng's retreat from Minorcan
waters led Murray to demand a peerage and his promotion to
the vacant post of Lord Chief Justice. Newcastle pressed him
to stay in the Commons, claiming that 'nobody but yourself
will or can support me; and . . . in this House of Commons,
support the King and his measures against such a formed
opposition and at such a critical conjuncture',[124] but Murray,
though suited to administration, lacked the temperament for
public adversarial politics. Willing to see the convicted
swing, he was not interested in bleeding on the floor of the
Commons. Murray was determined to resign and Newcastle's relationship with Fox was increasingly uneasy. Unwill-

---

[122] *Grenville Papers* I, 165, 168.   [123] *Grenville Papers* I, 171.
[124] Newcastle to Murray, 30 May 1756, BL Add. 32865 f. 143.

ing to rely totally on Fox, Newcastle feared that he would be unable to confront Pitt without help, especially as foreign policy, of which Fox knew little, was coming to the front of the political stage. The Duke sought to win the support of Leicester House, the court of the young Prince George. Fox was worried about the developing political storm over Minorca, which was not confined to the press. It was widely anticipated that when Parliament met the ministry would be blamed for the failure. The outbreak of war on the Continent, when Frederick II invaded Saxony on 28 August, in order to forestall a threatened Austrian and Russian invasion, aroused further concern. The British government had sought unsuccessfully to dissuade Frederick from his attack. It activated the provisions for mutual support in the event of attack contained in the recent Austro-French Treaty of Versailles of 12 May 1756. Britain now found herself allied to an unpredictable ruler whose forces were heavily outnumbered: by 1757 Prussia was to be at war with Austria, France, Russia and Sweden.[125]

Minorca dominated the domestic political agenda in the summer of 1756. The Duke of Chandos wrote to his heir on 26 August 'a strict scrutiny I think absolutely necessary next sessions; and the spirit of the kingdom seems to demand it'. Fox was worried. On 31 July he had written to the Duke of Devonshire about Minorca, 'the scene of action will be the House of Commons and I being the only figure of a minister there, shall of course draw all the odium on me'. Fox advised trying to win over Pitt, which he thought 'the surest means of getting Leicester House', though he feared it was impracticable. Fox presented the government as in a weak position as a result of a shift in public opinion, writing to Devonshire on

---

[125] K. W. Schweizer, 'The Seven Years' War', in J. Black (ed.), *Origins of War in Early Modern Europe* (Edinburgh, 1987) pp. 242–60; J. Black, *The Rise of the European Powers 1679–1793* (1990) pp. 109–14.

12 August, 'I do not think my offer with regard to Pitt in the least generous. – For this administration has, I think, lost the good will and good opinion of their country, (which they six months ago enjoyed to a great degree) and without them who can wish to be in administration.'[126]

Not all politicians were convinced that the ministry would have to bow before the political storm, Granville calling Newcastle and Fox cowards who were 'frightened with nothing'. However, Fox's anxiety about the situation, his inability to trust Newcastle, and what has lately been termed 'the insufficiency of his own ambition' led Fox to resign on 13 October 1756. He attributed this to Newcastle's refusal to provide him with the necessary support in the Commons and to the Duke's willingness to replace him with Pitt. Fox complained that he had

no power of making a friend or intimidating an adversary; and yet to attempt to lead a House of Commons with less help even in debate on our side than was known . . . I not only would not, but could not carry on the King's affairs without the Duke of Newcastle. It is absolutely impossible to go on with him. I therefore must get out of court . . . I find my credit in the House of Commons diminishing for want of support.[127]

These charges were symptomatic of an essential distrust in a relationship strained by deteriorating political circumstances and put under stress by the ambiguous nature of links between senior ministers in a system that lacked a prime minister, clear conventions for ministerial responsibility and a sense of stability.

Fox's departure led Newcastle to turn to Pitt as the only

---

[126] HL STB Box 10 (29); HP; Farmington, HW 63 ff. 41, 53–4.

[127] Luff, 'Fox' p. 43; Fox to Hanbury Williams, 7 August 1756, Farmington HW 61 ff. 58–9; Fox to Devonshire, 11, 13 October 1756, HP; Lady Betty Waldegrave to Viscount Trentham, 16 October 1756, PRO 30/29/1/17 f. 962.

politician who could lead the Commons, but George II was worried about an approach to such a vociferous critic. On 14 October Newcastle told the King, as the Duke reported to Hardwicke,

'there was but one of two things to do; – either to gratify Fox, in what he wanted, (which, said I, would, perhaps, be giving Mr Fox more power, than your Majesty would think proper); Or, to take in Mr Pitt.' 'But,' replied the King *peevishly*, 'Mr Pitt won't come.' 'If *that was done*', I said, 'we should have a quiet session.' 'But Mr Pitt *won't do my German business.*' 'If he comes into your service, Sir, he must be told, he must do your Majesty's business . . .' 'But I don't like Pitt. *He won't do my business.*' 'But, unfortunately, Sir, he is the only one, (in the opposition) who has ability to do the business.'[128]

Sackville responded to Fox's resignation by asking 'who is to do the business in the House of Commons, can Mr Pitt? I say no, without some alteration in measures which may not be convenient.' How far Pitt's demands would extend and whether he would be satisfied with office were now of central questions. On 15 October George authorised Newcastle to offer Pitt the Secretaryship in return for his support for government policy. However, Pitt was resolved to reject 'any plan with the Duke of Newcastle at the head of it, as well as any proposal for covering his retreat, in case he wishes to retire from being Minister'. He explained his refusal to serve under Newcastle by saying that 'he had a great regard for the Duke of Newcastle, but he had so engrossed the King's confidence that he could expect no share in it; and therefore never would come into his service whilst his Grace remained in it'. On the 19th Hardwicke offered Pitt the Secretaryship and a good reception from the King and posts for 'his particular friends', but Pitt sought not a reconstitution of the

[128] Newcastle to Hardwicke, 14 October 1756, BL Add. 35416 f. 100.

ministry but a rejection of the government and its policies, the course he had advocated in 1742, in contrast to that of those opposition Whigs who had then joined Newcastle and the Old Corps Whigs. In October 1756 Pitt demanded a rejection of the past. Newcastle must resign and an inquiry be established into setbacks in Minorca and North America. Foreign troops in British pay must be dismissed. Furthermore, a *cause célèbre* involving the Hanoverians deployed in England in the face of a threatened French invasion, the release from the custody of the civil authorities by the order of Holdernesse of a Hanoverian soldier arrested at Maidstone on suspicion of theft, must be resolved in accordance with the law and public outrage. Pitt was determined that he should not simply defend government policy. He insisted that a scheme of measures be adopted which he could approve and defend, pressed for a militia, and declared that his conditions were non-negotiable. On the 21st he went to see the Countess of Yarmouth, George's mistress, a Hanoverian now naturalised, who was also his political confidante, and presented to her a plan for a ministry nominally headed by the Duke of Devonshire. Devonshire was seen as conciliator of the disparate groups that would compose the new ministry.

George II rejected Pitt's terms, but Newcastle, unsuccessful in his attempt to find a Commons leader other than Fox or Pitt, told the King on 26 October that he could not engage to conduct business in the Commons. The Duke resigned the next day. He wrote to Gerlach Adolf von Münchhausen, the head of the Hanoverian ministry, explaining that setbacks in the war had created discontent and thus enabled several politicians to push their ambitious views. He added that though he had been certain of the firmness of the government's majority in the Commons, he had felt it necessary to find posts for those who had the talents necessary for parliamentary management.[129] Though usually associated with electoral patronage and parliamentary management, Newcastle had in fact fallen not because of any defeat in Parliament or at the polls but due to his failure at a time of crisis at the start of a major war to create and sustain what appeared to be a durable ministerial combination in parliamentary terms.

THE FORMATION OF THE PITT–DEVONSHIRE MINISTRY, OCTOBER–NOVEMBER 1756

the whole play is over and the curtain is dropped. The Duke of Newcastle has retired and left the whole ministry to be rebuilt from the ground . . . I believe there are at this instant among those expected to form the new ministry still more irreconcilable opinions and interests than subsisted under the former. Time and a short time will show this. (Charles Townshend, 30 October 1756)[130]

Since the Duke of Newcastle's retreat, it has been a most extraordinary scene and varied so often that it is hardly possible to relate all the turns it has had. (Henry Digby, 10 November 1756)[131]

On 27 October George II gave Henry Fox authority to form a Fox–Pitt ministry, but the next day Pitt rejected the idea that Fox should play any role in the new government, leading the latter's nephew Henry Digby to complain that Pitt had 'shown himself to be exceedingly impracticable and unreasonable throughout this whole transaction, and in all the

---

[129] Sackville to Sir Robert Wilmot, 17 October 1756, Matlock, Derbyshire Record Office, D 3155/WH 3450; Pitt to Grenville, 17 October 1756, *Grenville Papers* I, 178; Wilmot to Devonshire, 20, 21 October 1756, HP; Richard Rigby to Earl Gower, 21 October 1756, PRO 30/29/1/14; Newcastle to Münchhausen, 26 November 1756, Hanover, Des. 91 Münchhausen I Nr 24 ff. 2–3; Clark, *Dynamics of Change* pp. 268–75.

[130] Charles to George Townshend, 30 October 1756, Bod. MS Eng. hist. d. 211 f. 3.

[131] Digby to Hanbury-Williams, 10 November 1756, Farmington, HW 63 f. 45.

treaties that were carried on, he seemed rather determined to conquer than assist the King'. On the other hand, the previous March, Digby 'was not much surprised at Mr Pitt's great spirit choosing to quit rather than act a second part with any man'.[132] On the 30th Pitt told Devonshire that he could not serve in any ministry containing Fox, but he moderated some of his earlier demands, both over the case of the Hanoverian soldier at Maidstone and with regard to any inquiry into the conduct of the war. This compromising of Pitt's Patriot position paved the way for a Devonshire–Pitt ministry that would be able to rely on the backing of many of Newcastle's former supporters, for they would not be obliged to acquiesce in any punishing of the former ministry. Thus, in October 1756 Pitt accepted what he had not been willing to consider in the case of Walpole. Unlike the position in 1742, he now had the prospect of office, but it would be misleading to adopt too Olympian a perspective and too cynical a conclusion. In 1756 the need to win the support of the Old Corps if a viable government was to be created was clearer.

By 12 November the plan for the new ministry was largely complete. Devonshire and Temple were to be First Lords of the Treasury and Admiralty respectively, and Pitt was to be a Secretary of State. Pitt had initially sought to replace Holdernesse at the Northern Department, but an angry George II opposed the change, not welcoming the prospect of his taking responsibility for handling relations with the German powers. Pitt therefore took the Southern Department, which Newcastle had held from 1724 to 1748, receiving the seals on 4 December 1756. He was now clearly the leading government spokesman in the Commons and a

---

[132] Fox to Duke of Argyll, 28 October 1756, Farmington, Miscellaneous Manuscripts, Henry Fox; Digby to Hanbury-Williams, 10 November, 30 March 1756, Farmington HW 63 ff. 49, 61 f. 27.

minister holding one of the principal offices of business. However, the creation of the new government had not witnessed a ministerial revolution. Prominent members of the Old Corps continued in office and on 13 November Sackville noted 'how many people are provided for and how few absolutely turned out . . . everybody is considered either by new employments or peerages, so that three great Ministers retire without desiring anybody to follow them'. And yet the new ministry appeared unstable. Sackville wrote, 'Those who are apt to observe upon these transactions say that the late Ministers are rather stepped aside than removed for ever and that each would be glad to be recalled when real strength may be required by the undertakers of this new system'. Another, MP, Lord Carysfort, wrote to Earl Gower on 14 November 1756.

I think the present political system of administration seems too narrow and confined to last long. It is constituted principally of one single family against the united force of the principal nobility. Doubtless there are men of great abilities among them; but we have in our times seen that they alone will not do without powerful assistances from the great families in the country . . . Men of such character and principles as your Lordship, the Dukes of Devonshire and of Bedford are those that this nation must rely upon for its best security.[133]

Pitt had no such support. He had come to high office with the enthusiastic support of few politicians and he lacked a secure party and parliamentary basis. The King was unenthusiastic and most commentators saw the ministry as precarious, not so much because of the difficult international situation as due to unpropitious domestic circumstances. Popular expectations about the patriotic policies that would be adopted were high. Success abroad and reform at home

[133] Sackville to Earl of Loudoun, 13 November 1756, HL Loudoun papers 11617; Carysfort to Earl Gower, 14 November 1756, PRO 30/29/1/14.

were anticipated. Over the next eight months it was to be those who had predicted ministerial instability who were most accurate. Pitt himself came to office with some foreboding. On 19 November he wrote to his old friend Charles Lyttelton from Hayes,

I find it still difficult to use my pen . . . I am, in all senses, unfit for the work I am going to set my feeble hand to . . . the flattering expectation of good to the publick, in such a lost condition, and from such an aid as mine, sends me with a heavier heart than men use to bear to courts and high stations . . . some right intentions, I hope, I have: and were it as true a maxim, of abilities, as I think it is of virtue, that but to wish more is to gain, I might have a little better chance. Be the event what it may, as soon as I can crawl I will embark, perhaps on board a wreck; and trust I shall have your honest and kind wishes for a fair wind and favourable seas.[134]

[134] BL Add. 69288 no. 28.

Chapter 3

War Minister

I was always of opinion that the greatest strength and solidity
in His Majesty's councils would be wanting to carry on the
present unequal war with any prospect of success; but a still
greater strength will, certainly, be necessary whenever any
event shall fortunately make a peace practicable, and as, in
that peace, the King's German dominions must be included,
prejudices are to be combatted; popular clamour will be
raised, and ought to be withstood; but can only be conquered
by a solid and strong administration.

Earl of Holdernesse, June 1757

Fye Billy, so Naughtily thus to behave,
What just Dub'd a Freeman, and List for a Slave
With Pelham and Anson those true Packhorse Peers,
And Fox the Trained War-Horse, to draw in the Geers
The Presents of Britons, so meanly Abuse,
Turn again, a Court Hack, for a Stall in the meuse
As Sarah's ten Thousand, came just in the Nick,
Will you Play a whole Nation, the same scurvy Trick.
She knew not indeed, how Her Legacy Sped;
But the Nation is Living, tho' Sarah is Dead.

Anon., *The Poets Address to the Right Dis-honourable William Pitt*,

summer 1757[1]

[1] Holdernesse to Countess of Yarmouth, 11 June 1757, BL Eg. 3425 f. 48; BL Add.
63648 p. 220.

Pitt's claim to fame rests on British success during the Seven Years War and this chapter will concentrate on British policy and Pitt's role during that conflict, but it is first necessary to consider his position and strength as minister. This question can be divided chronologically into two sections: before and after the formation of the Pitt–Newcastle ministry in June 1757.

THE PITT–DEVONSHIRE MINISTRY, NOVEMBER 1756–MARCH 1757

By the Letter of the 23 of November *Dictator* Pitt had still the gout. Nothing could be done nor even thought without him. (William Bentinck, December 1756)[2]

In office without secure parliamentary support Pitt swiftly revealed a willingness to compromise that was necessary for a minister trusted by neither King nor the Old Corps Whigs and facing the danger that the other two major politicians, Newcastle and Fox, might, together or separately, take threatening steps. Pitt's position was made more difficult by his own ill-health and by the need to consider Devonshire, although the Duke was of less political consequence than Newcastle. An angry Fox, sulking in Holland House, presented Pitt as aggressive and unable to appreciate the limitations of his position,

Pitt is single, imperious, proud, enthusiastic; has engaged the Tories, who instead of strength are weakness; has Lord Bute and Leicester House absolutely. Upon these, and the belief that the Duke of Newcastle and I shall not join against him, and above all in the confidence he has in his own superiority over all mankind, he comes, or, having the gout, sends Legge and Grenville to talk

---

[2] Bentinck to Keith, 4 December 1756, BL Add. 35481 f. 158.

miserably to a majority set against them, and who only forbear dividing out of regard to public tranquillity.[3]

It is easy to appreciate how the firmness with which Pitt had maintained his insistence on refusing to share power with first Newcastle and then Fox had led to a general conviction that he was conceited, unwilling and unable to accept restraint and the exigencies of office, and therefore bound to fail. In fact he was relatively cautious once in office, sufficiently so for the *Test*, a London weekly launched on 6 November 1756 to propagate Fox's views, to claim on 18 December that since Fox's resignation nothing of conse-quence had been achieved by the sickly Pitt, 'since that period, I cannot hear of any one public measure, except the distribution of places, and chopping and changing, and turning in and turning out, and kissing hands, with other matters of equal importance'. The journal argued that nothing had been achieved in the war, and that the government had not been able 'to pursue lasting and solid measures'. Pitt did not achieve what some had feared. Had he sought to implement a Patriot agenda he would have pressed for an inquiry into military policy so far in the war, a step calculated to discredit both Newcastle and Fox, taken steps to have foreign troops withdrawn from England and to block subsidy treaties designed to obtain the alliance of Continental rulers and the support of their troops, created a militia and promoted the established opposition platform for domestic politics: shorter and therefore supposedly less corruptible Parliaments, free elections and moves against placemen.

These were not, however, the achievements of the Pitt–Devonshire ministry, a situation that reflected its political weakness, especially in the face of Old Corps strength in the

---

[3] Fox to Hanbury-Williams, 26 December 1756, Farmington, HW 63 f. 4.

Commons, and the exigencies of the international situation. Instead the ministry did not embark on a domestic reform programme, supported subsidies for an Army of Observation, composed mostly of Hanoverians and Hessians, designed to protect Hanover and cover Prussia's western frontier, and compromised its popularity by supporting leniency towards the convicted Byng because his punishment would make it more difficult to claim that the previous ministry was responsible for setbacks at the outset of the war. Nothing came of hopes that Pitt would introduce triennial elections.

Parliament met on 2 December 1756 and the King's speech, written by Pitt, promised that 'the succour and preservation of America cannot but constitute a main object of my attention and solicitude'. It also praised 'a national militia' and promised that the Hanoverian troops would be sent back to the Electorate. Pitt's cautious speech made it clear that the policy of the previous government would essentially be continued, Viscount Barrington writing,

The measures as declared and explained by Mr Pitt the first day of the session differ in nothing from those of the last administration. Every effort in America consistent with our safety at home, every effort at sea, and whatever this country can do besides, given to the support of our allies on the continent.[4]

Pitt was attacked for the ministry's continued commitment to the German war, the *Test* offering on 27 November 1756 a vision of the resolutions of a Pittite Parliament, including

That the doctrine of the accidental and immediate interest of a nation, be propagated through the kingdom to apologize for temporizing patriots. That to pay an extravagant subsidy to the King of Prussia, be not called a German measure, but that it shall fall under the denomination of accidental and immediate interest.

[4] BL Add. 6834 f. 5.

Pitt was to be attacked repeatedly for inconsistency over his German policy. *The Speech of William the Fourth, to both Houses of P—* a broadsheet of 1757 had Pitt declare, 'The Germans are now our natural enemies. I hate them and always shall, though I complied with immediate and accidental interest.' A pamphlet of the same year condemned Pitt for inconsistency and deplored German subsidies,

some three or four months ago, Great Britain was as naturally divided from the continent by her political interests, as by her situation . . . now the fruitfulness of her fields must be poured forth to enrich the barrenness of all Germany.

The Duke of Richmond on the other hand was angered in January 1757 by Pitt's failure to acknowledge the help provided by the Hanoverian troops,

You say you cannot blame Mr Pitt for not thanking the King for sending for the Hanoverians. If you will but consider one moment it is the absurdest of things. Whether it was right to desire the King to send for them or not it was certainly right in the King to do as he was desired by the Parliament and it is so contradictory in the same Parliament first to desire the King to do a thing and then a month after not thank him for doing the very thing you desired him to do.[5]

Such criticisms, however, exaggerated Pitt's political power, his ability to implement a consistent policy, as indeed Pitt's earlier attacks on former ministers had also done. On 26 November 1756 Holdernesse wrote to Andrew Mitchell, the envoy in Berlin, that he had been instructed by George II to inform him that there would be no change in policy and that Parliament would 'determine His Majesty, upon the means of carrying these salutary views into execution'.[6] At the end of 1756 the new ministry was still in a precarious condition and

[5] Anon., *The Constitution. With a Letter to the Author* no. 2 (1757) pp. 19–20; Anon. broadsheet, *The Enquiry is Not Begun* (1756); Richmond to Lord George Lennox, 25 January 1757, BL Bathurst Loan 57/103 f. 100.
[6] Holdernesse to Mitchell, 26 November 1756, PRO SP 90/67.

a number of options were discussed including a Pitt–Fox reconciliation. However, much appeared to depend on Newcastle's sufferance, for his backing seemed crucial if the Old Corps were to provide support. It was not realistic to think in terms of a dissolution and the election of a new House of Commons because there was no reason to believe that this would lead to a majority for the new government. Royal support was uncertain and, whatever the extent of Pitt's public support, it was unlikely to influence the result in more than a few constituencies, while Pitt's willingness to support the financing of an army to protect Hanover suggested that he would be attacked for compromising his views for the sake of office.

In addition, in early 1757 Pitt had bad gout. This was held partly responsible for the relative quiescence of the session and for a lack of energy in the business of government. The well-informed Sardinian envoy Count Viry reported on 18 January that Pitt's illness had stopped all essential affairs, 'the other ministers not daring to take anything upon them, domestically or diplomatically, without having first discussed the matter with him'. The regular reports that Richard Rigby MP, the Duke of Bedford's 'man of business', sent to his ducal patron reflect considerable interest in Pitt's health. Rarely good in earlier years, it was from now on to be a major theme of political correspondence. Thus, on 17 January 1757 Rigby wrote of Pitt's gout, that it 'is again grown much worse. He has it in his right arm and elbow and George Grenville told me in the House of Commons he felt it also last night in his left foot'; on 20 January 'Mr Pitt's illness I think contributes to this quiet, and his illness increases, and I have reason to think to such a degree that they imagined him last night in great danger from the gout's having attacked violently his head'; 25 January 'Mr Pitt, the Duke of Devonshire told me, is well enough to go out, but not to

Court or Parliament'; 7 February '. . . not well enough to see
the king'; 8 February 'Tomorrow the House of Commons
goes upon the Militia . . . Pitt neither goes there, nor to the
king, though I am told he is very well at home'; 9 February
'William Pitt still remains in obscurity'; and on 22 March
after an improvement in mid-February 'Mr Pitt is gone into
the country sick, not meaning to come to Parliament before
Easter holydays'.[7]

Such ill-health was not the basis for a stable government
nor likely to help Pitt develop and foster a parliamentary
following, a task to which he never really devoted much
time. He did not attend the Commons between 3 December
1756 and 17 February 1757. On the 17th, Pitt's first
appearance in the Commons as Secretary of State, he
delivered a message calling for extraordinary supplies to
meet the French threat 'against His Majesty's electoral
dominion, and those of his good ally the King of Prussia'.
Support for an army of observation to protect Hanover was
presented as a means to enable George to fulfil his
engagements with Frederick II, and on the 18th 200,000
pounds was asked for and obtained without any opposing
vote. On 18 February Pitt defended his consistency on the
matter in a fashion that he certainly would not have allowed
opponents, saying,

That if any gentleman had a mind to attack his consistency he hoped
that he would take another day and not enter into personal
altercations upon that great national question. That he did not insist
upon being literally and nominally consistent as long as he thought
he was substantially so; that he never was against granting
moderate sums of money to the support of a continent war as long
as we did not squander it away by millions.

[7] AST LM Ing. 61; Bedford vol. 33; MS Pitt/Bute correspondence nos. 11, 12, 24,
26, 34; Richard Potenger, Under-Secretary, to Mitchell, 25 January 1757, BL Add.
6823 f. 33; Charlotte Hanbury Williams to her uncle, 13 January 1757,
Farmington, HW 79.

Pitt's success was due to his skill in presenting support for Hanover as an essential prerequisite of assistance to Frederick, who at that stage was regarded very positively by most of those who had views on foreign policy, being seen widely as a Protestant Hero. There was indeed criticism of Pitt. Campbell observed, 'If he can do this with an unembarrassed countenance nothing can be too hard for him.'[8] The Test of 5 March 1757 saw him as hypocritical and referred to earlier claims in favourable newspapers, 'Did not the Monitor assure us that German subsidies should be entirely laid aside? that Great Britain and America should be the sole objects of our attention?' However, it was to be over Byng that Pitt exposed himself to serious attack. His hope that the failure to relieve Minorca could be used to discredit the previous ministry had been shaken by Byng's conviction by a court martial on 27 January 1757 on the grounds that he had failed to do his utmost to destroy the French ships. Neglect carried a mandatory death penalty, unless royal pardon was exercised, though the court martial had also recommended mercy. The issue of clemency was raised in Parliament and Pitt spoke in favour of mercy on the grounds that 'more good would accrue to the discipline of the navy and the good of the service than from the strictest justice'. He backed a special act to release the members of the court martial from their oaths of secrecy.[9]

Mercy was not the view of George II, nor was it a popular position outside Parliament. Pitt was seen as attempting to screen Byng and the failure to save the Admiral created an impression of ministerial weakness. Edward Owen, the printer of the Gazette, wrote on 5 March 1757,

The affair of Byng is looked upon in the City as a trial of the strength of the Old and New Ministry, in which the latter have greatly lost

[8] Campbell to his wife, 17 February 1757, Cawdor, Box 138.
[9] BL Add. 51341 f. 42.

themselves, and exposed their weakness. Old Velters Cornwall said in the House of Commons, that, probably, that was the last speech he should make in that House, for that he found himself breaking apace, but yet he thought he should hold out as long as the New Ministry; and looking Mr Pitt full in the face, said, that Mr Byng had been the means of throwing out the old Ministry, and certain he was, that Mr Byng would shortly be the means of turning out the New Ministry.

Pitt's attitude towards Byng was to lead to criticism for many years, and to be presented as evidence of his opportunism. In the 1780s George Johnstone, who had entered the Commons in 1768, noted down

a story of the late Earl of Chatham. Upon the taking of Minorca he undertook to support Byng and to play him against Mr Fox, the Duke of Newcastle and Lord Anson. They on the other hand so managed the court martial that the members agreed unanimously to condemn Byng and unanimously to recommend him to the royal mercy. When they applied to Chatham to obtain the pardon 'no no says he gentlemen I must not risk my popularity. As the court martial have condemned him I must execute him.' Old Doctor Campbell who was present and one of the solicitors for the unfortunate admiral and who told me the story said 'Sir if this is the way you treat your friends I hope you will always consider me as your enemy.'[10]

John Campbell was, as a propagandist for Bute, to attack Pitt in 1761 and what he said cannot be relied upon other than as evidence of the manner in which Pitt's reputation was compromised by his attitude towards Byng's trial and conviction.

Byng was shot on the *Monarch* on 14 March 1757, the most prominent of a long series of eighteenth-century admirals disgraced and prosecuted for failures, real and apparent:

[10] Owen to Edward Weston, 5 March 1757, Farmington, Weston papers vol. 4; Johnstone to Sir James Lowther [1780s], Carlisle, Cumbria Record Office D/ Lons/L 1/1.

unintentionally a powerful incentive to caution in naval operations, although boldness could bring striking victory, as Hawke demonstrated in 1759. To sustain his position Pitt needed to keep the initiative, to prevent those who did not like him from combining to create a new ministry. This initiative was lost in early 1757 because of ill-health and his mistaken prominence in attempts to save Byng, but his position had been weak anyway, because of the lack of support from George II and Newcastle. In late February the King approached Newcastle via Waldegrave, making clear his desire to dismiss the ministry. This set in train a course of complicated negotiations, in which Fox and his patron Cumberland played a major role, designed to produce a new ministry. Cumberland was not happy at the prospect of going to command the Army of Observation in Hanover while Pitt remained in office. George II's wish to part with Pitt was an important theme and on 6 April 1757 Pitt was dismissed.[11]

Pitt returned to the Secretaryship of the Southern Department on 18 June 1757. The intervening period was one of considerable complexity that can be approached in a number of fashions. It can be seen as essentially a high-political crisis in which a small number of individuals, principally George II, Newcastle, Pitt, Fox, and Bute, on behalf of Prince George, manoeuvred, seeking to create a viable ministry whose composition was most conducive to their views and connections. A wider political dimension can also be considered, by focusing attention on the role both of developments, specifically the course, real and anticipated, of the Seven Years War, and of the influence of political opinion. The departure of the Duke of Cumberland to command the Army of Observation in Hanover threw George II's commitment to the Electorate into prominence, while

[11] J. C. D. Clark, *Dynamics of Change* (Cambridge, 1982) pp. 335–53.

Pitt's dismissal was followed by the so-called 'rain' of golden boxes, the presentation to him of the freedom and compliments of thirteen cities. The shortcomings of Pitt in office were obscured to many by the circumstances of his departure, a development that helps to explain the controversy that was to surround the terms of his resignation in 1761. In 1757 the Common Council of London thanked Pitt for his attempt to 'stem the general torrent of corruption' and for his 'loyal and disinterested conduct'. Such motions were the consequence not simply of a spontaneous outburst of public zeal but also of manoeuvres by Pitt's supporters, but, nevertheless, it could be presented as a sign of his popularity and of the extent to which that had not been tarnished by his recent role in government and, in particular, his support of subsidies to Hanover. The 'rain' was clearly intended to demonstrate to George II Pitt's political importance, the critical Edward Owen writing from London on 30 April 'Newcastle upon Tyne is also sending up gold boxes and freedoms, but neither they, nor we, can give any reason why we do it, any more than to affront the King for dismissing Mr Pitt his service.'[12]

The consequence of this demonstration of support can be assessed variously. To treat Pitt as a conventional wheeler-dealer without trying to make sense of his rhetoric, his power base in commercial London, his patriotic aura and his press reputation would be misleading, an evasion of the question of why public reputation mattered in what can be seen simply as an age of oligarchy. On the other hand it is important not to exaggerate the extent, solidity and significance of Pitt's popularity. It is certainly possible to discuss the political manoeuvres of the period with little reference to

---

[12] N. Rogers, *Whigs and Cities. Popular Politics in the Age of Walpole and Pitt* (Oxford, 1989) p. 106; P. Langford, 'William Pitt and Public Opinion, 1757', *English Historical Review*, 88 (1973), pp. 54–80; Owen to Weston, 30 April 1757, Weston-Underwood.

opinion 'out of doors', in the contemporary phrase, and there is no doubt that the essential agenda was set by the personal interrelationships of a small group, of whom the King was the most important. However, rulers were most obliged to accept ministerial combinations that were to some degree unwelcome during periods of war or international tension. Then the political system was least susceptible to control and it was felt necessary to consider the views of those who did not hold power. George I had had to accept the return of Walpole to office in 1720, George II the loss of Walpole in 1742 and his inability to sustain Carteret in 1744 and 46; George III was to lose Lord North and be obliged to abandon his American policy in 1782.

In 1757 Britain had only one ally, Frederick the Great, who was heavily outnumbered. Hanover was vulnerable to French attack, while, hitherto, British success against French colonies had been limited. Assistance to Hanover was politically controversial and the success in obtaining parliamentary support on 18 February 1757 did not lessen governmental vulnerability on this score. Any moves that could appear to accentuate either Pitt's political support or the prominence of the Hanoverian issue would thus have to be considered in the high-political manoeuvres of the period. On 17 May 1757 Viry reported that there was little enthusiasm for a vote of credit for the extraordinary expenses of the Army of Observation, adding 'the anger of the people on the recent change of government has lessened the eagerness that some people had shown at the beginning of the session to help Hanover'. According to Viry, who had good relations with Devonshire, this led the ministry instead to ask for a vote of credit in general terms to back the extraordinary expenses of government, a measure that was passed.[13]

---

[13] Viry to Charles Emmanuel III, 17 May 1757, AST LM Ing. 61.

Aid to Hanover was the King's vulnerable point. He hoped that Frederick the Great would send Cumberland military assistance, but Frederick was himself hard pressed. In the debate on the Vote of Credit Pitt 'added some hints on his own popularity, and on the independence of the country gentlemen who favoured him'.[14] The potential importance of such support can be variously assessed. Alongside Viry's report can be noted the opinion of George Townshend, who had proposed in April 1757 in the Commons inquiry over the conduct of the government at the beginning of the war a number of critical resolutions, only to see them rejected. Owen reported Townshend saying

That as there were 260 members of that House who always voted with the minister in all his measures, he foresaw, as there was no stemming the general torrent of corruption, that the ruin of his country was near at hand, and therefore he thought the best thing he could do, was to go with his little fortune and family into some other country.[15]

Such an analysis necessarily minimised the possible role of public opinion, but it rested on the ministry being united and certain of its intentions. This did not describe the situation in the second quarter of 1757 as a number of individuals manoeuvred in order to influence the composition of the King's ministry, while groups that could not hope to be comprised in it, the Tories and those who expressed Patriot opinion, sought to affect policy or were used for the purposes of political stratagems. The two key political players were George II and the Duke of Newcastle and, concerned about the alternatives, both of those were prepared to accept that Pitt should play a major role in a new ministry provided that he adopted an acceptable position in the composition and

[14] Horace Walpole, *Memoirs of King George II*, edited by J. Brooke (3 vols., New Haven, 1983) II, 258.
[15] Owen to Weston, 28 April 1757, Weston-Underwood.

policies of the ministry. Initially unwilling or reluctant, Pitt changed his mind, his position in the crisis of 1757 thus repeating his earlier shift over joining the government in 1746. As a recent detailed study has demonstrated ably, there was a range of ministerial options available in 1757,[16] but the eventual solution, a Newcastle–Pitt government, had been a possibility long before it was eventually formed, although Newcastle was not really prepared to concede genuine power to Pitt until the autumn of 1756 at the earliest.

Both men had earlier sought co-operation, Pitt after the death of Pelham, Newcastle in the autumn of 1756, but in 1757 it was Pitt who had to make the major concession of agreeing to retreat from his position of not serving with either Newcastle or Fox. George II was certainly prepared to entertain such a solution, provided that Pitt adopted a reasonable position on help to Hanover, but a Newcastle–Pitt government seemed to guarantee that, for Newcastle was both sensitive to royal views and had recently supported an active policy of Continental commitments. In May 1757 Devonshire reported on a conversation in which George II had told him that 'as to Pitt he had not so much objection to him but he thought him too impracticable to act with anybody'. The Duke replied 'that if Mr Pitt would consent to act an under part and confine himself to Secretary of State under the Duke of Newcastle and Mr Fox Paymaster etc., I thought it would be the surest means of giving ease to His Majesty and restoring strength and consistency at home'.[17] Pitt's terms in May were indeed too sweeping: Newcastle was to leave the Commons and foreign policy to Pitt and to accept Pitt's allies in the Treasury. However, as a result of further political negotiation it became clear that a Newcastle–Pitt combination was essential. An attempt to form a Walde-

---

[16] Clark, *Dynamics of Change* pp. 355–443.
[17] Devonshire to Cumberland, 5 May 1757, quoted Clark, *Dynamics of Change* p. 374.

grave–Fox ministry failed and on 11 June 1757 Waldegrave told George II that such a government would be defeated when Parliament met,

for that the Duke of Newcastle had a considerable Majority in the House of Commons, whilst the popular Cry without doors was violent in favour of Mr Pitt: and tho the Duke of Newcastle hated Pitt, as much as Pitt despised the Duke of Newcastle, they were united in one Particular, that nothing should be done for the public service, till they were Ministers.

Waldegrave also suggested that Pitt was not as stubborn as he could seem and that if the King treated him well he would respond, a recommendation that, while perceptive, was not one that Pitt's actions had always smoothed the path for,

That I was not ignorant that Pitt could be guilty of the worst of actions whenever his ambition, his Pride, or his Resentment were to be gratified; but that he could also be sensible of good Treatment; was bold and resolute; above doing things by halves; and, if he once engaged, would go farther than any Man in this Country. Nor would his former Violence against Hanover be any kind of Obstacle, as he had given frequent Proofs that he could change Sides whenever he found it necessary, and could deny his own words with an unembarras'd Countenance.[18]

The next day Henry Digby commented,

this union between Leicester House, Newcastle, Pitt, and the Tories was too strong for anything to stand against . . . the Duke of Newcastle by his very strange conduct has brought about the thing he least intended; he has made Mr Pitt the minister. They will I suppose come in together, but as the Duke of Newcastle has offended the King in so open a manner, I fancy Pitt will be the best received, and as he has got Leicester House, I think the Duke of Newcastle will be in his power.[19]

---

[18] J. Clark (ed.), The Memoirs and Speeches of James, 2nd Earl Waldegrave 1742–1763 (Cambridge, 1988) pp. 205–6.

[19] Digby to Hanbury-Williams, 12 June 1757, BL Add. 69093.

Pitt finally accepted office in a ministry that included Newcastle as First Lord of the Treasury, Fox as Paymaster, and Anson, First Lord of the Admiralty at the time of Minorca, back in office, a government committed to supporting the defence of Hanover. Having looked to Tories, Patriots and Leicester House for his political support, Pitt was now the member of a ministry dominated by the Old Corps, a step that placed his relations with his former supporters under threat[20] and, in particular, undermined his links with Leicester House, rather as he had broken those with Prince Frederick in the 1740s. The allocation of posts was clearly a central theme in the negotiations that led to the formation of the new ministry. In a memorandum drawn up on 4 June 1757 Newcastle wrote, 'The two great difficulties that seem to arise in forming a plan of administration with Mr Pitt and his friends are First the King's promise of the Pay Office for Mr Fox . . . Secondly the difficulty of removing My Lord Winchelsea and reinstating the other Lords of the Admiralty.' Eleven days later, the Duchess of Newcastle saw the same points as crucial, 'the King insists upon Mr Fox's being Pay Master, and keeping the Admiralty as it is and says he will yield in everything else'.[21]

Such considerations led some to argue that the entire crisis was simply a matter of quarrels over office. Edward Owen suggested on 20 May that Pitt's attitude towards assistance for Hanover 'has prevented all hopes of a coalition; and indeed it seems to me impossible for any such thing to be brought about, except we had about 50 more places of one or two thousand a year to dispose of; for I am such an odd fellow, as to be very jealous, that therein chiefly consists the good of the country on all sides'. Reacting to the Earl of Halifax's anger

[20] Monitor 2 July 1757.
[21] NeC 3158; Duchess of Newcastle to her father Francis, Second Earl of Godolphin, 15 June 1757, Northampton, County Record Office F(M)G 808.

when he was not made a Secretary of State, the Duchess of
Newcastle wrote 'it is provoking to find that the seeming
friendship and strong professions for eight months that he
has made, had no meaning in them, but to serve himself'. The
Duke of Cumberland, disappointed in his hope of seeing Fox
at the head of the ministry, suggested, as did some other
commentators, that certain politicians were manoeuvring
with an eye to the accession of George III, 'the proper shop
for future bargains', and attacked Pitt's hypocrisy,

With what face can that popular great man Pitt, with his humble
follower Legge, appear with the Duke of Newcastle Treasurer and
poor Anson Admiral when they have built their faction on the
heinous crimes and omissions of those two persons in those very
offices.[22]

These manoeuvres over place had an obvious political
resonance in terms of parliamentary management and
ministerial stability, and the pressure to create a viable
government can be seen in those terms as much as in any
struggle for place. Cumberland wrote to Devonshire on 23
May 1757 'the only material point is an administration and
almost any one is better than none'.[23] The viability of such a
ministry would it was believed be tested in Parliament and it
was there that Pitt's position was seen as crucial, despite the
fact that he did not control or lead anything recognisable as a
parliamentary party, comparable to the Old Corps. With tears
in his eyes, Newcastle's nephew the Earl of Lincoln told Viry
at the end of May that Newcastle was resolved to try to form a
government without Pitt, and that the Duke's friends did not
see how it could survive the winter.[24] It was not parliamen-

[22] Owen to Weston, 20 May 1757, Weston-Underwood; Newcastle to Godolphin,
21 June 1757, Northampton F(M)G 809; Cumberland to Devonshire, 1 July 1757,
Chatsworth HP.
[23] Cumberland to Devonshire, 23 May 1757, Chatsworth HP.
[24] Viry to Charles Emmanuel III, 31 May 1757, AST LM Ing. 61.

tary arithmetic that was seen as crucial but likely ministerial disunity, a disunity that the prospect of failure and recrimination helped to create and foster. The Old Corps political system could not cope with failure. The absence of a reliable party unity on which government could rest left politicians feeling vulnerable to attack. It was in this context that Pitt in opposition was an obvious threat for, although enjoying a measure of Tory support, he was a Whig able to exploit adverse developments in the war, and it was difficult to feel confident of political success against such a figure. And yet such success was vital if the Prussian alliance was to be maintained and the war continued. Concerned at the prospect of a Fox ministry, Holdernesse resigned on 9 June 1757, only to return to office when the Newcastle–Pitt ministry was formed. His resignation was seen as understandable. Two days later the Duke of Richmond wrote to his brother George asking 'what must be the consequence, if the measures taken this summer are not confirmed by Parliament at the opening of the Sessions' and suggesting that had he been Secretary the prospect would have seemed bleak,

From the nature of my department, I must have carried into execution the King's orders, upon the most important objects, either of war or peace, and upon the very points where the stress of the future opposition will certainly lie, and that, without seeing sufficient strength in the Minister, efficaciously to support the King's views in Parliament, and without being sure that even the small assistance he could give me, would be exerted in my favour, if I should be attacked, but must have stood the shield of a minister with whom I have no connection, and be wounded by the shafts that are aimed at another.

Holdernesse made the same point,

Nor would my safety admit of my remaining in so answerable a station as that of Secretary of State for the Northern Department, joined with persons of whose parliamentary strength to conduct the King's affairs I was doubtful, without a certainty or even an assurance that that little strength would have been asserted in my favour had I been attacked by an able opposition for executing the King's commands upon those points whereon the stress of their animadversions would chiefly have been laid so that I might have ruined myself but could not possibly have been of any real service to the King.[25]

Without testing his parliamentary strength and without referring to the limited success of opposition in divisions in recent sessions, a hostile Pitt was presented as a fundamental question-mark against the stability of any ministry that did not include him. In part this was tactical, the obvious point to be made by any politician who wanted Pitt in the government or who sought to block any move that he might be thought to oppose. In part, however, it reflected the manner in which Pitt's reputation had developed since 1754. He was able to present himself as the spokesman of opinion 'out of doors' and yet was willing to manoeuvre as other politicians did, retracting or compromising his stated views in order to further his ends. The last was a particular skill as most politicians were not taking part in politics to such a public extent: the political milieu and modus operandi of say Devonshire or Waldegrave was very different from that of Pitt, and possibly, partly as a result, Pitt's political skills and potential importance were overrated. In many respects Pitt benefited from being able to act as an apparent link between the world of court and high politics and that out of doors, an ability that owed much to his being in many respects temperamentally a political outsider. In 1757, though Secretary of State, Pitt still did not control or influence any important parliamentary

---

[25] Richmond to Lord George Lennox, 11 June 1757, BL Bathurst Loan 57/103 f. 49; Holdernesse to Bentinck, 12 July 1757, BL Eg. 3481 ff. 64–5.

connection. And yet it was difficult to imagine any who did being described as Pitt was in the spring of 1757 when he supported a financial proposal of Sir John Barnard, one of the City MPs, 'Mr Pitt and Mr Beckford seconded him, roaring out against Jobs, Ingrossers, Jews etc. though Sir John had 2 in his own list of 14.' Similarly, Pitt alone was capable of acting the part of the 'theatric valetudinarian', described by Walpole with a perceptive glance at his ambition, 'no aspiring cardinal ever coughed for the tiara with more specious debility'. Pitt alone could be presented with some credibility in the eyes of many contemporaries as the saviour of his country, the Tory pamphleteer John Shebbeare explaining in 1757 'If Mr Pitt long held his place in complacency, it was still in expectation, that, at length understood by the ministers, he might gain the opportunity of being heard by his sovereign, and save the land: from this jealousy excluded him. If he held it in silence, he both held and renounced it with honour, to open his lips for the preservation of his country.'[26]

His apparent indispensability in the Commons had allowed Pitt to set Newcastle and Fox at defiance in October 1756, and, despite all Pitt's weakness in the Closet, neither Newcastle nor Fox seemed to have a good chance of forming a government that could survive in the Lower House without Pitt; in large measure because it would be vulnerable to devastating oratory from Pitt if anything went wrong with the handling of the war, Minorca all over again. Fox did not have the stomach for the fight, and Newcastle had no-one of sufficient stature or courage to take Pitt on. There seemed to be no alternative, and Pitt knew it. His position may have looked weak, but it was stronger than anyone else's, though

[26] Owen to Weston, 28 April 1757, Weston Underwood; Walpole, Memoirs . . . George II II, 253; [Shebbeare], A Fifth Letter to the People of England (1757) p. 62.

not strong enough for him to run a government all by himself. The approach of the parliamentary session had destroyed the Newcastle administration in October 1756 and the creation of a viable leadership in the Commons was the key issue thereafter. Pitt had indeed succeeded, a triumph that owed a lot to Fox's weaknesses, and yet it was a triumph circumscribed by Newcastle's power in the new ministry and by Pitt's need to take responsibility for a war that was going badly, not least with regard to Hanover, the defence of which he could not now dissociate himself from. Pitt subsequently claimed that the situation he had inherited was dire, and it certainly seemed so at the time. On 13 July 1757 Charles Townshend wrote to his mother,

How do projectors, for all ministers are little more in times of so much danger and national weakness, propose to continue even a disadvantageous war for another year; when the siege of Prague shall be turned into the siege of Berlin: Hanover garrisoned by France: Ostend, a French port; and England sinking under its own debt and expences, shall be the only fund and purse for carrying on every other Prince's war in our alliance? Indeed, Lady Townshend, we are undone, and, as Mr F says . . . no genius is equal to the distress and danger of the times.[27]

THE NEWCASTLE–PITT MINISTRY

Things go on perfectly well with Pitt. (Newcastle, 3 September 1757)

how much Mr Pitt is already disappointed. (Charles Townshend, 6 September 1757)[28]

[27] Pitt speech, BL Add. 32932 f. 81; Charles Townshend to Lady Townshend, 13 July 1757, BL Add. 63079.
[28] Newcastle to Hardwicke, 3 September 1757, BL Add. 35417 f. 43; Charles Townshend to Lady Townshend, BL Add. 63079.

British policy in the Seven Years War will be examined in the next section for it is first necessary to consider the question of how much power and influence Pitt enjoyed during the Newcastle–Pitt administration. The problem will be addressed afresh for the reign of George III, because the new King's views and the particular position of his favourite, Bute, led to a new political situation. During the last years of George II, however, it is clear that Pitt did not wield the degree of power that is sometimes attributed to him. It is for these years, 1757–60, that the positive re-evaluation of the abilities and influence of both George II and Newcastle that has characterised some recent work is possibly most pertinent. This has led to a corresponding diminution in Pitt's reputation.[29] By stressing the extent to which government was departmental, and Pitt as Southern Secretary had limited influence only in the conduct of other offices, it is possible to query his importance in directing the implementation of government policy. By arguing that Newcastle was concerned about more than patronage and that George II still exercised considerable power, it becomes clear that Pitt's role in the formulation of policy was not unchallenged. Furthermore, the wisdom of the policies with which he was most closely associated and the skill with which they were executed can be assessed critically. Such questioning has not had to await a modern world supposedly not given to heroes, or at least preferring to slight the champions of the past. In 1834, in the course of a critical review of an eulogistic work on Pitt that extended to an attack on the minister, Macaulay wrote,

Even as a war minister, Pitt is scarcely entitled to all the praise which his contemporaries lavished on him. We, perhaps from ignorance,

---

[29] S. B. Baxter, 'The Conduct of the Seven Years' War', in Baxter (ed.), *England's Rise to Greatness 1660–1763* (Berkeley, 1983) pp. 335–44; R. Middleton, *The Bells of Victory. The Pitt–Newcastle Ministry and the Conduct of the Seven Years War 1757–1762* (Cambridge, 1985).

cannot discern in his arrangements any appearance of profound or dexterous combination. Several of his expeditions, particularly those which were sent to the coast of France, were at once costly and absurd. Our Indian conquests, though they add to the splendour of the period during which he was at the head of affairs, were not planned by him.[30]

Macaulay's impression of Pitt's contemporary reputation was in fact mistaken. His conduct of the war was criticised because there was room for controversy; the conduct of the war was located in a political sphere that the outbreak of the hostilities had made more contentious, not suspended; and also because the means for propagating critical views, especially the press, were subject neither to new restrictions nor to self-censorship.

It is no longer credible to argue that Pitt was concerned with measures, Newcastle with patronage. The importance of consultation at the highest level of government makes such a claim inaccurate, while the crucial importance of the financing of the war ensured that Newcastle's post as First Lord of the Treasury was a key one. Furthermore, Pitt cared more about patronage than he liked to show,[31] for a disdain for such considerations and for the obligations of connection and clientage was a central feature of the political image Pitt worked so hard to sustain in office. However, a valuable unpublished recent thesis has restated the case for Pitt's prominence, arguing that, while he did not interfere in the detailed work of the departments, Pitt, nevertheless, dominated the Cabinet. The claim, also recently advanced, that only Almon among contemporary writers made sweeping claims for Pitt's influence and that the myth of Pitt as the sole directing minister only grew up among later historians is dismissed by reference to numerous sources from the

[30] Edinburgh Review 58 (1834) p. 543.
[31] Baxter, 'Conduct of the Seven Years' War' p. 337.

period.[32] Fraser suggests that Pitt's very political weakness, his lack of secure backing in Parliament or the Closet, enabled him to reconcile the disparate tendencies in his political position. These were principally his role in formulating and executing government policy, especially controversial policies such as backing for Hanover and the dispatch of British troops to the Continent, and his desire to retain the support of Tory and Patriot opinion. He had fostered this support while critical of the government and it enabled him to enjoy a power base, limited and precarious as it might be, that was independent of Newcastle's supporters and that therefore allowed him to maintain his bargaining position in the coalition. Fraser stresses,

Pitt's outstanding ability as a politician and his use of this ability to ensure that political factors deflected to the minimum extent the course of war policy he wanted to pursue. He cleverly exploited the weakness of his own position in the government; took advantage of Newcastle's majority in the House of Commons while retaining Tory support by disclaiming any responsibility for the control of the Commons and retaining an apparently independent attitude; took advantage also of Newcastle's favour in the closet as a means of enforcing disagreeable policies on the King; and frequently contrived to put the blame on Newcastle for decisions unpopular with his own supporters but which were in reality of his own devising ... combination of a willingness to avow leadership in the cabinet with a disclaimer of royal confidence or control of Parliament.[33]

The situation did not always work to Pitt's advantage for the conspicuous steps he took to please Tory and Patriot opinion, such as his unsuccessful attempt in the spring of 1758 to expand the definition of habeas corpus by the Habeas Corpus

[32] E. J. S. Fraser, 'The Pitt–Newcastle Coalition and the Conduct of the Seven Years War 1757–1760' (unpublished D.Phil., Oxford, 1976) p. 53 n. 1.

[33] Fraser, 'Pitt–Newcastle Coalition' iv–v, 55. On Tory support for Pitt, L. J. Colley, In Defiance of Oligarchy. The Tory Party 1714–60 (Cambridge, 1982) pp. 271–85.

Bill,[34] could make it more difficult for him to enjoy good relations with George II and his ministerial colleagues, and thus kept him an outsider as far as the Old Corps were concerned, dependent for his political strength on assessments of his popularity, competence and indispensability. Thus in April 1758 Hardwicke reassured Newcastle,

As to the part Mr Pitt may take in the House of Commons, I much doubt whether it will be such a one as will greatly increase his credit in the Closet. I rather apprehend that he will accompany the shining parts with such limitations and saving clauses, and with such strong declarations against going further, in order to make what he says palatable to his Country-Gentlemen, that the favour, he may gain by it in a certain place will not be to be envied.[35]

Newcastle complained about Pitt's efforts to win his support for the Habeas Corpus Bill, 'a greater rhapsody of violence and virulence could not be flung out', while his wife reported that Pitt had told Lady Yarmouth that 'if this Bill did not pass, it was impossible for him to act with much confidence with those, that took away the Liberty of the People . . . he told her, he did not mean this, to the Duke of Newcastle: but God knows, that will make little difference in regard to their acting together'.[36] Clearly Pitt had lost none of his vigour with language, his willingness to misunderstand the motives of others nor his capacity to cause offence, but the bill failed. The sense of outrage and the bullying that were so inextricably and confusingly intertwined in Pitt's language and approach did not have to prevail. They could have as little effect, in terms of influencing policy rather than gaining attention, as some of his parliamentary rhetoric of earlier years.

[34] Walpole, Memoirs . . . George II III, 11–12; Baxter, 'Conduct of the Seven Years' War' p. 337.
[35] Hardwicke to Newcastle, 13 April 1758, BL Add. 32879 f. 151.
[36] Newcastle to Hardwicke, 14 April 1758, BL Add. 32879 ff. 157–8; Duchess of Newcastle to Earl of Lincoln, 23 May 1758, NeC 3154.

Fraser's positive assessment of Pitt as a minster can in part be reconciled with the more critical approach of Richard Middleton by noting that the latter is stressing the execution of policy and drawing heavily on administrative papers, while Fraser adopts a more political perspective, but there is still a considerable gap. It is possible to cite instances of both Newcastle and Pitt getting their way, which is scarcely surprising. Newcastle clearly retained his influence in the field of patronage and was important in the formulation of policy. However, he clearly felt that he needed Pitt and it is in this respect that Middleton's approach possibly offers a less than fully rounded picture. Over three years of political infighting had in some measure exhausted the participants, but it had also convinced them that a Newcastle–Pitt ministry was the best combination. Pitt had gained office by being both stubborn and flexible: stubborn in repeating ideas and demands that he knew to be unacceptable, or barely acceptable, to George II and likely ministerial colleagues, and flexible in being prepared to negotiate on these points. Fraser's portrayal of an astute politician able to exploit the weaknesses of his position and maintain links in different political directions, albeit at the cost of charges of hypocrisy, accords with any reading of the 1754–7 governmental crisis that places a premium on Pitt's skill.

Nevertheless, it is also, as ever, necessary to stress the role of circumstances, especially the outbreak of an unexpected conflict with France, the collapse of Britain's alliance system in 1755 as Austria made it clear that she would not assist Hanover against a possible French attack, the failure to retain Russian support, the unexpected outbreak of fighting on the Continent in 1756 and Britain's dismal performance in the opening stages of the war. As in 1718–20 and 1739–46, the Whig system seemed fragile and heavily under pressure in the event of war. Newcastle's crucial weakness was the lack of satisfactory and reliable leadership of the Commons, ever since the death of Pelham. The deterioration in Britain's position in 1755–6 exposed both a general weakness in the political system, the difficulties of coping with adverse developments, and the more specific problem of Commons leadership. Newcastle, Fox and Murray, all experienced politicians, hurried to dissociate themselves from the possible political consequences, Pitt's rise to high office, despite his lack of strong party backing, can therefore in part be seen as the consequence of the bankruptcy of a political system: the inability of Newcastle's Old Corps Whigs to cope with a serious crisis. During the last stages of the War of the Austrian Succession Horatio Walpole had similarly warned that control of Parliament by the Pelhams was not enough to enable them to cope with the difficulties facing them, but the crisis had been averted by France's willingness to negotiate a compromise peace in 1748. In 1756–7, in contrast, France was a member of a coalition that appeared to face the happy prospect of Continental invincibility and at the very time when the limitations of parliamentary superiority in Britain seemed frightening. It was against this background that Newcastle had accepted Pitt's rise to office and thus a measure of responsibility, and this set the background to the co-operation between the two ministers during the war. Newcastle did his best to win the approval of the King for Pitt.

Pitt's importance can also be grasped in another, more amorphous, sphere. Macaulay, who was no champion of the minister, claimed 'that the national spirit rose to the emergency – that the national resources were contributed with unexampled cheerfulness, – this was undoubtedly his work. The ardour of his spirit had set the whole kingdom on fire.'[37] This was not actually the case, as any detailed study of

[37] *Edinburgh Review* 58 (1834) p. 543.

the press debate of the period would reveal. On the other hand it was certainly true that British commitment to Hanoverian concerns was accepted far more readily once Pitt had become Secretary than it had been during the Carteret ministry. In addition, the political consequences of limited success in the early stages of the Seven Years War were surmounted with less difficulty than might have been anticipated. The contribution that Pitt and 'Patriot' opinion made to British victory may be questioned and qualified, but there seems little doubt both that Newcastle's task would have been more difficult had Pitt remained in opposition, especially in terms of finding adequate leadership for the Commons, and that he believed that this would be the case. War accentuated a central feature of the political system, namely that successful parliamentary management required competent leadership and acceptable policies, as well as patronage, and that, especially in periods of real and apparent crisis, such policies tended to take note of opinion 'out of doors', however manipulated and whatever the arithmetic of parliamentary strength was.

Given this situation, it was not surprising that Pitt played a central role during the Newcastle–Pitt ministry, a role that does not need to be explained solely in terms of his ability or of Newcastle's indecisiveness and desire to share responsibility. Pitt's importance was accentuated by his clear views in policy and in December 1761 he told the Commons, 'I am much obliged to the gentleman who lent me the same majority to execute the plan which he lent to the minister who went before me.' As so often with new colleagues, Newcastle was initially happy with Pitt. The Duke wrote to an ally and protégé, the Marquess of Rockingham,

Nothing can go worse than they do *abroad* in every respect . . . Things however go well amongst us at home, some little [word obscure]

from my new colleague, (which I verily believe are more the effect of constitution and humour than design,) and which pass over; The King is quite civil, and behaves very well to him, and indeed he deserves it, and His Majesty is satisfied. I have laboured all I can do to produce this good humour, and I have succeeded, and I must do them justice they have both done their parts well.[38]

However, the relationship between Pitt and both George II and Newcastle was not free from strain, and this caused Pitt stress. In December 1757 he wrote to John Pitt, 'I am worn with constant fatigue, and broken-hearted with the wretched interior of our condition, worse than all the foreign ills that threaten us. But I will not grow morose if I can help it, or utterly despair of better days.' This situation was exacerbated by Pitt's health, which continued poor. It was from personal experience as 'a veteran invalid' that he wrote to his sister Ann to 'recommend to you, above all things, to use this returning strength and spirits very sparingly at first'. In August 1758 he informed her that he knew of nothing able

to renovate and brace up a sickly constitution of thought but that mild and generous philosophy which teaches us the true value of the world, and a rational, firm religion that anchors us safe in the confidence of another, but I will end my sermon and come to the affairs of the world I am so deeply immersed in.

British troops had landed near Cherbourg, and Pitt referred to the stress he was under, 'I am infinitely anxious till we hear again.' Later that year he wrote to Ann, 'I am just going to Hayes for some hours recess, that I want much.'[39] Concern about his popularity ensured that the question of sending British troops to the Continent, which Pitt opposed when out of office and was unhappy about after he re-entered the

---

[38] Newcastle to Rockingham, 1757, misdated 1751, WW R1-5.
[39] Georgiana, Lady Chatterton, *Memorials of Admiral Lord Gambier* (2 vols., 1861) I, 81; BL Add. 69289 nos. 44, 46, 48; BL Add. 69289 nos. 44, 46, 48.

ministry, caused much tension. In January 1758 he wrote to Newcastle denouncing Andrew Mitchell, the envoy in Berlin, and alleging that British policy was being distorted,

I find to my extreme concern, Mr Mitchell's letters so constantly in the same strain, with regard to sending British troops, to reinforce the army in the Electorate; and his chief and favourite object seems to be so particularly to nourish the King of Prussia's mind, with the fitness and practicability of that impossible measure, that I can't forbear, on reading his last letter from Breslau, to express to your Grace my strong alarm at so extraordinary a proceeding. I love to speak plainly, Andrew Mitchell is not a fool, and therefore he must be something not fit to be the instrument of the present system of administration . . . it is evident to whom he belongs, and whose work he is doing. Thus it is, My Lord, in every part of government, the tools of another system are perpetually marring every hopeful measure of the present administration. In a word, if your Grace is not able to eradicate this lurking, diffusive poison a little more out of the mass of government, especially from the vitals, I think it's better for us, to have done. I do not intend for one, that Andrew Mitchell shall carry me, where I have resolved not to go.

Such a letter explains why Newcastle found Pitt so difficult: his rhetorical and aggressive style and his tendency to exaggeration were not solely for public display in Parliament. The letter also reveals Pitt's paranoia, but, possibly as seriously, his failure to accept that in a state in which the practice as well as the principle of government was to a considerable extent monarchical, the King was unlikely so to purge his servants and so entrust himself to one set of ministers and give them authority in all spheres, that only one 'system' would appear to prevail. Like many long-standing opponents of Walpole, he attributed to the King's ministers more power than they actually possessed. This was especially the case in diplomacy. Envoys were the personal representatives of the monarch, chosen and paid by him. To demand the replacement of Mitchell, who was also a supporter of Newcastle in the Commons and was anyway not a diplomat in Pitt's department, was therefore a bold step. Pitt clashed with George II on the matter and threatened to resign.[40] Berlin was a crucial embassy, Pitt's dominant role was accepted by his Secretarial colleague, Holdernesse, Pitt had to take responsibility for carrying government business through the Commons. That was made more difficult if he felt he could not rely on such a key envoy, and on earlier occasions ministers had sought to influence British diplomatic representation. Furthermore, George II did conduct negotiations with foreign powers without reference to the Secretaries of State and it was understandable that Pitt should be concerned about this. In addition, Pitt's German policies placed him under particular strain and pressure. For psychological as well as political reasons Pitt needed to show that he had not decisively broken with his Patriot past, and that he was demonstrating a realistic grasp of the problems facing the country, not ambition. In appealing for support he stressed his concern for the general good. Thanking the Mayor of Bath for his election as MP there, Pitt wrote in 1757,

In discharge of this public trust, vested in me by such a general and free concurrence I shall endeavour to the best of my judgment constantly to pursue the great object of general and national good and thereby best consult the particular interests of my several constituents.

Accepting the freedom of the society granted him by Bristol's Society of Merchant Adventurers, Pitt wrote that he would be glad 'if a sincere zeal for the true commercial interests of my country obtains the approbation of so valuable a society'.[41]

[40] Pitt to Newcastle, 28 January 1758, BL Add. 35417 ff. 187–8; Viry to Charles Emmanuel III, 14 March 1758, AST LM Ing. 63.
[41] PRO 30/8/6 ff. 2, 12.

Pitt's ability to see and present himself as furthering true interests was vital to his self-respect and political reputation, but many disagreed with his interpretation of these interests and queried the means by which he sought to further both them and his own career. In addition, there was a tension between the parliamentary aspect of government – (ministers) taking responsibility for successful management of the Commons in particular – and the departmental one, where different spheres were focused on the Crown and ministerial influence was more a consequence of personality than office. This was an inherently unstable situation that Pitt, like other ministers before him, found frustrating. He naturally stressed his own importance in order to acquire as much influence as possible and this has been criticised as egocentric although it was far from unprecedented. Pitt's demands were clearly not easy to take. In 1771 Holdernesse recalled that in the Cabinet Pitt 'used to harangue, as in Parliament'. The Test of 8 January 1757 presented Pitt as a doctor whose 'zeal for his patient's constitution is so vehement and warm, that he is apt to be rather overbearing in a consultation'. He took care to ensure his own importance, Lady Essex noting in May 1758, 'Mr Pitt undertakes to carry all the Admiralty dispatches in to the King instead of suffering the eldest Lord [of the Admiralty] to carry them as is the custom'. In April 1758 Hardwicke replied to a complaint by Newcastle, expressing understanding of the Duke's desire to retire, but presenting Pitt in a strong position,

The complaints, which your Grace has so much reason to make, give me great concern. The behaviour is certainly intolerable, but what can be done at present? I always feared it would be bad, and, from the beginning, your Grace saw my opinion upon the question about your coming in again. I don't however pretend to have foreseen the *manner* and *extent* of the disagreeableness; but advantage has been taken from the low and desperate state, to which *other persons* have reduced themselves since the Coalition was made; and some pride is taken from the success of the measure of breaking the Convention [of Klosterseven], which this Gentleman so much pressed. In short I do not at present know any other Connection, to which resort can be had. The money must be got in Parliament, or the nation is undone.[42]

In 1766 Pitt referred to his success in establishing a new militia system, under acts passed in 1757 and 1758, despite the opposition of ministerial colleagues, telling the Commons that 'the late King had become a convert to it from its utility, but that some of the ministers were then its latent enemies'.[43] The Habeas Corpus Bill caused particular difficulty in 1758. The bill made it compulsory for a judge to grant habeas corpus where a man had been wrongly detained because of the Press or Recruiting Acts, a measure that was popular with the Tories but opposed by most of the ministry on the grounds that it might harm recruitment. The bill, first read in the Commons on 8 March 1758, received its third reading on 24 April, passing without any division, but it was blocked in the Lords in May and June, as a result of ministerial action, Newcastle speaking against it 'in the full vigour of his nonsense'. The Duke complained to Cumberland,

our distress here is greater than ever; impracticability, or, at least the greatest difficulty in pursuing, with care, and success, one system, which alone can, at present, serve the King and the Country; and at the same time, no possibility of adopting any other. This is too much our case.[44]

Pitt's pressure on his colleagues over the issue angered George II and his threats that the defeat of the measure would

---

[42] HP Harris, 9 February 1771; Farmington 71 ff. 245–7; Hardwicke to Newcastle, 6 April 1758, BL Add. 32879 f. 76.

[43] HP Harris, 14 April 1766.

[44] Walpole, *Memoirs . . . George II* III, 19; Newcastle to Cumberland, 4 May 1758, BL Add. 32879 f. 415.

create difficulties for the ministry proved abortive. The episode can therefore be presented as a defeat for Pitt, as can the fact that although Mitchell was recalled the envoy remained in Berlin as a result of Frederick II's support. However, the fact that the Habeas Corpus Bill was defeated in the Lords was a reminder of Pitt's strength in the Commons and his support there was clearly important. James West, Joint Secretary to the Treasury, wrote to Newcastle in April 1758 about the Commons' discussion of ways and means, that it was 'the easiest day I ever remember on voting such ways and means'. Although angered by the defeat in the Lords, Pitt refused to support Beckford in trying to use the Commons' financial strength to put pressure on the Lords, he

could not agree with Mr Beckford that the money ought to be denied because the Lords had thrown out the Bill . . . flattered Beckford most violently, and declared that he had rather be an Alderman and representative of the opulent City of London . . . than the greatest Peer in the Realm: At the same time he see-sawed in some things, disclaimed distinctions between parts of the Administration – believed all deserved confidence – and talked in short a great while.

In July 1758 Holdernesse saw the ministry as stormy but stable, an assessment that was related to the success abroad he also noted,

Notre interieur continue comme par le passé, ferme dans le fond and with some little rubs now and then we jog on. I am still the entremetteur [intermediary] when I see any clouds arising, I look upon myself as a sort of electrified wire used to draw particles of thunder from black clouds whenever a storm threatens. You may believe from what you saw when you was amongst us that I do not want work. The whole face of foreign affairs are so changed in our favour since you left England that it seems a new world.

Holdernesse added in November 1759, 'In private we have still some jarrings, but not considerable or important enough to impede the great work we have in hand; we shall have a most unanimous session.'[45]

The Monitor claimed that Pitt had brought unanimity,

The immense sums granted by Parliament this year are a proof of it . . . The unanimity, with which the great sums necessary for answering these great ends were granted, is a proof that a minister, whose actions entitled him to the confidence of the people, is alone capable of carrying this nation happily through such a war, as we are now engaged in.

. . . at present all party-disputes seem to be laid asleep: those old distinctions of Whig and Tory, which have so long distracted the nation, and to perpetuate which, even after the spirit of them was lost, some late ministers have so successfully laboured, are no more heard of: but the whole body of the nation seem to be inflamed with one common spirit, and to pursue one common interest.[46]

Unanimity in this context is relative: there were serious differences within the ministry and criticism of its conduct. 1759 is usually remembered as a year of victories, but in March Charles Townshend, embittered by his exclusion from favour, could see only a crisis, for which he held Pitt responsible,

The causes of the want of bullion are these. 3 millions in specie exported to pay the army on the Rhine and Prussian subsidy and one million to North America; at a time when the return of bullion from Portugal has been prevented and no Spanish captures as in the last war: you then broke when your expences were less, your importation of bullion greater, and therefore how can you expect to survive now, when your charges are so much higher, your resources so much less, and your debt so much increased? Mr Pitt feels this and has lost all temper. In the House he has lost all parties

---

[45] West to Newcastle, 28 April 1758, BL Add. 32879 f. 331; Lady to Lord Anson, 2 May 1758, Stafford, County Record Office D615/P(S)1; Holdernesse to Robert Keith, 25 July 1758, 2 November 1759, BL Add. 35482 f. 112, 35483 f. 40. Robert Keith had been appointed the envoy to Russia the previous October.
[46] Monitor 13 May, 17 June 1758.

by his opposition to Mr Legge, his servile adulation of Beckford, his flattery to Sir Robert Walpole's ashes, his declaration for an excise, and his contempt of the country gentlemen. Yesterday the House groaned as he spoke: your friend Vyner attacked him roughly upon his Martinique expedition and continental measures: and all, of that party [Tories], stand amazed and disgusted. Northey has retired from the House, Sir John Philipps openly opposes Mr Pitt, Mr Legge professes to resign, and all hastens to confusion. I have not seen the Duke of Newcastle: but Pitt gives him no quarter, with the hopes, I believe, of being turned out, that he may run away from present embarrassment, be absent when the crush comes, and come in again when the storm is passed.

Townshend added that the hitherto unsuccessful campaign in the West Indies, where Martinique had proved too difficult to capture and the expedition to Guadeloupe had become bogged down, had led to parliamentary criticism of Pitt, who 'hung down his head and was silent. The grounds of the expedition and the unequal force are much blamed.'[47] The consequences of the weakening of Tory support in 1759 have not been probed. More generally, public attacks on Pitt at the height of the war have generally been overlooked, but it serves as a reminder both that the controversy that surrounded him did not cease and that he was therefore under continuous pressure. The Monitor of 14 July 1759 deplored press criticism of Pitt and argued that 'his connections with the powers at war on the continent, are necessary to preserve religion and liberty'. However, despite divisions within the ministry and attacks on Pitt, the political situation was far more favourable than it had been both before the formation of the government and during the last war.

---

[47] Charles to George Townshend, 13 March 1759, Bod. MS Eng. hist. d. 211 f. 5–6.

THE CONDUCT OF THE SEVEN YEARS WAR 1757–1760

From a distant prospect the Seven Years War (1756–63) appears a remarkable triumph, an obvious contrast to the indifferent result of the War of the Austrian Succession and the defeats of the War of American Independence. It was indeed the most successful major war that Britain fought during the eighteenth century and it witnessed the decisive defeat of French power in North America and India. When, in the War of American Independence, French forces returned to challenge the British position in North America they did so because the British had been defeated in 1777 already by the American revolutionaries at Saratoga, and because they had allies: the revolutionaries and the prospect of Spanish help. The British victories in the Seven Years War ensured that France could only act thereafter in North America if they had allies. Supporters of Pitt argued that the government's commitment of resources to the struggle against France in Germany was in the national interest because it contributed to success elsewhere, and was therefore different to the policies and achievements of pre-Pittite ministries. The *Monitor* of 12 May 1759 claimed that Pitt did so 'no farther than the nation is obliged by treaty; and is consistent with good policy to reduce the common enemy to sue for peace; though there had been no right to demand our aid'. The paper stated that troops and money were sent to Germany 'to reduce the French . . . to an incapacity of acting' and that Pitt was 'always in a condition to improve the arms of his country's allies to the national interest, by feeding them with such succours and supplies only, as the connection of their war influenceth the measures to be pursued, in favour of his own country; and to keep clear of those ruinous continental measures, which were taken in favour of the Dutch and the House of Austria'.

In discussing why in the earlier war Britain defeated France, also a great maritime and colonial power as well as being a far more populous country, there is a tendency today to concentrate on 'structural' factors, the inherent strength and character of the two states, such as the sophistication of British administration and specifically of the system of public finance which raised substantial sums of money at a lower rate of interest than that paid by the French government. These are of considerable importance but they lend an appearance of inevitability to the outcome of the conflict. So also does the argument that Britain 'won America in Germany', that the British financial and eventually military contribution to the war in Germany diverted France from making a sufficient effort to defend her colonies.[48]

Both these arguments treat the war as a single unit and each offer a somewhat schematic interpretation that diminishes the role of circumstances and individuals. In the space of a short work it is not possible to study the war in sufficient detail to bring out adequately the play of contingency, but by adopting a narrative rather than a schematic interpretation, it is easier to show that the fate of the conflict was not a foregone conclusion and thus to throw more light on the problems and choices facing Pitt.

1757: The collapse of Hanover

It is sad that the prejudices of only one man, well-intentioned in other respects, can prevail over the clearest and best-demonstrated truths. I see, however, that these prejudices are too engrained to hope to destroy them, and therefore it is necessary to renounce all

---

[48] P. Kennedy, *The Rise and Fall of the Great Powers* (1988) pp. 146–8; J. Brewer, *The Sinews of People. War, Money and the English State, 1688–1783* (1989), esp. pp. 174–5. For a different interpretation, see J. Black, *A System of Ambition? British Foreign Policy 1660–1793* (1991).

hope of British troops. (Count Finckenstein, Prussian minister, March 1758)[49]

The Seven Years War, like all major wars, was an umbrella conflict: beneath the single title lay a number of different struggles. The two most prominent were the Anglo-French conflict, waged in Germany, the colonies and on the high seas, and that between Frederick the Great and his enemies; by 1762 the agenda of hostility had lengthened to include war between Spain and Britain and Spain, with French assistance, and Portugal, and confrontation between Russia and Denmark. At the outset of the Newcastle–Pitt ministry Britain had formally been at war with France for a year, but hostilities had actually begun in North America in 1754. The scope of the British commitment had widened in 1756 with the outbreak of war and the loss of Minorca, which ensured that some countervailing gain would have to be made, if Britain was not to lose at the eventual peace settlement; and with the beginning of fighting on the Continent. Hanover was clearly vulnerable and the outnumbered forces of Britain's ally Prussia offered only a precarious prospect of support. In 1757 the departure of the Duke of Cumberland to take command of the Army of Observation, a German force partly financed by Britain, formed to protect Hanover, focused attention on the issue of possible British military assistance, a sensitive matter for Pitt who had contradictory obligations towards the government and towards Patriot and Tory opinion, the *Monitor* of 30 July 1757 having warned against being involved 'in a war on the Continent for the pretended preservation of the balance of power'.

Unfortunately for those who propounded this view Cumberland was defeated by the French at Hastenbeck on 26

---

[49] Finckenstein to Gerlach Adolf von Münchhausen, 18 March 1758, Hanover, Des. 91 Münchhausen I No. 41 f. 4.

July. The Duke was heavily outnumbered and felt abandoned by the ministry in London. He complained to Fox, 'I hear you send two thousand men more to North America, what for, God knows. Here I am sure you'll send none, though perhaps they would be more necessary than anywhere England can employ them.' Pitt resisted the idea of sending British troops to Germany to reinforce Cumberland. He had already on 20 May 1757, while out of office, argued that if any subsidy should be given to help the war in Germany it should go to Frederick II, who alone appeared capable of mounting the offensive operations necessary for success. Pitt told the Commons that it was pointless to 'go on subsidising little princes here and there and fancy that all together they will make a King of Prussia', an accurate prediction of the fate of Cumberland.[50] Hastenbeck, like Byng's conduct off Minorca, was to lead to the loss of some of George II's territory, but the political consequences were smaller because in part of Pitt's entry into the ministry and the consequent weakening of opposition. The retreating Cumberland signed on 10 September 1757 the Convention of Klosterseven by which he agreed to the disbanding of the Army of Observation and the French occupation of Hanover, thus giving the French a powerful negotiating counter in any future peace settlement with George II.[51] The seriousness of this move was exacerbated by the prospect of the disintegration of the Anglo-Prussian combination. As Elector, George, concerned about the lack of British support for Hanover, had shown an interest in negotiations with Austria for a neutrality for the electorate, much to the concern of his British ministers. Pitt was totally against such negotiations and helped to stiffen the resolve of

---

[50] Cumberland to Fox, July 1757, Earl of Ilchester (ed.), Letters to Henry Fox . . . With a Few Addressed to his Brother Stephen (Roxburghe Club, 1915) pp. 116–17; W. J. Smith (ed.) The Grenville Papers (4 vols., 1852–3) I, 206.

[51] W. Mediger, 'Hastenbeck und Zeven', Niedersächsisches Jahrbuch für Landesgeschichte, 56 (1984).

other ministers. Newcastle noted, 'Mr Pitt said the application to the Court of Vienna . . . implied a change of system, by flinging off the King of Prussia, and returning to the Queen of Hungary', which Pitt opposed. The Duke commented, 'if something cannot be found out to put a short end to this separate measure, Pitt, I am persuaded, will quit the King's service, and I cannot blame him'.[52] Newcastle had no doubt that Pitt did not simply seek office and that there was a limit to his willingness to compromise his views. If the Convention was accepted there was a danger that Frederick, his western flank exposed, might accept peace terms and abandon Britain.

Pitt took a firm line in the crisis of 1757, insisting on the repudiation of the Convention, and thus vindicating Fox's prediction that 'those who were most against assisting the Electorate, will be most angry at this neutrality'.[53] Pitt also pressed for an attack on the French port of Rochefort, and displayed a willingness to take a potentially more risky step, an approach to Spain, offering her Gibraltar in return for help in reconquering Minorca and thus a breach between France and Spain. His dispatch of 23 August 1757 to Benjamin Keene, still envoy in Spain, the diplomat who had negotiated the Convention of the Pardo which Pitt had savaged in the Commons in 1739, provided a gloomy account of Britain's situation, but also a defence of interventionist policies and an identification of the plight of Hanover with that of Europe,

. . . the formidable progress of the arms of France, and the imminent dangers to Great Britain and her allies resulting from a total subversion of the system of Europe . . . it is impossible to pass in silence that affecting and calamitous part of the subversion of Europe, namely the French conquests and desolations in Lower Saxony, which affords the afflicting spectacle of His Majesty's

[52] Newcastle to Hardwicke, 10 September 1757, BL Add. 35417 f. 54.
[53] Fox to Bedford, 20 September 1757, Bedford vol. 35.

ancient patrimonial dominions, transmitted down with glory in his most illustrious house through a long series of centuries, now lying prey to France . . . nothing can shake His Majesty's firmness, or abate . . . concern for . . . his crown, and the rights of his kingdoms; nor can any events withdraw the necessary attention of his consummate wisdom from the proper interest of Europe, or divert his generous cares from endeavouring to prevent the final overthrow of all system and independency among the powers of the Continent.

On the same day Pitt wrote to the Earl of Home, Governor of Gibraltar, 'to have particular regard to our engagements with His Catholic Majesty'.[54] Despite the rhetorical language of his instruction to Keene, Pitt was acting as a pragmatist. He sought, however unrealistically, to purchase Spanish support, appreciating that Bourbon disunity was crucial to Britain (which was certainly the case in naval terms), and, in the meantime, tried to ensure that Spain was not provoked. The approach was a failure, which was scarcely surprising as Britain had little to offer: as Secretary of State Pitt found Britain's international position poor, her diplomatic options limited and he was obliged to concentrate on what he was temperamentally more suited for: military planning.

The Rochefort expedition was as unsuccessful as the approach to Spain. It was supported by Pitt as a means to employ forces that had to be retained in or near Britain for defensive purposes, as a way to resist pressure to send troops to Germany and yet reduce French pressure on Germany, and as a demonstration that in joining the ministry he had not abandoned traditional Patriot views on foreign policy. Pitt adopted the idea of an attack on the naval base of Rochefort, proposed by an officer in the Engineers, and supported it against Newcastle's suggestion that the forces be employed in a fashion that might more directly assist the war in

[54] Pitt to Keene, 23 August, Pitt to Home, 23 August 1757, Beinecke, Osborn Files, Pitt.

Germany. However, after the British force reached the approaches to Rochefort on 21 September 1757 a combination of poor intelligence, inadequate co-operation between naval and army commanders, and indifferent generalship led to a failure to attack the port. The consequence was public disquiet, the setting up on 1 November of a Commission of Enquiry into the conduct of the generals on the expedition and the unsuccessful court martial of the army commander, Sir John Mordaunt on 14–20 December 1757.[55] Pitt set up the inquiry in order to assuage public discontent and he showed his concern about opinion in London and the danger of a hostile address from the City, by sending a message to the Lord Mayor of London through one of the Privy Council clerks to inform the City that an inquiry had been set up. Horace Walpole, conservative on social and constitutional matters like his colleagues in the Commons, complained about the step, arguing that 'confusion may follow from incorporating the mob of London with the other parts of the legislature'.[56]

As so often in his career, Pitt's demonstrative public moves were resented by other politicians, who considered not so much the reasons for particular steps as the rejection of what were felt to be the prevalent norms of political behaviour. In late 1757 he evaded blame for the Rochefort expedition by setting up the Commission of Enquiry. Pitt played an active role in the subsequent court martial of Mordaunt, appearing before it in order to criticise the generals. He had earlier told Viry that the failure at Rochefort was due to Cumberland's

---

[55] Lady Betty Waldegrave to Earl Gower, 17 October 1757, PRO 30/29/1/17 f. 969; George Quarme to Marquess of Rockingham, 18 October 1757, WW R1–111; Monitor 22 October, 5 November 1757; Dr Akenside to Sir Francis Drake, 27 October 1757, Exeter, Devon County Record Office 346 M/F 18; George Ross to Brigadier Forbes, 10 November 1757, Edinburgh, Scottish Record Office GD 45/2/20/4; Earl of Ilchester (ed.), *Letters to Henry Fox . . . With a Few Addressed to his Brother Stephen* (Roxburghe Club, 1915) p. 125; Viry to Charles Emmanuel III, 6 December 1757, AST LM Ing. 62. [56] Walpole, *Memoirs . . . George II* II, 291.

hostility to the scheme and his influence in the army, probably an example of his paranoia, but a view that Newcastle appeared to share,[57] while Cumberland himself espoused the cause of the generals. The acquittal of Mordaunt reflected the court martial's view that the expedition had been misconceived, and was therefore a criticism of Pitt, but by encouraging the process of inquiry and the atmosphere of recrimination he avoided any serious consequences for himself.

In 1757 operations were no more successful in the New World. The Earl of Loudoun had been placed in command and Pitt had written to him on 4 February pressing the need for action. He hoped to see Canada conquered that year, which would have been a great triumph for both nation and ministry. Loudoun was told that he should be able to

form, early in the spring, an army of near 17,000 men, His Majesty doubts not, but with such a force, supplied with artillery, and supported with a strong squadron, your Lordship will find yourself in a condition to push, with the utmost vigour, an offensive war, and to effectuate some great and essential impressions on the enemy. The King is of opinion, that the taking of Louisbourg, and Quebec, can alone prove decisive; but as the success of both these enterprises may depend on circumstances, not to be known here, His Majesty is pleased to leave some latitude to your Lordship's discretion and judgement, to decide on the time, and manner of carrying these attempts into execution. Nevertheless, I am to acquaint your Lordship, that the King, depending on your known ability, and great zeal for his service, expects the utmost activity, and vigour, in this critical and important campaign; It is therefore His Majesty's pleasure, that your Lordship should forthwith so dispose the forces, now in America, and make all such necessary preparations of victuals, and transports, and all other requisites, for the same; as well as obtain, by all possible means, the best

---

[57] Viry to Charles Emmanuel III, 7 October 1757, AST LM Ing. 62.

intelligences, and informations, relative to Louisbourg and to the navigation of the River St Lawrence to Quebec, as may enable your Lordship, on the arrival of the reinforcement from Ireland, immediately to attack Louisbourg with such a force, by sea and land, as may be judged sufficient to carry that important fortress. And as there is the highest probability, in case the troops from Ireland arrive, by the time intended, in the month of April, that this attempt may have its issue, by about the end of May, or the beginning of June, the season will be then the properest for the navigation of the River St Lawrence to Quebec; to the attack of which place, it is the King's pleasure, your Lordship should, without loss of time next proceed.

At the same time the governors of the North American colonies were ordered to provide military assistance.[58] It however proved easier to plan victory than to secure it. Poor weather helped to ensure that the British force did not assemble at Halifax until July. By then the French had succeeded in assembling a superior fleet at Louisbourg, a result of the failure of the British to block the departure of French squadrons from Brest. In the face of the larger French fleet, the council of war summoned by Loudoun decided not to risk disaster by landing on Cape Breton Island. On 9 August, while the British forces in North America were concentrated for the Louisbourg expedition, Fort William Henry at the head of Lake George fell to the Marquis de Montcalm, the French commander at Quebec. The Hudson valley was thus exposed to attack, though Montcalm decided not to press his advantage. Pitt was not exaggerating when he wrote that December of 'the losses and disappointments of the last inactive and unhappy campaign'.[59] There were therefore no victories elsewhere to compensate for or distract attention from the situation in Germany.

[58] HL Loudoun papers 2765 A, 2764 A.
[59] G. S. Kimball (ed.), *Correspondence of William Pitt when Secretary of State with Colonial Governors and Military and Naval Commissioners in America* (2 vols., 1906) I, 143.

In the winter of 1757–8 Pitt played a major role in securing a political settlement that tied the defence of Hanover to British direction and identified it with the Prussian alliance, a policy he had anticipated in Parliament when supporting the grant for the Army of Observation. This was crucial to the disavowal of the Hanover neutrality convention which George II rejected after some persuasion, leading to a resumption of active Hanoverian intervention in the war. Pitt had pressed George II hard for the rapid disavowal of the convention, refusing in October 1757 to pay the Hanoverian troops while they remained inactive. Cumberland's disgrace helped to increase Pitt's influence within the coalition, ensuring that Newcastle, who did not want the coalition to appear disunited, felt greater pressure to accept Pitt's views and defend them to the King. In defining a common response to the neutrality convention, the two men had also come closer together. The Duchess of Newcastle was told by her husband that 'Mr Pitt is very reasonable and acts extremely well, if the word happiness may be named in such a time as this surely it is one that the administration is what it is'. Nevertheless, Pitt was far from pliant. A month later Newcastle referred to Pitt's 'usual fierte' (haughtiness) and noted that when the two Secretaries of State had discussed the need for a commander-in-chief of the army to replace Cumberland, only Pitt of the Secretaries had spoken.[60]

Pitt's success in helping to establish Hanover's role as an active member of the anti-French alliance posed political problems in Britain, as Carteret's comparable success in 1742 had done. Unlike then, Pitt was responsible for supporting the new commitment, seeking to make political capital within the government by doing so successfully, rather than hoping to win fame by opposing the policy. In 1757 Pitt

---

[60] NeC 3156; Newcastle to Hardwicke, 23 October 1757, BL Add. 35417 ff. 126–8.

committed himself to obtaining parliamentary funds for the Army of Observation, while a subsidy of £670,000 for Prussia was also required, in order to support Frederick the Great and prevent him from negotiating a separate peace. At the Cabinet on 7 October Pitt's suggestion that Britain agree to pay the entire cost of the Army of Observation provided the Convention was disavowed was adopted.[61] The government relied for parliamentary backing for this policy on Pitt. Holdernesse wrote that the King relied 'on the signal zeal of His Parliament' to finance the Prussian subsidy, while Henry Fox observed 'all this, I hear, Mr Pitt can get the Common Council, etc. etc. (he thinks), to come into'.[62] And yet, even while these new commitments were being adopted, there were warnings about possible future problems. Newcastle made it clear that he saw the Prussian subsidy as the means to peace; 'These measures, though expensive, I rejoice to concur in. There is safety and sound politics in them; and these are the only, or, at least, the most likely ones, to bring us to our grand object, a solid peace: For these immense expences cannot be long supported anywhere, and peace must soon become the object of all parties.' Holdernesse sought to warn about the possible dangers of sending British troops to Germany, writing of

the unanimity with which the present session of Parliament has been opened; the zeal with which the Protestant cause is supported; and the cheerfulness with which people, in general, will bear the heavy load, that must necessarily be laid upon them, for the support of the war, this year. An attempt to send British troops abroad would put the continuance of this happy situation of things at home to the greatest hazard, and it is past doubt, that a unanimity in

[61] Cabinet minute, 7 October 1757, PRO SP 90/70, 30/8/89 f. 52; Hardwicke's notes, BL Add. 35870 f. 284.

[62] Holdernesse to Mitchell, 23 September 1757, PRO SP 90/70; Fox to Bedford, 14 November 1757, Bedford vol. 35; Campbell to Fox, 21 October 1757, Ilchester (ed.), *Letters to Fox* p. 126.

Parliament is, in this critical session, of much more consequence to the interests of Germany, than a few British troops joined to the armies there could possibly be.[63]

Frederick had crushed a Franco-German army at Rossbach on 5 November 1757, sending Pitt to dinner with a better appetite when he received the news.[64] However, the Prussian situation remained difficult and Frederick pressed for the dispatch of British troops to cover his western flank. Newcastle was willing to agree, but Pitt refused, in Hardwicke's eyes because of his concern about Tory views. The Cabinet decided on 23 February 1758 not to send any.[65] British policy was being framed in light of what Pitt thought practicable in parliamentary terms.

1758: Troops to Germany; Louisbourg falls

this country is to send to the continent four millions, which the greatest authority last year declared could not afford above two hundred thousand to that service. (Earl Gower, April 1758)[66]

Both during the course of the conflict and subsequently the claim was to be made that Britain conquered 'America', i.e. Canada, in Germany. It is easy to present this as arising from some long-held plan, but in fact the decision to send troops to Germany was seen as an unfortunate necessity, arising from the need to keep Hanover and Prussia in the war. Soon after he resigned in October 1761 Pitt justified his policy during the war in the Commons, declaring that when he had joined the government,

---

[63] Newcastle to Mitchell, 8 December, 1757, BL Add 6832 f. 33; Holdernesse to Mitchell, 12 December, 1757, PRO SP 90/70.

[64] Grenville Papers I, 230.

[65] Newcastle to Hardwicke, 29 January, Hardwicke to Newcastle, 29 January 1758, BL Add. 32877 ff. 271, 276; K. W. Schweizer, England, Prussia and the Seven Years War (Lewiston, 1989) p. 64.

[66] Gower to Bedford, 14 April 1758, Bedford vol. 36.

it was my opinion that we being once engaged in the German war, there was nothing to be done but to make the best of it after the principal objects of this country should be provided for . . . the point was to consider whether it was not possible to make the German war useful to the interests of this country as a subordinate measure, while our marine and colonies should be the principal object. These were my ideas and I have had the happiness hitherto of seeing them succeed upon my plan, in both views – of Germany and of our maritime interests.[67]

With the benefit of victorious hindsight, Pitt chose to overlook the risks of this plan and its questionable logic. It is unlikely that had her army not been committed in Germany, France would have been able to devote substantially more resources to the maritime struggle with Britain: army and naval resources were not so interchangeable as this suggestion assumes.

British troops were committed initially to defend the North Sea port of Emden, a limited goal pressed by Frederick, and by Ferdinand of Brunswick, Cumberland's replacement in Germany. Pitt realised the military necessity of the step, although he took care to ensure that he would appear to have accepted it reluctantly, rather than to have instigated the move. In political terms he covered himself by supporting with fresh determination the 'popular' issues before the Commons: the Habeas Corpus Bill and the bill introduced by George Townshend to amend the Militia Act. This conduct in the spring of 1758 angered George II and depressed Newcastle, but it prevented any strong parliamentary opposition to the decision to commit troops to Germany. On 19 April the Commons voted a subsidy to Frederick and money to support 50,000 men in Ferdinand's army without a division. Pitt presented the dispatch of troops to Emden as a necessary step that did not divert manpower from North

<hr />

[67] BL Add. 38334 f. 34.

America, and this proved generally acceptable. In practical terms Pitt had brought unanimity and this was amply demonstrated by the ease with which Parliament granted the ministry's substantial financial requirements.

In May 1758 Pitt persuaded the Cabinet to agree on another expedition to the French coast. Such an attack fulfilled traditional Tory notions of a maritime war and also limited the possible British commitment to the defence of Hanover. The original plan was for an attack on St Malo, but this was abandoned in June 1758 due to the apparent difficulty of the task. However, though such expeditions were seen by some critics as a futile distraction of British resources, they did not mean that Pitt was unprepared to accept a greater commitment to Germany. Though in June 1758 he blocked the idea, pressed by Frederick and Ferdinand, and supported by George II and Newcastle, that the expeditions should be directed towards the Austrian Netherlands, specifically Nieuport, rather than to ports further distant from the German battlefields, Pitt agreed to the dispatch of substantial British reinforcements to Ferdinand's army. As with many contentious decisions in eighteenth-century government, this was taken soon after the beginning of the parliamentary recess. Pitt's move was eased also by the successful attack on Cherbourg on 8 August, a vindication of the strategy of coastal expeditions, and by the care he took to persuade Bute to abandon his hostility to the idea of sending troops.

Better news was soon to come. Pitt had had the commanders he blamed for failure in North America in 1757 replaced and he took a prominent role in planning a three-pronged offensive on Canada. Separate forces were to attack Ticonderoga and Crown Point en route to Montreal, as well as Louisbourg and Fort Duquesne. The largest army was sent under General James Abercromby against Ticonderoga, but it was the smaller force under Generals Jeffrey Amherst and

James Wolfe and Admiral Edward Boscawen that attacked Louisbourg that was successful.[68] British forces landed on Cape Breton Island on 8 June and after a short siege Louisbourg surrendered on 26 July, 3,000 Frenchmen becoming prisoners of war, while the French had also lost five ships of the line and four frigates. There were also defeats: the attempt on 8 July to storm the French position at Ticonderoga was a costly failure. The French fortifications were stronger than anticipated and the British lost nearly 2,000 men, a very high figure for a British army in trans-oceanic operations. In Europe a force landed in September for a second attempt on St Malo had to re-embark in the face of a superior French army with the loss of 750 men. Those responsible for the latter failure were protégés of the court of George, Prince of Wales at Leicester House and anger with their subsequent treatment, especially that of Robert Clerk, helped to damage relations between Pitt and Leicester House seriously,[69] as did a growing sense that Pitt was failing to consider the views of the young court sufficiently.[70]

Despite these setbacks, a more optimistic note character-ised British ministerial thinking about the war by late 1758. Far from the conflict being seen as primarily defensive, plans were now readily advanced to seize French possessions, not only in North America, but also in the West Indies, where Pitt proposed an attack on Martinique, and West Africa, where the capture of Goree was seen as a necessary complement to the recent gain of Senegal. It fell that winter. Pitt stressed the determination of the government to go onto the offensive

[68] Pitt to Abercromby, 30 December 1757, Kimball I, 143–9; Richmond to Lennox, 21 January 1758, BL Bathurst Loan 57/103 ff. 123–4.
[69] John Calcraft to Fox, 19 September 1758, Ilchester (ed.), *Letters to Fox* p. 132; Viry to Charles Emmanuel III, 22 September 1758, AST LM Ing. 63; R. Sedgwick (ed.), *Letters from George III to Lord Bute, 1756–1766* (1939) pp. 10–11.
[70] Viry to Charles Emmanuel, 27 September, 17 October 1758, AST LM Ing. 63; Sedgwick (ed.), *Letters* p. 18.

with all vigour possible in America, the Caribbean, Africa and Germany, and on the oceans of the world.[71] At the same time there were obvious dangers. Frederick was still outnumbered and, although Ferdinand's army in Westphalia had been far more successful than that of Cumberland, there was the danger that this achievement would be reversed. Diplomatically Britain had had little success, failing to win the alliance of the United Provinces or to sow dissension among the anti-Prussian coalition. Government finances and credit were both weak. Newcastle complained that Pitt's ideas about finance were absurd and ignorant.[72] There was little suggestion that Britain was on the eve of a year of victories.

The year 1758 was when Pitt first came to be associated widely with victory. His role in pressing for and organising a substantial military effort in North America designed to conquer Canada was well known and he was given much of the credit for British success. The Reverend Samuel Pullein took time from his publications on silk cultivation to write the poem 'On the Taking of Louisburgh', which was published in *Owen's Weekly Chronicle* on 9 September 1758, as well as in the *Gentleman's Magazine*. Pullein saw the capture of the fortress as a decisive moment in world history, the war as part of a struggle against tyranny and superstition presided over by the unlikely figures of the elderly George II and the sickly Pitt.

> Hail, western world! begin they better fate,
> Hence let they annals take a happier date . . .
> GEORGE, fear'd in arms, belov'd for gentle sway,
> And PITT, the vestal guard of freedom's ray;
> Prompt to consummate heav'n's supreme decree,
> They give the mandate, and thy realms are free . . .
> Thus liberty, releas'd by heroes hands . . .

[71] Viry to Charles Emmanuel, 27 September 1758, AST LM Ing. 63.
[72] Newcastle to Hardwicke, 17 September 1758, BL Add. 35418 f. 23.

gives the new-known worlds a second birth . . .
when the fated ages shall have run,
And shewn new empires to the setting sun,
Each rising Aera shall its date restrain
To PITT, and LIBERTY, and GEORGE's reign.

George II was convinced, as he told Pitt, 'that we must keep Cape Breton, and Canada', which had not yet been conquered, and regain Minorca by exchanging it with a yet to be captured Martinique. Newcastle thought both men unrealistic, argued that it would be difficult to find the funds to continue the war in 1759 and impossible to do so for 1760, and he pressed the need for peace.[73] However, others who met Pitt were impressed by him. The long-serving Bavarian envoy Baron Haslang reported in October 1758, 'Pitt makes things go very differently to his predecessors. He acts with vigour and, although crushed by gout, his mind is always clear and continually active.' He also found Pitt firm and incorruptible. The Austrian Chancellor Count Kaunitz wrote in May 1758 that he could see no likelihood of the British wishing to make peace 'not least because Pitt has his hand on the tiller. His former conduct has furnished convincing proof that he does not live from day to day, but goes to work in a systematic fashion, and knows how to direct the decisions in his part of the world towards a single aim.'[74]

The wisdom of his policies was more questionable. Aside from the problems facing coastal attacks on France, which reflected the difficulties of staging amphibious operations, they had little effect on the French and did not distract them from their operations in Germany. The attempt to hinder French maritime operations, especially to prevent her from

---

[73] Newcastle to Hardwicke, 17 September, 19 October (quote) 1758, BL Add. 35418 ff. 21, 45.
[74] Haslang to Count Preysing, Bavarian foreign minister, 3 October, 8 December 1758, Munich, Bayr. Ges. London 234; Kaunitz quoted in C. Duffy, The Military Experience in the Age of Reason (1987) p. 154.

reinforcing her colonies, by maintaining a British naval presence off Brest had been unsuccessful. The French navy had sailed from its west-coast ports relatively freely, saving Louisbourg in 1757, and their merchant and supply convoys had continued to operate. It was in the crucial financial sphere that the French navy was increasingly handicapped in 1758.[75] In North America the three-pronged British offensive had not led to the conquest of Canada. The prongs had not been mutually supporting and Montcalm had been able to concentrate his efforts against Abercromby. The surrender of Louisbourg on 26 July had not been followed up successfully. James Wolfe wrote thence on 9 August,

I don't well know what we are doing here – with the harbour full of men of war, and transports – and the fine season stealing away, unenjoyed – I call it so because we should use it for the purposes of war. We have enemies close at hand, and others at a greater distance, that should in my mind be sought after . . . Our fleet, it seems, wants anchors, and cables, and provisions and pilots, pretty essential articles you will say . . . I am sure Abercromby wants assistance – we have it to spare.

Given the serious logistical difficulties of operating on the Hudson–Lake Champlain axis, it would have been wiser to make Louisbourg and the St Lawrence the principal sphere of operations in 1758, as it was to be in 1759, as Britain could have used her control of the sea to most effect there.[76] This might not seem too serious if it is assumed to be the case that a lengthy war providing the British with opportunities for

---

[75] P Mackesy, 'Problems of an Amphibious Power: Britain against France, 1793–1815', *Naval War College Review*, (1978), pp. 16–25; R. Middleton, 'British Naval Strategy, 1755–1762. The Western Squadron', *Mariner's Mirror*, 75 (1989), p. 359; R. Harding, *Amphibious Warfare in the Eighteenth Century* (1991) p. 195; J. Pritchard, *Louis XV's Navy 1748–1762* (Kingston, Ontario, 1987) pp. 184–205.

[76] Wolfe to Colonel Charles Hotham, 9 August 1758, Hull, University Library, Hotham papers, DDHo/4/7; Kimball (ed.), *Correspondence of William Pitt* I, 365; S. Pargellis, *Military Affairs in North America 1748–1765* (New York, 1936) xviii–xxi.

successive campaigns in which they took the initiative, as in fact happened, was inevitable; but that was not so. There was the continual danger that Frederick might be forced to end the war on his opponents' terms, forcing the British to negotiate peace. It is not surprising that Pitt reacted with such emotional intensity to Prussian victories, writing in September 1758 of

the King of Kings, whose last glories transcend all the pasts. The modesty of His Prussian Majesty's relation, his silence of himself, and entire attribution of the victory to General Seidlitz, are of a mind, as truely heroick, as His Majesty's taking a colours in his own hand, when exhortations failed, and forcing a disordered infantry to follow him or see him perish. More glory can not be won, but more decisive, final consequences we still hope to hear, and languish for farther letters from the Prussian army.

The following month he claimed, 'this heroick monarch's happy genius never fails him when he wants it most'.[77] Discussions over likely peace terms reflected the possibility that the war might end soon, while Newcastle, repeatedly drew attention to the cost of continued conflict and the danger of a drying up of the credit essential to Britain's war effort. The window of opportunity for major gains could not be expected to last. Against this background the failure to capture Louisbourg in 1757 and conquer Canada in 1758 appeared more serious.

Before Pitt is judged too harshly, however, it is worth pointing out that he laboured under considerable difficulties in planning campaigns at such a distance, difficulties that were to help to lead to failure in the War of American Independence.[78] The French might be heavily outnumbered, but the concentration of overwhelming British forces at crucial points faced serious logistical problems. Contempor-

---

[77] BL Add. 69289 nos. 45, 54.   [78] J. Black, *War for America* (Stroud, 1991).

aries contrasted British success with the less brilliant trans-oceanic operations of the War of the Austrian Succession, when the colonial campaign was clearly a sideshow compared to the war in the Low Countries. The contrast was to be even clearer by the end of 1759.

1759: Year of victories

No one will have a majority at present against Mr Pitt. No man will, in the present conjuncture, set his face against Mr Pitt in the House of Commons. (Newcastle, October 1759)[79]

It would be inaccurate to claim that domestic politics were suspended during the Newcastle–Pitt ministry. There were political differences and rivalries and tension within the government could be acute, as over Pitt's eventually successful pressure in late 1759 that Temple be made a Knight of the Garter, a conspicuous display of royal favour and therefore a jealously guarded aspect of royal patronage. However, certainly compared to the Nine Years War (1689–97), the War of the Spanish Succession (1702–13) and the War of the Austrian Succession, Britain was remarkably united. This was not simply a matter of a secure ministerial majority in Parliament. That had existed in 1747–8, but then Frederick, Prince of Wales was sponsoring opposition activity, whereas, after the formation of the Newcastle–Pitt ministry, Leicester House supported the government, albeit with considerable and growing misgivings. 'A simile', a manuscript poem, compared the Tories to rural Corinna, seduced by a cornet of horse,[80]

[79] Newcastle to Hardwicke, 25 October 1759, BL Add. 35419 f. 36.
[80] Newcastle to Hardwicke, 15 October 1759, BL Add. 32897 ff. 91–4; Middleton, Bells of Victory pp. 139–42, 145; Stafford, County Record Office D615/P(S) 1/2/15.

So have I seen the Tory race
Impatient long for want of place,
Never in humour, never well,
Wishing for what they dar'd not tell,
Their heads with country notions fraught,
Notions in town not worth a groat;
All their old-fashioned tenets quit,
And step by step at last submit
To reason, eloquence, and Pitt.

This widespread reconciliation and consensus owed much to the political developments of 1754–7 and to Pitt's subsequent skill in retaining the confidence of those outside the ministry, but military success was also important. Had British moves in Canada in 1758, 1759 and 1760, the years when respectively Louisbourg, Quebec and Montreal fell, been unsuccessful, then it is difficult to see how there would not have been more criticism of the commitment to Germany. In addition, there might have been more pressure for peace, which would have raised tension over the terms that should be proposed and accepted. The war was expensive, the maintenance of domestic political harmony difficult. Thus, as the conflict continued it became more important to obtain success, increasingly so as Frederick II was placed under greater strain.

The year 1759 was one of triumph, of victories that were celebrated with ringing bells and other public celebrations. The ringers at York Minster were paid four times between 21 August and 22 October for celebrating victories, beginning with the triumph at Minden and ending with the capture of Quebec.[81] There were in fact two great years of victories during the Seven Years War: 1759 and 1762. The victories of 1762, principally the seizure of Havana and Manila, have

---

[81] G. E. Aylmer and R. Cant (eds.), *A History of York Minster* (Oxford, 1977), p. 247.

been overshadowed because by that stage the war was won and peace was being negotiated, secondly they were won at the expense of Spain rather than France, thirdly the Bute ministry was unpopular and somewhat embarrassed by its gains and fourthly the 'heroic' stage of the war, certainly in the view of later commentators, was the struggle with France in 1758–9, which was associated with Pitt, specifically the conquest of Quebec culminating in the death of General James Wolfe on 13 September 1759 at the moment of glorious victory on the Heights of Abraham outside the city. That appeared a pivotal moment in both the war and the history of North America, whereas both Havana and Manila were returned to Spain under the Peace of Paris of 1763. This concentration of attention is less than fair to the skilful planning and bravery displayed in 1762, when Britain provided a formidable display of power, for neither expedition was of the nature of a raid. The very geographical divergence of the two successes indicates the extent of Britain's commitment to the war. Furthermore, in 1762 British military assistance helped to prevent Spain overrunning Portugal. A pamphlet of 1765 claimed that after Pitt's resignation, 'vigorous measures were pursued in regard to the war; and Mr Pitt himself, far from opposing, strengthened the hands of government with his hearty concurrence in raising the supplies for the service of the year 1762'.[82]

However, 1759 was without a doubt a more serious crisis than 1762, because it was the decisive year in the conflict with France, the sole power able both to challenge Britain at sea without assistance and to threaten invasion. This was planned for 1759. 'The '59' is not a phrase that comes readily to mind, unlike 'the '15' or 'the '45', but it was a serious threat, as indeed earlier had been the too-often neglected

---

[82] Anon., *A Full and Free Enquiry into the Merits of the Peace* (1765) p. 146.

French invasion schemes of early 1744 and early 1746. In 1759 the French planned landings in the Clyde, and at Portsmouth, a destination altered to Essex, because of the British blockade of the intended invasion port of Le Havre.[83] The scheme was wrecked by the British navy. The French navy was divided into two fleets, based on Brest and Toulon, a division that limited the chance of achieving the concentration of force necessary to cover any invasion attempt. British blockading squadrons sought to maintain this division. Though the Toulon fleet under La Clue managed to get out of first Toulon and then the Mediterranean in August 1759, it was defeated by Boscawen near Lagos on the Portuguese coast on 18 August. Bad weather forced Hawke to lift the blockade of Brest in November, but the French fleet under Conflans was unable to sail for Scotland via the west coast of Ireland. While still off the French coast, Conflans was trapped by Hawke. Conflans took refuge in Quiberon Bay, expecting that Hawke would not risk entering its shoal-strewn waters in such poor weather, but he was wrong. On 20 November Hawke boldly attacked and in a confused engagement the French fleet was scattered with several ships captured or sunk.

The naval victories were the decisive triumphs of 1759, because it was naval power that enabled Britain to make colonial conquests, naval strength on which the security of the country depended. Victories on land, such as that at Minden in Germany on 1 August 1759, or the capture of Quebec, were important, not least in terms of the economy of making gains and preventing losses which played such a major role in determining the content of eventual peace settlements. However, without the maintenance of naval

[83] C. Nordmann, 'Choiseul and the Last Jacobite Attempt of 1759', in E. Cruickshanks (ed.), Ideology and Conspiracy. Aspects of Jacobitism, 1689–1759 (Edinburgh, 1982) pp. 201–17.

superiority such victories could only be precarious. The surrender of Cornwallis' hitherto undefeated army at York-town in 1781, the step that led to the fall of the North ministry and to the acceptance that the American colonies could never be recovered, was due to loss of control of the sea to the French. In 1759 the stakes were even greater. A successful French invasion was designed to drive the British to peace. The forces the French planned to land were by no means small. The plan outlined at the French council on 14 July 1759 called for the landing of 48,000 men, a force far larger than the British coastal expeditions of the previous two years. It was unlikely that this army could be defeated by untried militia. In August 1757 Cumberland had mocked Pitt's support for these poorly trained soldiers. 'I have wrote my humble opinion for the raising more troops, but I don't know whether the dauntless Man Mountain will think it proper, or perhaps intends to meet the enemy at their landing in person at the head of his new valiant militia. If so, what has Old England to fear.' In November 1759 the Marquess of Rockingham recorded, 'I had some conversation a few days ago with Mr Pitt, who I find still continues desirous that no strength (that can be had) should be now neglected for the security of this country. All the militias which are in readiness are called out.' However, despite all Pitt's praise of the militia, especially at politically opportune moments when Tory support was being wooed, he was aware that it was not as effective as the army.[84]

By focusing attention on the navy, less consideration is necessarily devoted to Britain's overseas campaigns and Pitt's role in planning and sustaining them. There is no doubt that

[84] Cumberland to Fox, 29 August 1757, Ilchester (ed.), *Letters to Henry Fox* p. 118; Rockingham to Sir George Savile, 15 November 1759, Bod. MS Eng. Lett. c144 f. 280. On the militia, J. R. Western, *The English Militia in the Eighteenth Century* (1965) pp. 127–61.

the navy was at a higher pitch of effectiveness in 1759 than it had been in 1756. That was only to be expected as the transition from peacetime arrangements to a major mobilisation for war could not be achieved overnight. Similarly the navy was stronger and more effective by the unsuccessful end of the War of American Independence than it had been earlier during the conflict. The state of the navy in 1756 can be criticised, as indeed it was, on the grounds of the failure to relieve Minorca, and the condition and success of the force during the Pitt ministry praised in comparison, but there is little doubt that the navy would have reacted forcefully to any attempt to invade Britain in 1756: that was why Byng was sent to the Mediterranean with so few ships.

The most recent study of the period states that, 'Pitt had only marginal responsibility for naval administration and any attempt to explain the British success must focus on Anson and his Admiralty colleagues.' This is indeed the case. Naval success owed less to any bold new strategic conception than to the ability of the new administration to keep a large number of ships at sea and to the quality of the ships. In part this reflected a political consensus in favour of paying to sustain Britain as a powerful naval state, but that was a consensus that was not in need of Pitt's support. Britain had triumphed at sea similarly in 1747 in the two battles of Cape Finisterre: the Newcastle–Pitt ministry did not bring naval victory. The origins of the western squadron designed to guard the western approaches to the Channel, a policy that led to the victory of Quiberon Bay, are to be found in 1745–7. It has recently been pointed out that 'whatever the changes in personnel on the formation of the Pitt–Devonshire ministry, there was to be no change in planning at the Admiralty'.[85]

[85]   R. Middleton, 'Naval Administration in the Age of Pitt and Anson, 1755–1763', in J. Black and P. L. Woodfine (eds.), The British Navy and the Use of Naval Power in the Eighteenth Century (Leicester, 1988) p. 109; Middleton, 'Naval Strategy' pp. 349–50, 355.

Pitt's contribution was greater in so far as the land campaigns were concerned. Naval victory presupposed the retention of much of Britain's maritime strength in or near home waters, but success on land required the dispatch of forces from Britain. Pitt was determined to maintain substantial forces in North America and to send sufficient troops to prevent the defeat of Prince Ferdinand in Germany. After the Prince's victory at Minden Pitt suggested that Ferdinand be provided with 10,000 new men, including two men out of every company in Britain and 600 Highlanders. Newcastle, more concerned by the prospect of invasion, was unenthusiastic.[86] To secure these ends Pitt actively pressed for the raising of fresh troops in Britain and refused to be distracted by the prospect of invasion in 1759. He was against withdrawing any troops from America or Europe.[87] Pitt's policy can be interpreted in a number of lights. It can be seen as a reckless response to French preparations. Equally it can be argued that Pitt's determination had helped to free Britain from the mesmerised state of 1756 when the prospect of French invasion had led to an essentially reactive strategy. By 1759 the situation appeared less threatening. The militia could bear a share in national defence, freeing regulars for the field army, although Pitt was in fact reluctant to rely on the militia. The degree of domestic harmony in 1759 ensured that the political atmosphere was less jittery. The ministry was also helped by not having to bear the responsibility for defending the Low Countries from a French invasion. In contrast, during the previous war plans to follow up the capture of Louisbourg in 1745 by an invasion of Canada had been abandoned.

---

[86] Memoranda for George II, 14, 16, 21 August, Newcastle to Hardwicke, 31 August 1759, BL Add. 32894 ff. 182, 237, 333, 32895 f. 81.

[87] Newcastle to Andrew Stone, 1 August 1759, BL Add. 32893 f. 404; G. Marcus, Quiberon Bay (1960) pp. 26–7.

The plan for an attack on Quebec was scarcely novel. Its risky nature was amply demonstrated by the fact that the French were defeated only late in the campaigning season and then only after a hazardous ascent of the cliffs near Quebec. The strategic situation favoured Britain: her naval power enabled her to cover amphibious operations while the French were unable to reinforce their colonies. On the other hand it was necessary to gain as many territories as possible, because the war would not last for ever. In 1759 there was active discussion of the possibility of peace within the government. In light of Pitt's later criticism of the terms of the eventual peace settlement, the Peace of Paris of 1763, it is worth noting that in 1759 he was willing to consider a conciliatory settlement that would not involve the gain of all of Canada. This was in line with his willingness in 1757 to accept the possible cession of Gibraltar. In August 1759 Pitt adopted the attitude that it would be sensible to negotiate peace while still in a position to make war. Two months later he told the Prussian envoy that although he supported the retention of the Great Lakes, Crown Point and Niagara, he did not intend to press for that of Louisbourg, or Quebec if captured, and would return the West Indian sugar island of Guadeloupe, captured that summer, or the African trading station of Goree, which had fallen the previous December. Newcastle, who thought peace necessary for financial reasons, was pleased with Pitt's 'reasonable way of thinking'.[88]

Clearly Pitt faced a difficult prospect. In 1748 he had been a member of a ministry that had returned Louisbourg, but the situation in the Low Countries had been serious while Pitt was not then in a position to bear responsibility for the terms. In 1759, in contrast, he was suggesting terms that would

---

[88] BL Add. 32897 f. 90.

compromise his political position, and yet, as the spokesman of the ministry in the Commons, he would have to take prime responsibility for any peace. Furthermore, as eighteenth-century conflicts between major powers commonly ended in compromise settlements, there was generally a political cost to taking such responsibility. This was especially so in Britain where mistaken notions of national capability, engendered in part by opposition polemic, such as the parliamentary attacks on Walpole in which Pitt had participated, made any peace contentious.

When Parliament met on 13 November 1759 Pitt warned that it would be impossible to negotiate a peace that pleased everyone in Britain. His speech was widely welcomed, Rockingham reporting that he 'spoke wisely and honestly to the satisfaction of everybody'.[89] In late 1759 he actively pressed for negotiation, and it was not until the following February that Pitt decided both that it was worth fighting on for another campaign and that Britain should seek to retain the whole of Canada. Pitt's willingness to negotiate in late 1759 is worth stressing because he was subsequently to be accused of seeking a continuation of the war, indeed of personally benefiting from it, a charge that had also been directed by political rivals at the Duke of Marlborough in the last years of the War of the Spanish Succession.

In June 1759 Richard Cox, Secretary to the Master General of the Ordnance, had observed, 'Whilst the war lasts Mr Pitt will in all human probability be an Timon des affaires, and bear the burden of the day and its consequences.'[90] Such statements became increasingly common in 1759, reflecting anew what was such a characteristic feature of Pitt's career: the contrast between the public reputation and more

---

[89] Rockingham to Savile, 15, 22 November 1759, Bod. MS Eng. Lett. c. 144 ff. 280–1; *Walpole . . . Memoirs George II* III, 77–9.

[90] Cox to Weston, 7 June 1759, Farmington, Weston papers vol. 3.

complex reality. Political insiders were well aware of Newcastle's role in bearing the burdens of financial administration, while in other departments Pitt played scant part. More significant was Pitt's willingness to consider terms, a willingness not shared in late 1759 by George II who wanted to fight on in order to obtain the best peace possible for Hanover. Pitt's readiness to return Louisbourg and other gains was not common knowledge, but it helped to ensure that when he subsequently adopted the pose of firm opponent of national sell-out, his attitude commanded little respect among other ministers.

Pitt also differed from the King over reinforcements for India. The struggle there with France was conducted by the East India Company, but the government provided some military support. This process was not begun by Pitt, nor was he responsible for Robert Clive's victory over the Indian Prince, Surajah Dowla, at Plassey on 23 June 1757. A regiment and six warships had been sent to India in 1754, four companies of artillery following in 1755. They helped Clive to victory in 1757, and thus laid the basis for the virtual control of Bengal, Bihar and Orissa by the East India Company. However, in face of the arrival of French reinforcements in 1757 and 1758 and of a French revival in southern India that led to an unsuccessful siege of Madras in early 1759, Clive asked Pitt for assistance in February 1759. Pitt was responsive, and reinforcements were sent in 1759 and 1760. As a result Eyre Coote was able to defeat the French at Wandewash on 22 January 1760, while the remaining French possessions in India were captured in 1760 and early 1761, Pondicherry surrendering on 16 January 1761. Pitt was more aware of the importance of India than George II or Newcastle, and in October 1759 the Duke wrote of the East India Company, 'Mr Pitt is mightily for sending them two battalions', and of a Scottish regiment that was to be raised,

'The King wants it for the army in Germany. Mr Pitt rather designs it, at present, for the East Indies.'[91]

The breakdown of Pitt's good relations with Leicester House was more ominous than tension between George II and the minister. Both Prince George and Bute felt neglected by Pitt. The treatment of a Leicester House favourite, Lord George Sackville, who had refused to order the British cavalry to charge at Minden, aroused resentment, while Pitt was concerned about Holdernesse's approaches to the young court, but the essential problem was one of failure of adequate consultation. Pitt did keep Bute informed about developments. His correspondence among the Bute papers at Mount Stuart includes letters referring to the diplomatic situation, and the two men met to discuss events at Pitt's initiative, one undated letter of 1759 reading 'Mr Pitt would be particularly desirous of half an hour with Lord Bute, on the subject of the intelligence of the French preparations, in their ports, particularly at Havre.' Robert Wood, one of Pitt's Under-Secretaries, recalled in 1767 that Pitt,

during the late King's reign, had the most intimate connection with Lord Bute, and that he [Wood] was the person who communicated between them – that Pitt had at that time the total direction of the old King under Lady Yarmouth, and by her means, and had quite subdued the Duke of Newcastle . . . he said the connection between Bute and Pitt had gradually lessened, and at length come to perfect dislike.[92]

Bute and Prince George expected to be consulted as well as informed, but Pitt was not really interested in any consultation that was more than a formality. By the late 1750s there was a substantial difference over strategy between the minister and the young court. An undated letter of Prince George to Bute, preserved at Mount Stuart, revealed the

[91] Newcastle to Hardwicke, 15 October 1759, BL Add. 32897 f. 87.
[92] HP Harris, 13 May 1767.

Prince's opposition to the dispatch of troops to Germany, as well as his related hostility to his grandfather, 'I shall soon be going to that hateful Drawing-Room, which I suppose will be fuller than usual, on account of last Monday's news from the foreign dominions; I fear the troops will now with greater ardour be demanded to keep the French from returning.'[93]

As so often in Pitt's career, the observer cannot but sympathise with him in one sense while feeling he was reaping his own whirlwind on the other. It was obviously impossible for him to serve two masters – George II and the Prince – especially when they had such fundamentally opposed views over Hanover and operations in Germany;[94] and in that sense his testy comments about not being answerable to Bute and the Prince for every step before he took it are perfectly understandable. But he had used Leicester House as a stepping stone to power and thus contributed to his future difficulties. The differences between the young court and Pitt were to become more serious as peace became an increasingly central issue and the minister adopted a less conciliatory line towards the Bourbons.

1760: Last year of the age of George II

After the triumphs of 1759, 1760 was in some respects an anti-climax for contemporaries. The major success was the capture of the remainder of French Canada and the capitulation of the French there. This was achieved with considerable skill by Amherst, Montreal surrendering in September, but the campaign lacked the drama of Wolfe's attack on Quebec. Initially it went badly for Britain, as the French nearly recaptured Quebec, the British being defeated on the Heights of Abraham on 28 April. However, British command of the

[93] MS; see also R. R. Sedgwick (ed.), *Letters from George III to Lord Bute 1756–1766* (1939) p. 11.   [94] Sedgwick, *Letters* pp. 11, 17–19, 25–8, 45.

sea permitted the dispatch of vital reinforcements. In Germany Ferdinand and Frederick were essentially obliged to adopt a defensive position, much to the disappointment of Pitt, who had expected a better return from the dispatch of more British troops. Ferdinand defeated the French at Warburg, but was in turn beaten at Klostercamp, with heavy British casualties. In December 1759 and January 1760 Pitt had supported the sending of reinforcements, though he made it clear in February 1760 that he saw little point in meeting Prussian demands for an extra 10,000 men. In so doing, Pitt not only drew attention to the domestic political context, pointing out that the Tories wanted 'to make us depend upon the militia only', but also stressed his determination to follow what he thought best, 'that he had been for sending troops, when the run was against it, and should be equally against it, when the run might be for it'.[95] This self-righteous stress on the value of his own views and his sense that his integrity required that he assert and follow them was a characteristic feature of Pitt and was to be demonstrated fully in the controversy over relations with Spain that led to his resignation in October 1761.

The defeat of a French raid on Northern Ireland early in 1760 helped to quell fears of invasion and in the summer of 1760 Pitt took an active role in supporting the dispatch of more troops to Ferdinand's army. He was concerned to prevent the French regaining their colonial losses at the peace by conquering Hanover during the war: blocking the French invasion plans of Britain increased the pressure on Ferdinand, as more French troops were sent to fight him. It was a matter not so much of conquering America in Germany, a claim often made, but one that overlooks the limited extent to

[95] Memorandum by Newcastle, 18 February 1760, BL Stowe 263 f. 16.

which the French could intervene in North America; but rather holding onto America in Germany. In June and July 1760 Pitt played a major role in sending sufficient infantry and cavalry to raise the British contingent in Ferdinand's army to 22,000, a figure that would have astounded the Duke of Cumberland and Pitt's other critics in 1757.

This was not a commitment that would please the young court. In April 1760 Bute expressed his regret at 'the long chain of unfortunate circumstances now subsisting' between him and Pitt, adding his hope that their former 'fraternal union' could be renewed.[96] He approached Pitt via Gilbert Elliot and proposed a Bute–Pitt ministry, with Bute replacing Newcastle. Pitt rejected the idea and made it clear that he could not accept the young court's view on the relationship with him. Elliot, a Lord of the Admiralty who was loyal to Pitt as well as being a confidential adviser to Bute, recorded Pitt's powerful declaration of self-sufficiency,

As to want of confidence and communication so much complained of: I have acted upon the concerted plan, I have effectually barred the entrance to those who were meant to be excluded, carried on the war on its plan, armed the country even Scotland when every other Minister threw out suspicions on that quarter, but have not carefully transmitted every little scrap of paper, all the little paltry detail, I have not waited for direction and approbation, but seized the moment when I could to secure these measures: my health, infirmity's, temper don't admit of making such court: neither would; I would never have been Minister to act in collusion with any Prince and Minister. I will not be rid with a check rein, nor postpone measures or delay business till I hear from the King: such being the case I know it is impossible for me to act in a responsible ministerial office with Lord Bute; he has all confidence, all habitude, gives hourly indications of an imperious nature, I can't

[96] MS 6/131.

bear a touch of command, my sentiments in politicks like my
religion are my own, I can't change them . . . I cannot be dictated,
prescribed to etc.[97]

This was not the declaration of a courtier, nor did it augur
well for any stable relationship between Bute and Pitt. Pitt's
reference to his health is important. He was ill for much of his
period as minister, laid up for weeks in the early spring every
year, except in 1758. An undated anecdote from this period
recorded that.

Mr Pitt's plan, when he had the gout, was to have no fire in his
room, but to load himself with bedclothes. At his house at Hayes he
slept in a long room; at one end of which was his bed, and his lady's
at the other. His way was, when he thought the Duke of Newcastle
had fallen into any mistake to send for him and read him a lecture.
The Duke was sent for once and came when Mr Pitt was confined to
bed by the gout. There was, as usual, no fire in the room; the day
was very chilly and the Duke, as usual, afraid of catching cold. The
Duke first sat down on Mrs Pitt's bed, as the warmest place; then
drew up his legs into it, as he got colder. The lecture unluckily
continuing a considerable time, the Duke at length fairly lodged
himself under Mrs Pitt's bed clothes. A person, from whom I had
the story, suddenly going in, saw the two ministers in bed, at the
two ends of the room, while Pitt's long nose and black beard
unshaved for some days, added to the grotesqueness of the scene.

When he was not physically ill he was under tremendous
mental stress, asking Bute at the end of one letter in 1759 to
pardon 'extreme fatigue'.[98] In the spring of 1760 he was
certainly ill, and this affected his ability to discharge his
duties, both in seeing foreign envoys and in conducting the
correspondence of his office. On 15 April he wrote to the Earl
of Kinnoull, envoy at Lisbon, 'A severe fit of the gout has
prevented me from sooner acknowledging the honor of your

[97] L. B. Namier, England in the Age of the American Revolution (2nd edn, 1963) pp. 106–7.
[98] Walpoliana I (1799) pp. 33–4; MS Pitt/Bute corresp. no. 40.

Excellency's letter of the 10th past.' On 30 May Pitt wrote again referring to Kinnoull's of 14 and 16 April, 'A severe attack, with which I have been confined to my bed ever since, and of which I am still ill, having, to my extreme regret, disabled me from executing His Majesty's commands on matters, so highly interesting, and of such peculiar moment' as those in the dispatches. He added that he would have to defer writing on commercial affairs with Portugal, a subject of great importance, because of 'the present state of my health'.[99] Pitt's frenetic tendencies, his irritability and his hyperbolic statements that so often appear egoistic, can be attributed to the pressure of poor health and stress on a volatile and opinionated personality. By the spring of 1760 the cumulative strain of several years of war, of competing demands, both military and political, was considerable. The reply to Bute's approach can be seen in this context, but it was scarcely propitious for good relations after George III succeeded to the throne. Pitt sketched out to Elliot an acceptable path if the new King wished to rely on Bute,

my age, infirmitys, turn of mind make it impossible for me to undertake new oppositions, the heats and colds of the House of Commons are too much for me, neither will I retire peevish and discontented but recur to the Prince and Lord Bute friendships to put me in some honourable bystanding office where I have no responsibility but aid counsels if called upon.[100]

This was not without precedent. Carteret, by then Earl Granville, was Lord President of the Council from 1751 until 1763, influential, but without real power or responsibility. Pitt stressed the dangers of driving ministers from office in February 1760, Newcastle recording, 'Mr Pitt talked very

---

[99] Pitt to Kinnoull, 15 April, 30 May 1760, PRO SP 89/52 ff. 19, 108, 114; Viry to Charles Emmanuel, 7 March, 11 April 1760, 13, 20 February 1761, AST LM Ing. 65, 66.

[100] Namier, *American Revolution* p. 107.

plainly of the insufficiency of my Lord Holdernesse for his
office – that he had no intimacy or confidence with him; But
that he was extremely against his going out – that he would
be considerable out who could not be so in'.[101] However, it
was by no means clear that Pitt would agree to remain in on
acceptable terms. He wrote to his wife in the summer of 1760
of 'the great object of a happy peace'.[102] Securing that was to
complete the breach between Pitt and George III, but judging
from the future King's angry response to Pitt's reply to Bute's
approach there was little prospect of good relations. George
wrote, 'I can never bear to see him in any future Ministry.'[103]

THE NEW REIGN

some months ago . . . I said that I thought Mr Pitt would never make
peace, because he never could make such a peace, as he had taught
the nation to expect. I suppose he now sees that we are within a year
or two of an impracticability of carrying on the war upon the
present footing; and may think, by going out, upon a spirited
pretence, to turn the attention, and dissatisfaction of the public,
upon those, who at a ruinous expence, are to carry on his wild
measures, and whom they have been taught to dislike, by a total
abandonment of the press to him and his creatures. (George
Dodington, Lord Melcombe, to Bute, 8 October 1761)[104]

Mr Pitt has brought his bark into a happy port. A barony for his wife
and a pension of 3,000 a year for three lives are agreeable
circumstances in a retreat, which delivers him from the difficulty of
carrying on the war, or making the peace, and keeps all his laurels
green and unfading on his brow. No minister in this country has
ever known so well the times of seasons, of going in and coming

---

[101] Memorandum by Newcastle, 18 February 1760, BL Stowe 263 f. 17.
[102] Pitt to his wife, undated, summer 1760, Beinecke, Osborn Files, Pitt.
[103] Namier, *American Revolution* p. 108.
[104] Dodington to Bute, 8 October 1761 MS 2/85.

out with advantage to himself . . . I hear that all over this country since first we have had the news of his resigning the seals, the cry of the people in the taverns and alehouses is *no Pitt, no King*. However, I imagine, that, as he has condescended to accept of this mark of royal favour, he will be so good as to let the King remain on the throne. (George Lord Lyttelton, 14 October 1761)[105]

George II's opposition had delayed Pitt's rise to office and yet by the end of his reign, the King's relations with his minister were on the whole good, and they were well used to each other. George III had little favour for Pitt but the minister served the King as a Secretary of State from George's accession on 25 October 1760 until his resignation a year later, and again as Lord Privy Seal in 1766–8. Far from George's determination both to rely on Bute and to end the war-making rivalry and Pitt's speedy fall inevitable, the minister accepted Holdernesse's replacement by Bute in March 1761, while Pitt was the minister principally responsible for unsuccessful Anglo-French peace negotiations that summer. And yet Bute's position and British relations with the Bourbons were to be the crucial issues that drove Pitt from the ministry, although the fundamental cause was his unwillingness to compromise, his refusal to accept the views of others. In the last years of George II's reign Pitt had become used to a measure of royal support and to a government in which his policies were followed. He was not suited temperamentally to the world of court politics, not adept at seeking approval, soliciting support and judging the currents of court favour in order to further his views. In November 1760 he wrote to his sister Ann that 'having never been a solicitor of favour, upon any occasion, how can I become so now without contradicting the whole tenour of my life?'[106] Fortunately for Pitt the ministry remained essentially

---

[105] Lyttelton to Elizabeth Montagu, 14 October 1761, HL MO 1297.
[106] BL Add. 69289 no. 61.

unchanged in October 1760. Pitt offered to support Bute at the Treasury, but advised a continuation of the current ministry, and Bute agreed. Hardwicke urged Newcastle to retire, but Pitt, Bute, Devonshire and others persuaded him to continue in office.[107] Instead of Bute replacing Newcastle, he became Groom of the Stole, a court appointment, and a member of the Cabinet Council, a position with political possibilities, but without any matching responsibilities.

Pitt was not prepared, however, for the uncertainties that were to characterise politics over the next few years: uncertainties both over the extent to which George III would seek to implement his views and over the likely response of leading politicians. The political world appeared unusually volatile and kaleidoscopic, not simply because of the start of a new reign, as ever the episodic beginning of a new world in a high-political system dominated by the institution and practice of monarchy, but also because of the challenge of negotiating peace and the disappearance of the remaining signs of Whig–Tory division. George III's ostentatious displays of favour towards individual Tories, who had been denied access to the benefits of court approval since the Hanoverian accession in 1714, reflected his support for the ideas and ideals of non-party government that had character-ised attempts over the previous thirty-five years to create a united opposition, an attractive alternative to both Old Corps Whiggery and Jacobitism. George III could therefore be seen in a tradition that went back, via Bolingbroke's *Patriot King* and the Leicester House opposition around Prince Frederick, to 'Country' and 'Patriot' hostility to Walpole.

Although on occasion Pitt had sought to play on Whig suspicion of the Tories, he had also been prominent in the opposition to Walpole, had in government benefited from a

---

[107] P. Yorke, *Life and Correspondence of Philip Yorke, Earl of Hardwicke* (3 vols., Cambridge, 1913) III, 305–7.

measure of Tory support and had employed anti-party rhetoric, declaring in the debate over the Qualification of MPs Bill 'I am neither Whig nor Tory.' In 1760–1, however, he was fundamentally opposed to any disruption of a governmental system that appeared to be operating in a satisfactory fashion. Pitt made it clear to Bute on the evening of 25 October 1760 that he would accept no changes,

That he must act as an independent Minister or not at all, that his politicks were like his religion which would admit of no accommodation. That if the system of the war was to undergo the least change or even shadow of a change he could no longer be of any service.[108]

Walpole had made no such conditions in 1727 when George II had come to the throne with his own ideas and his own men. Instead, he had successfully set out to demonstrate his indispensability, by managing the general election and obtaining a substantial Civil List from Parliament. Pitt also appeared indispensable in late 1760. He was the minister most clearly associated with victory and the harmonious management of the Commons. He was also popular outside Parliament, a factor of some importance given the need to sustain support for a costly war. At the electoral meeting at the Crown in Blandford Forum held on 13 January 1761 to introduce the candidates for the county for the forthcoming general election the toasts included

May the Unanimity of the County never be Interrupted.
A speedy safe and honourable peace.
And the National Pilot proposed by Captain Barber which from the laugh which it occasioned from several gentlemen I concluded meant Countrey Matters – but the Captain after a little pause said he supposed it was to any of this company quite unnecessary to explain this toast to be Mr Secretary Pitt.

[108] Namier, *American Revolution* p. 121.

That Pitt could be toasted at such a meeting indicated the range of his appeal or rather the extent to which he was automatically, and possibly without any real deliberation, associated with national interests, albeit with the addition of the bawdy that reflected the widespread delight in puns. The two candidates, the sitting MPs, were both Tories, one his kinsman George Pitt of Strathfieldsaye, who had opposed the government ever since elected to Parliament in 1742. Dorset was a Tory county, and there had been no poll for the county seats since 1727, scarcely the sort of constituency that is often associated with Pitt. However, George Pitt's colleague, Humphry Sturt, in a largely incomprehensible speech, shortly before the meeting turned towards the serious business of drinking bumpers, mentioned 'independency',[109] a characteristic that William Pitt had continued successfully to associate himself with, despite his years in office. William Pitt might have received drunken praise in Dorset in January 1761, but of the two MPs elected George Pitt cleaved to the Crown after the accession of George III and supported Bute, while the independent Humphry Sturt apparently never spoke in his thirty years as an MP. Neither was to resist the dropping of the 'national pilot'.

George III, like many other newly acceeded monarchs, was not prepared to accept the guidance of someone who saw himself, or was seen, in this role. Pitt's attitude towards Bute was unacceptable to George III. He took few pains to sooth the Earl's susceptibilities and clearly felt contempt for the man. Bute himself was not as malleable an intermediary with the King as Newcastle had been with George II. Furthermore, the basis of Pitt's position was unstable. A minister trusted with the conduct of war would find it more difficult to control negotiations for peace, especially once compromise

---

[109] Bod. MS Don. b 20 f. 2.

was placed on the agenda, and the balancing act of appealing to Tory and Patriot opinion, while Newcastle managed the Whigs, was threatened by the redefinition of political groups that George III's accession threatened. The problems of being 'an independent Minister' were considerable.

Pitt triumphed in the first clash of the new reign. He insisted that the King's first speech to the Privy Council, delivered on the 25th and drawn up by Bute, should be altered. Instead of referring to 'a bloody and expensive war' and 'obtaining an honourable and lasting peace', the phrases were changed in the printed copy to 'an expensive but just and necessary war' and after the words 'honourable peace' should be inserted 'in concert with our allies'. These changes were symptomatic of fundamental differences of opinion about the war and reflected the indifference if not suspicion of George III and Bute towards the Prussians, an attitude that was to be transformed to hostility.

The King neither trusted nor felt close to any of his principal ministers and, although Bute was not initially appointed to high office, George III clearly intended that his favourite should enjoy predominant influence, a recipe for disagreement. On 27 October 1760 Devonshire recorded in his diary 'Lord Bute told Mr Pitt that the King would have no meetings held at which he [Bute] was not present, and that for the future everything should be considered and debated in his presence, and then His Majesty would determine as he thought proper.'[110]

Ten weeks later Pitt saw the well-connected Sardinian envoy, Viry, and told him that the King did not have the confidence in him that he should, adding 'my situation is such that I am hindered and impeded in the dispatch of most of my work'.[111] Pitt reacted angrily in January 1761 to the idea

---

[110] P. D. Brown and K. W. Schweizer (eds.), *The Devonshire Diary* 982) p. 43.
[111] Viry to Charles Emmanuel, 13 January 1761, AST LM Ing. 66.

that Bute replace Holdernesse, and thereby gain power in the crucial field of foreign policy and responsibility for Anglo-Prussian relations. Two months later, however, the change took place with the approval of Newcastle. The Duke told George III 'that Mr Pitt's ill health was such as rendered it impossible for him to do business with the King for weeks and months at time' but added 'that his credit and influence were a great service to H.M. and therefore nothing ought to be done that should give him offence'. This was not an argument Bute accepted. He also told Newcastle that Pitt's 'popularity was sunk', that 'he never would go into opposition' and that he 'would never gain the King'. In the end Bute agreed to leave 'Pitt master of foreign affairs, except where' Newcastle, Hardwicke and Devonshire thought 'he goes too far'.[112]

Pitt did not take an active role in the ministerial change. He had been ill with gout since January 1761, and his health continued to trouble him until the end of April, on the 28th of which he wrote to Bute 'I was too lame to be at court today as I intended.' Relations between the two Secretaries were uneasy. Pitt made little effort to win the confidence of the inexperienced Bute, who complained that he was told nothing about the affairs of the Southern Department.[113] This lack of trust was of growing importance as peace became a pressing subject for consideration. Pitt was to try to bring to the work of peace the determination and impatience with obstacles that had characterised his conduct of the war. Relations between Newcastle and Pitt were already poor as the result of a dispute that sprang up over Ferdinand's claim that his operations in Germany had been obstructed due to commissariat problems which Pitt blamed on the Treasury.

---

[112] *Devonshire Diary* pp. 88–90.
[113] MS; Viry to Charles Emmanuel, 31 March, 7 April 1761, AST LM Ing. 61.

Pitt was isolated within the ministry, Charles Jenkinson, Under-Secretary to Bute, writing on 2 May 'the long draught to Prince Ferdinand when it was brought into the Cabinet, Pitt again objected to the same sentiments in it which he opposed at the Council, but they unanimously overruled him, and the whole of the draught was approved. This however produced rather an angry letter from him to My Lord'.[114] Pitt certainly had not learned how to take defeat gracefully or without recriminations. Although 'Pitt was coming round to the attitude towards Prussia which Bute was to adopt as policy a year later', he displayed no willingness to deal with the problems in Anglo-Prussian relations,[115] and he was alone in excusing Frederick II's lack of assistance to Ferdinand. Pitt was therefore already in a weak position on the eve of peace negotiations with France, a dramatic shift from the situation when high politics had been essentially a matter of his relations with George II and Newcastle.

Pitt's reputation as a supporter of efficiency, an able war minister can be seen in the correspondence of Major General Studholme Hodgson, who commanded the land forces in the expedition that seized Belle Isle, an island off the west coast of France, that spring. When Hodgson saw the minister before he left, Pitt 'recommended me not to stay for trifles if the wind was fair, nor confine myself to forms; and has promised to support me in all stretches of power whatever and against whomsoever'. Hodgson found he had been supplied with inadequate cannon and engineers, but clearly thought that Pitt was the minister to turn to, 'I have been most cruelly treated by the Board of Ordnance. If I take the place and live to come home, and find Mr Pitt a minister, I think I shall be able

[114] Jenkinson to Weston, 2 May 1761, Farmington, Weston papers, vol. 3.
[115] P. F. Doran, *Andrew Mitchell and Anglo-Prussian Diplomatic Relations during the Seven Years' War* (New York, 1986) p. 261.

to make him hang Sir Charles Frederick [Surveyor General of the Ordnance] in his red ribbon.'[116] Hodgson certainly saw Pitt as an animating force within the government, a minister who was not confined by forms or departmental boundaries.

The capture of the island, which had been long pressed by Pitt, acted as a tonic on him, Richard Rigby writing sardonically, 'Pitt, who was before confined, carries the letters to the King himself. Saint Lambert could not have done more, if he had bid him rise, take up his bed and walk.' However, the value of the acquisition was questioned in political circles. Doubting that it would lead France to accept peace, Rigby, in addition, feared that the capture would 'confirm us in our Knight Errantry'. Rigby had already warned the pacific Bedford that the ministers were afraid of standing up to Pitt over peace negotiations, and, repeating Newcastle, written of the danger that they would be 'bullied out' of their peaceable dispositions'.[117] Pitt was not viewed as a friend of peace, either in Britain or abroad. The Russian envoy in London, Prince Galitzin, wrote to the Duke of Choiseul, the leading French minister, in April,

Pitt, being the minister of the people, cannot maintain his position unless he possesses their favour; and as a result he can only want either the continuation of the war or a peace that is extremely advantageous to Britain.

He also informed Choiseul that Bute, Newcastle and the sanest part of the nation would take a different view. Richard Wall, the Irish-born Spanish Secretary of State, who had met Pitt while envoy in London, thought that Pitt would resign rather than consent to terms he deemed unacceptable, while Choiseul was dubious about the chances of successfully

---

[116] Hodgson to Earl of Albemarle, no date, 17 May 1761, T. Keppel, The Life of Augustus, Viscount Keppel (2 vols., 1842) I, 299, 320.
[117] Ilchester (ed.), Letters to Henry Fox p. 146; Bedford.

negotiating peace between Britain and France in light of Pitt's character and views.[118]

Pitt certainly adopted an aggressive attitude in Cabinet discussions over negotiations, threatening to resign on 27 April 1761 when he found himself in a minority. To a considerable extent he got his way, in part because Bute did not take a decided stand against him. Bedford complained on 11 July that the Council were all giving way to one man. By then the negotiations had already begun, in both London and Paris. As these were the most important negotiations Pitt was involved in, it is worth considering them despite their failure, because a discussion of their course is crucial in assessing whether he was only suitable for high office as a war minister, whether in short he had to fall both for peace to be negotiated and because he personally could not act as a bringer of peace.

The French envoy François de Bussy, who had earlier in his career as a diplomat and foreign office administrator acted as British agent 101, supplying crucial information on French plans to act on behalf of the Jacobites, arrived in London on 31 May 1761 and saw Pitt next morning. Pitt very sensibly told him that Anglo-French negotiations should be handled separately from those involving the German belligerents in order for progress to be made and Bussy found that, at least as far as relations with France were concerned, the other ministers, with the exception of Bedford, appeared to support Pitt. Pitt told him that peace could be made in eight days if France was sincere, and, when Bussy pressed for an equivalent for French conquests of Hanoverian territory in the shape of the return of British conquests, Pitt told him that, although that claim would have made a considerable impact during the reign of George II, the situation was now very

---

[118] AE CP Ang. 443 f. 89, Espagne 533 ff. 235, 259, Ang. 444 ff. 226–8.

different, because George III was less concerned about
Hanover. Pitt contrasted the ephemeral gains that France had
made in Germany, where, he claimed, she had essentially
fought for the benefit of her ally Austria, with the 'considerable and permanent advantages' Britain had secured from her
'sea war', adding 'it is clear that our expences and debts are
excessive, and that we very sincerely seek peace in order to
end them, but if we are obliged to fight on we will find all the
money we need . . . that there are no longer any factions or
parties in opposition, and the royal council is united'. Pitt
thus outlined two of his principal claims: that Britain could
fight a major war successfully and that it was possible to fight
one for national interests and to the national gain. Bussy
replied that Pitt's attitude did not seem very peaceful, but he
was clearly impressed by the minister and did not portray
him as a stubborn demagogue,

This minister seems to me to have great talents, a singular firmness,
much method and consistency of spirit. Though he speaks harshly, I
know that he can be master of himself when he wishes and that he
knows how to conduct affairs with all imaginable politeness. In that
respect he was very attentive to me. He told me that he did not wish
to offend the French government, and he asked me to warn him if
he said anything too harsh . . . Pitt dominates the government by his
genius, eloquence, courage and honesty.[119]

In June 1761 France offered the cession of all of Canada bar
Cape Breton Isle, which would be retained unfortified so that
French fishermen could dry their catches from the valuable
Newfoundland fishery. Minorca would be exchanged for
Guadeloupe and Goree, while Hanover would be returned.
Pitt was unhappy with the proposals. He did not want to
return Goree, leading Bussy to accuse him of wishing to
monopolise the valuable supply of Negro slaves, and he made

[119] Bussy to Choiseul, 11 June 1761, AE CP Ang. 443 ff. 180–1, 184–5, 187.

it clear that he was opposed to France retaining her fishing off Newfoundland, which was seen as a crucial training ground for sailors and thus a vital source of naval manpower in wartime. By July Bussy could refer to Pitt insisting on his plan 'with all the stiffness that is natural to him'. When Bussy raised the issue of Dunkirk on 8 July, Pitt told him that he did not share to the same extent the public's concern about the danger to Britain if the port was re-established, 'but that he knew the views of the nation and that they would never pardon a government' that did not enforce the stipulations of the Peace of Utrecht on this point. Later in the month Pitt returned to the theme that no British minister would dare to make peace without satisfaction over Dunkirk. As so often in his career, Pitt's response to public opinion was ambivalent. He could cite it with approval or disapproval, explain why he had to heed it or must reject it. Devonshire recorded an instructive exchange with Pitt after the Cabinet meeting of 14 August 1761,

He then took notice that I had mentioned the word unpopular; that for his part he was not guided by it and that he did not call popularity what arose in the City from the cry of stockjobbers and those that were interested in subscriptions.

I replyed I was glad he had not intimated as if I had charged him with it; that I mentioned it as a reason why we should be explicit on the terms on which we would make peace, as I was convinced the breaking off the peace would be very unpopular; that I did not take my notions from the cry of the City but from the universal voice of every part of England I had gone through this year; that I did not charge him with being governed by popularity, and that I believed I was in no danger of being suspected of it.

Pitt's ambivalence thus reflected a more general uncertainty within the political system towards the importance of opinion 'out-of-doors', one that was particularly difficult for ministerial Whigs. It was unclear what they could base their position on if they could not appeal to the constituency of popularity. Pitt's inconsistent response towards public opinion was partly a matter of the tactics and pressures of specific political situations, but also a product of the tensions within him: an outsider who wanted to belong, yet rejected much of the ethos of the political establishment, a man convinced of his own integrity and ideas but more eager to have them applauded, heeded, or at least appreciated than he generally suggested, someone for whom popularity, especially in the sense of a good public reputation, was a psychological as much as a political necessity.

These were not the best bases for conducting contentious negotiations, but Bussy was offered reassurance. He was told that the ministers who were in favour of peace, headed by Bute, would force Pitt's hand if he resisted reasonable propositions.[120] As so often happened when peace was negotiated in the eighteenth century and compromise was in the air, the ministry was divided over terms, but the failure to maintain a common line towards France was undercutting Pitt's position. Bedford argued that fighting on would expose all of Hanover to conquest and he challenged Pitt's long-standing support of coastal operations, claiming that they could make little impact in France. Bedford argued that the French terms were very good and that if Britain gained a monopoly of naval power it would lead to a European reaction.[121]

France meanwhile had begun to argue that a satisfactory settlement of Anglo-Spanish maritime and colonial differences would have to be part of any Anglo-French agreement,

---

[120] Bussy to Choiseul, 9, 26 July 1761, AE CP Ang. 443 ff. 336–8, 342–3, 444 ff. 68–9; *Devonshire Diary* pp. 112–13.

[121] Bedford to Bute, 9 July 1761, MS 1761 papers no. 478.

an idea Pitt rejected in late July. He told Bussy that in his view France should be totally excluded from the Newfoundland fishery, that he wished to leave France no access to the Gulf of St Lawrence by land or sea, though he stressed that the decision was up to the council. Pitt offered to return Belle Isle, Guadeloupe and Martinique, but he insisted on Minorca, the French evacuation of Germany, the retention of Goree and the demolition of the fortifications at Dunkirk. Pitt added that the fall of Pondicherry, the principal French base in India, would have consequences. However, Bussy reported that conversations with councillors he did not name led him to think that if French yielded over Dunkirk and the evacuation of her forces from Germany, which the British were pressing for, the French would be left a share in the Newfoundland fishery and some nearby islands from which to conduct it.[122] This advice may have influenced Choiseul, who regarded Pitt's replies as unacceptable in their form as well as in their content. He argued that Pitt was acting as if he was a conqueror dictating terms. Pitt indeed may have been influenced by the continuing series of fresh triumphs. He wrote to his nephew on 21 July of 'joyful accounts being just arrived of the surrender of Pondicherry and of the taking of the Island Dominique'.[123]

On 5 August 1761 Choiseul presented Hans Stanley, the British envoy in Paris, with the French demands that she retain her Newfoundland fishery and with her refusal to evacuate Prussian territory. The Cabinet debated this on 19 August and agreed that they would accept the right of the French to the fishery and offer them a suitable place for drying their catches. Bute was now willing to support

---

[122] Bussy to Choiseul, 26 July 1761, AE CP Ang. 444 ff. 62–70.
[123] Choiseul to Bussy, 29 July, Choiseul to Ossun, envoy in Spain, 30 July 1761, AE CP Ang. 444 f. 84, Espagne 533 f. 173; BL Add. 69288 no. 30.

Newcastle. Given his resignation from the ministry eight weeks later, it is interesting that Pitt was willing to go along with the decision, Devonshire recording 'Pitt said he disapproved but would for the sake of unanimity come into it.'[124]

However, it was too late to be conciliatory. On 15 August 1761 France and Spain had signed the Third Family Compact. Their separation had been a crucial goal of British policy since 1748, one that Pitt had striven to maintain as Secretary of State. United, they were both now in a stronger position to press their claims on Britain. Spain was committed to helping France militarily after eight months, a period long enough to permit negotiations, but there was little incentive now for France to be conciliatory. In fact Spain's entry into the war was to make little difference: Britain was to triumph in the subsequent conflict; but the failure of the Anglo-French negotiations necessitates an assessment of Pitt's skill in wartime diplomacy, just as the 1759 invasion scare raises questions about his military strategy of dispersed effort. In 1761 there was no shortage of critics, both domestic and foreign, of Pitt. Bedford's sister-in-law, Lady Betty Waldegrave, wrote to her brother Earl Gower on 2 July 1761,

Why carry on the war any longer against the opinion of all the great men of the kingdom (not omitting the principal), the general sense of the nation and every individual that has not as insatiable an ambition as Mr Pitt . . . only to indulge one may really now say the chimerical policies of one man which God knows has already cost lives and money enough to this country. Lose a fair opportunity of settling and making Europe happy, and running the risk of losing our present advantage in the war, by failing and making unsuccessful attempts, hereafter . . . this monster should be overruled . . . let him reason and bellow.

---

[124] Devonshire Diary p. 116.

Rigby referred to Pitt in June as 'the Dictator'.[125] Choiseul was offended by Pitt's 'hauteur' and by his 'shocking' projects, which he suggested would arouse the anger of the European powers and possibly that of some of the British. Wall, also angered by Pitt's 'hauteur', told the French envoy that Pitt was a devil. Bussy offered a more rounded portrait on 30 August,

This minister is, as you know, the idol of the people, who regard him as the sole author of their success, and they do not have the same confidence in the other members of the council. The court and its partisans are obliged to have the greatest regards for the fantasies of a fiery people, whom it is dangerous to contradict.

Pitt joins to a reputation of superior spirit and talent, that of most exact honesty ... with simple manners and dignity, he seeks neither display nor ostentation. He neither makes his own court, nor receives people. Unless one wishes to discuss affairs one is not admitted to see him at his house. He is very eloquent, specious, wheedling, and with all the chicanery of an experienced lawyer. He is courageous to the point of rashness, he supports his ideas in an impassioned fashion and with an invincible determination, seeking to subjugate all the world by the tyranny of his opinions, Pitt seems to have no other ambition than to elevate Britain to the highest point of glory and to abase France to the lowest degree of humiliation ... he has few friends in the Council, but there is no one there strong or bold enough to try to replace him and the only way to stop him will be if Britain is defeated by France or in her new war with Spain, caused by the refusal of the opinionated Pitt to accept France's reasonable conditions.[126]

[125] A. Soulange-Bodin, La Diplomatie de Louis XV et le Pacte de Famille (Paris, 1894); A. Bourguet, Le Duc de Choiseul et l'alliance Espagnole (Paris, 1906); PRO 30/29/1/17 f. 977; Bedford vol. 44.
[126] Choiseul to Bussy, 29 July, Ossun to Choiseul, 10, 13 August, Bussy to Choiseul, 30 August 1761, AE CP Ang. 444 f. 84, Espagne 533 ff. 235, 259, Ang. 444 ff. 226–8; W. L. Grant, 'La Mission de M. de Bussy à Londres en 1761', Revue d'histoire diplomatique, 20 (1901), p. 351. On the negotiations, K. W. Schweizer, 'Lord Bute, William Pitt and the Peace Negotiations with France, April–September 1761', in Schweizer (ed.), Lord Bute (Leicester, 1988) pp. 41–55.

These were harsh charges, but they can be divided into essentially two categories, only one of which can be fully supported. The claim that Pitt was opposed to peace can be questioned, although it is more reasonable to argue that in his negotiations he lacked a mastery of the conciliatory diplomatic arts. While informing Hardwicke on 1 August 1761 that Pitt was not, according to Bute, sincere for peace, Newcastle wrote that Pitt's letter to Stanley of 25 July and the accompanying paper of points contained 'some very offensive expressions', a view shared by Hardwicke, who thought them 'inelegant and awkward and full of rough and offensive expressions', the paper 'in a very haughty and dictatorial style, more strongly so than any which I remember to have seen of Louis the 14th in the height of his glory and presumption . . . there runs thro' both the air of a man not disposed to conciliation'. Choiseul complained of the 'imperative tone, scarcely appropriate for a negotiation' of the pieces, and at a Council meeting on 14 August 1761 a draft reply by Pitt was criticised as 'too long and too irritating'. Pitt refused to alter it, leading Hardwicke to comment that nations might 'be writ . . . into perpetuating a war'.[127] Bedford was so angry that he refused to attend any more Cabinet meetings.

The aggressive and long-winded style that made Pitt's parliamentary speeches so distinctive was not suitable for diplomacy. Bedford was out of sympathy with Pitt's goals, but he clearly also thought his method of conducting negotiations inappropriate, and Bedford had, like Newcastle, been a Secretary of State. They had been the two Secretaries responsible for the peace negotiations that had ended the War of Austrian Succession in 1748, while Hardwicke had been consulted during numerous negotiations. At the

---

[127] Yorke, *Hardwicke* III 318–21; *Devonshire Diary* p. 111. Middleton misdates the meeting to 15 August, *Bells of Victory* p. 191.

meeting on 14 August Granville, on the basis of his diplomatic and Secretarial experience, criticised Pitt's draft as too offensive and oratorical. Just as many of Pitt's parliamentary speeches had echoes of classical oratory, so too, in this case at least, did his writing. Granville 'called the letter a fine piece of oratory, a classical and elegant performance; that all his experience had taught him that in negotiation plain language and style did best'. He thus backed Hardwicke's view that the piece had 'rather the appearance of a manifesto'. Thus, the public, demonstrative aspect of Pitt's personality and politics and his wish to win popular support, were seen as having too much effect on his ministerial conduct.[128] Pitt had no experience as a diplomat and his instinctual distrust of the Bourbons may have exacerbated the consequences of his naturally autocratic temperament. Suspicion was mutual: Bussy was concerned lest anything be said or written that could be subsequently used against France by Pitt, and he referred to Pitt's public and demonstrative style of diplomacy when he warned of the danger of Pitt using any French mistakes as the basis for an anti-French manifesto.[129]

Accepting that Pitt's style could be excessively harsh, it is nevertheless worth pointing out both that that would have mattered less had the Bourbons been prepared to settle, and that Pitt moderated his attitude during the negotiations. The first point was clearly made on 14 August when Bute interrupted the disputes over Pitt's draft to read a letter from Choiseul to the French envoy in Stockholm, a copy of which had been provided by the excellent postal interception system that served Britain so well in the mid-eighteenth century. Choiseul stated that France was determined to continue the war but would continue to negotiate with Britain in order to conceal her purpose. This led Devonshire

[128] *Devonshire Diary* p. 111.
[129] Bussy to Choiseul, 19 June 1761, AE CP Ang. 443 f. 247.

to tell the Council that he found Pitt's letter too offensive, but that 'the letter read by Lord Bute rendered it of less consequence'. Newcastle drew attention to another difficulty when on 2 July he expressed his concern that there were 'so many things to be adjusted'.[130]

The same day Pitt wrote to his wife then at Stowe, providing a reminder that he was not simply a public figure, but concerned in the midst of these crucial negotiations with his family.

I have gone through the labours of the *corps diplomatique* from ten this morning till past two . . . I have just received . . . a continuation of good accounts from the nursery. All are in perfect health. I propose to see them tomorrow evening, and to devote Saturday to children and to hay-making; and I hope Sunday will prove a day of rest from business – a day of impatience, but of a sweeter kind, it is sure to prove, big with the dear expectation of receiving again my delight and comfort on Monday.[131]

Pitt's attitude was not the central question in the diplomacy of the summer of 1761: rather it was whether France would be able to win Spanish support and thus, it was generally thought, fight on with more success and oblige Britain to be more accommodating. Pitt can be criticised for his failure to prevent a deterioration in Anglo-Spanish relations, but, under the new King, Charles III, Spanish policy had become less conciliatory in 1760. Spain claimed rights under the Peace of Utrecht to the Newfoundland fishery and stated that she would no longer accept what she saw as the illegal British cutting of logwood in Honduras, part of Spanish Central America, a long-standing cause of dispute. Pitt was not accommodating on either head, although he did seek to avoid provocations, pressing the Admiralty to respect

---

[130] *Devonshire Diary* p. 112; Choiseul to Marquis of Havrincourt, 30 July 1761, BL Add. 32926 f. 67; Newcastle to Rockingham, 2 July 1761, WW R146–1.
[131] *Chatham Corresp.* II, 130–1.

Spanish territorial waters and arranging for the release of a Spanish ship held at Portsmouth. Given the willingness to offer Gibraltar in 1757, Pitt could be criticised for a lack of bold initiatives to solve Anglo-Spanish differences in 1760–1, but he felt the Newfoundland fishery important and Spanish claims in the matter undeserved, while British victories over France made Spanish views appear less serious than in 1757. Pitt's relations with Fuentes, the Spanish envoy, were not good, and his position was undermined by the Spanish belief that his opponents would overthrow him. Fuentes reported that a numerous party, led by Bedford, Fox and Cumberland and secretly supported by Newcastle and the Whigs, was opposed to Pitt and inclined to peace.[132]

Pitt was to break with his ministerial colleagues in October 1761 over relations with Spain, not the previous summer over negotiations with France. That reflected his willingness to settle with France if satisfactory terms could be obtained. Arguably Pitt delayed the offer of reasonable terms until too late, but the lengthy negotiations that had marked the end of the wars of the Spanish and Austrian Successions suggest that a quick peace was difficult to obtain and the following year, without Pitt, the pacific ministry was still to find peace negotiations with the Bourbons difficult and very divisive. To a certain extent Pitt was castigated in the summer of 1761 as a result of his reputation, rather than as a consequence of his actions, a common and not inappropriate fate for a politician whose political strength was derived from his reputation. Far from being consistently isolated within the ministry, Pitt found a measure of support, winning the vote on 14 August over his draft by 6 votes to 5, Devonshire abstaining. On 14 August Bute told Devonshire that 'he never could nor would unite himself with' Pitt, but he voted with him that day and

---

[132] Ossun to Choiseul, 13 July 1761, AE CP Espagne 533 f. 48.

Viry pointed out eleven days later that Bute did not dare oppose Pitt.[133]

Nevertheless, the clashes of the summer had been unsettling for all involved, including Pitt. His tendency to believe that he alone could be relied on to defend national interests had been accentuated, as had his distrust of the Bourbons. Conversely the divisive consequences of Pitt's determination to defend his position had been demonstrated, while he had failed to secure the goals desired by the government: an acceptable peace with France and the continued separation of Spain from France. Although Bourbon duplicity could be blamed, there was a clear sense that Pitt had failed, a conclusion that it was difficult to separate from criticism of his methods. These views were largely held only by political insiders, but they help to explain the contrasting response to Pitt's resignation: relief within the ministry, but shock 'out-of-doors'.

The failure of the negotiations forced the ministry to confront the possibility of war with Spain. In the council in September 1761 Pitt, supported by Temple, the Lord Privy Seal, pressed for an immediate declaration of war stating on the 18th that 'loss of time [is] loss of opportunity. Whatever is dangerous will be more so 6 months hence; no safety but acting with vigour. Procrastination will increase the danger . . . an immediate action gives us the best chance to extricate ourselves.' The other ministers disagreed. They did not want to widen the war, were especially concerned about the possible financial burdens and hoped that Spain would not take action against Britain. They doubted that Britain had sufficient grounds to attack and proposed pressing Spain to deliver a categorical assurance of her friendly intentions. The exact details of the Family Compact were unknown and there

---

[133] *Devonshire Diary* p. 110.

was the danger that to attack Spain would only drive the Bourbon courts closer together. Unwilling to agree with their colleagues, Pitt and Temple declared that they would draw up a separate minute for George III, an unconventional step.[134] This stated that the combination of the Bourbon powers in enmity to Britain required 'necessary and timely measures', namely the breaking of diplomatic relations.[135] Three days later the issue was debated again. Devonshire recorded, 'Mr Pitt proposed the recall of Lord Bristol [envoy in Madrid] again and to follow it with an immediate declaration of war. Those that had opposed it the 18th continued of the same mind. In that meeting, he [Pitt] said, that though he should enter his protest, yet he would execute any resolution we should come to: now he said he would not do it, that the other Secretary or other Lords used to the business might'. Pitt and Temple then signed their paper and withdrew.[136]

It is clear from Newcastle's account of the episode that although Temple not unusually lost his temper, being 'very passionate' and 'very abusive', Pitt did not behave in an histrionic fashion, speaking instead 'very well and very determined but with great politeness and candour'. He, however, made it clear that he could not depart from his opinion, regretting indeed that he had done so during the negotiations with France.[137] The other ministers concluded that Pitt would quit and it is indeed from mid-September that his effective departure from the ministry should be dated, although he did not resign until the following month. On 24 September 1761 the members of the Council gave George III their reasons for differing from Pitt and Temple and on 2

---

[134] *Devonshire Diary* pp. 127–31; W. Hunt, 'Pitt's Retirement from Office, October 5, 1761', *EHR*, 21 (1906), pp. 126–7.

[135] *Grenville Papers* I, 386–7.   [136] *Devonshire Diary* p. 135.

[137] Yorke, *Hardwicke* III 326.

October Pitt attended the Council for the last time as Secretary. He argued that Britain must attack Spain while she was unprepared for war and, then the other ministers reiterated their views, claiming that it was not the moment to attack and that to do so would consolidate the Family Compact, Pitt delivered his valedictory assessment of his years as Secretary, Newcastle recorded,

Mr Pitt in his speech recapitulated his own situation, called (as he was without having ever asked any one single employment in his life) by his Sovereign, and he might say in some degree by the voice of the People, to assist the State, when others had *abdicated* the service of it; that he accordingly came, had gone thro' more difficulties than ever man did: that (tho' he supposed it might be good fortune) he had succeeded in his measures taken for the honour and interest of the nation; that in the execution of these measures, he had met with great obstructions from some (hinting at principal persons) who did not wish the success of them; that there was hardly one expedition which he had proposed, tho' the most probable and at last attended with the best success, that had not been before treated as chimerical and ridiculous; that he was loaded with the imputation of this war being *solely his*; that it was called *his war*; that it had been a successful one, and more than hinted that the success was singly owing to him; that the case was otherwise now; he saw what little credit he had in the Council from an union of opinion of some of the greatest persons in this Kingdom; he knew the little interest he had, either in Council or Parliament; that he had but one Lord in Council who agreed with him, with whom he would live and die; that the papers he had in his bag (meaning my Lord Bristol's letter and Mr Wall's paper) fixed an eternal stain on the Crown of England, if proper measures were not taken upon it; that it would be criminal in him, as Secretary of State, to let this affair sleep in his office ... that he could not acquiesce in sending no answer to Spain; that he could agree to no answer, but what was contained in his paper. That in his station and situation he was responsible; and would not continue without having the direction;

that this being the case, nobody could be surprised that he could go on no longer; and he would repeat it again, that he would be responsible for nothing but what he directed.

Granville's mild rejoinder was that Pitt 'could not justifye withdrawing himself from the service of his country at this crisis, declaring he was to have the direction of the whole, [Pitt] was taking more upon himself than any man had a right to, approaching to infalibility.' Pitt certainly had not heeded the advice of Charles Townshend 'that animation of language and sentiment, which is allowed to the orator in political conflicts ... has no place in a sober discussion'.[138] His attitude made the words ascribed to him by Elizabeth Montagu, a prominent blue-stocking, as well as the wife of an independent MP, in an unpublished dialogue of about 1760, appear appropriate. They also testified to disenchantment with Pitt's image. The Secretary in the dialogue, Pitt, declares 'My disinterestedness, my zeal for liberty, my ardor for my country's glory made me a first minister', and says of miracles,

I did really work them. I made Papists and Jacobites raise a militia to keep out the Pope and Pretender. I persuaded Republicans to give money to the King of Prussia. I convinced the House of Commons that troops sent to Emden were not designed for Germany. I made Anti-Hanoverians and the enemies of Germany send men we could ill spare, and money we could ill raise to the aid of Prince Ferdinand. Before I came into power, one Clive, by the help of I do not know who, won a battle I do not know where, and by calling him a Heaven-born general all his conquests have been ascribed to me. I gained honour every day by disgrace being thrown upon measures to which I assented, in which I assisted. The oftener I altered my opinion the more I was esteemed for my consistency,

---

[138] BL Add. 32929 ff. 21–2; Yorke, *Hardwicke* III 279–80; *Devonshire Diary* p. 139; [Townshend], *Remarks on the Letter Address'd to Two Great Men. In a Letter to the Author of that Piece* (1760) p. 5.

and the oftener my present actions contradicted my former promises the more I was praised for my probity. Had I not miraculous powers?[139]

Pitt's resignation on 5 October 1761 stemmed from his unwillingness to follow a policy that he believed to be wrong. As was predicted at the time, Pitt was to be vindicated in part by the outbreak of war with Spain that winter. George Lyttelton, who had broken with Pitt when the latter went into opposition to Newcastle in November 1755, identified that on 8 October 1761 as likely to be the key element in the public response to the resignation,

I want much to know whether it is probable that by Pitt's going out we shall be saved from a war with Spain. The opinion of the Publick as to the wisdom of his conduct will greatly depend on that question. For, if it be inevitable, some will think he was in the right to desire to act à la Prussienne and strike first, while the enemy was unguarded and more vulnerable than afterwards. Our people naturally love violent and spirited measures, without troubling themselves much about forms. But if Spain is not determined to make war upon us few persons I believe will approve of our making it upon them.[140]

In 1718 the British had defeated the Spanish fleet off Cape Passero in Sicily without declaring war. The step had been relatively popular in Britain, where Pitt's uncle James, First Earl Stanhope, who used to call Pitt 'the young marshal', was one of the leading members of the ministry. In 1755 Boscawen had similarly attacked the French fleet en route to Canada. Pitt's proposal was not therefore without precedent. However, his attitude to the conduct of government was unacceptable. The co-operative nature of British ministries was the product of the absence both of party government

[139] Elizabeth Montagu, '[A Dialogue between] Simon or Simeon Stylites and Mr Secretary', HL MO 2997.
[140] Lyttelton to Elizabeth Montagu, 8 October 1761, HL MO 1296.

based on a party organisation and of unchallenged royal direction that could be delegated to a favourite. This co-operative element produced stress for ministers who found the process of winning support difficult, as Newcastle had done frequently, and as Pitt did in the summer of 1761. Judging Anglo-Spanish relations as both a source of danger and an opportunity for victory, Pitt did not appreciate that he might have to yield to the views of colleagues whose assumptions were not dishonourable. In light of a growing national desire for peace and the individual grievances of particular ministers against him, Pitt's determination to force the pace for war was inappropriate. On 5 October 1761 George Lyttelton described him as 'a man who (in a political sense) fears neither God nor Devil'.[141] Fearing none, he was also unwilling to concede in order to win co-operation. That determination, both egoistic obstinacy and honourable single-mindedness, was to make him a difficult man to work with and collaborate with, both in office and out of it.

[141] Lyttelton to Elizabeth Montagu, 5 October 1761, HL MO 1295.

≈ Chapter 4 ≈

'Greatness going off'? Pitt
1761–1778

I think the best way to ruin Pitt would be to make him once
more minister and I'd be hanged if in a twelve month he was
not the most unpopular man in the kingdom.

George Macartney to his patron Henry Fox, Lord Holland,
14 October 1763[1]

OUT OF OFFICE: OPPONENT OF THE PEACE OF PARIS
1761–1763

Mr Pitt is as great a bruiser as any orator whatsoever. He has hard
words of all sorts, and I do not wonder that Mr Grenville, who has
but a soft lisping eloquence should be afraid of him. A man of great
wit might be a match for Mr Pitt. Ridicule is the only weapon with
which he can be subdued, false eloquence and fictitious patriotism
are fine subjects for raillery. The affected greatness of this
gentleman's sentiments, and the gigantesca sublimita of his oratory
expose him to it. One may beat a bladder full of wind long enough
without making an impression, a pointed weapon and a pointed
word would make the football and the orator shrink to their native
size. (Elizabeth Montagu, 21 October 1762)[2]

The events of 1761–3 helped to foster a set of assumptions
about Pitt that played a major role in creating the myth that he

[1] BL Add. 51388 f. 141.
[2] Elizabeth Montagu to Earl of Bath, 21 October 1762, HL MO 4547.

226

was to be associated with. Though war with Spain soon broke out and was prosecuted with success, the terms of the Peace of Paris of 1763 that ended the conflict with the Bourbons were criticised by Pitt and others as too conciliatory, thus fostering the identification of Pitt with the vigorous defence of national interests. Though the Bute ministry easily carried the terms through Parliament, Bute, unnerved by the political struggle, resigned in 1763, helping to create the misleading impression that no ministry without Pitt could be stable. In November 1763 Pitt took a major role in the debate over parliamentary privilege and the arrest of John Wilkes, an MP, political supporter and polemical journalist, thus allowing himself to be presented as the defender of supposedly endangered liberty. In a manner that was sometimes at variance with his actual views and actions, Pitt became a totem of the new 'patriotism', the cause of national integrity and honour, supposedly threatened by sinister desires to weaken national liberties on the part of Bute, a Scot and a Stuart, and therefore easy to castigate as malevolent, and possibly George III. This totemic quality was to give Pitt a significance to Americans resisting British authority that was clearer than his more complex views on Anglo-American relations really justified.

On 5 October 1761 Pitt resigned, telling George III that it would only create problems if he remained in office when he disagreed over policy towards Spain, but also stating that he would neither oppose the King's measures nor attend the Commons except to defend his own policy or support supplies for the armed forces. As an acknowledgement for his services he was offered the Governor-Generalship of Canada or the Chancellorship of the Duchy of Lancaster. The former would have been a definite challenge, but Pitt declined both, accepting a peerage for his wife and an annuity of £3,000. The combination of the resignation and this grant helped to produce a bitter public debate about Pitt's merits and motives. Pitt was accused of allowing himself to be bribed; self-interest was seen as the key to his career. It was suggested that the grant to Pitt was made with the specific purpose of compromising his public reputation and providing the basis for a press attack on him. The most recent study of the episode, one written admittedly by a scholar who is concerned to reassess Bute's reputation positively, suggests that Bute sought to minimise domestic tension in the autumn of 1761 and that Pitt's reward was seen as a way to pacify parliamentary and popular opinion. Newcastle referred to 'the great favour intended for Mr Pitt'. The 'press war' that broke out over Pitt's position has been traced to the attempts of Pittite supporters to suggest that the minister's departure was an unfortunate step, and Bute's moves are presented as reactive.[3]

Feeling obliged to explain his position, Pitt defended himself by writing to one of his most prominent supporters, William Beckford, both explaining why he had resigned and stressing that he had not sought his pension. This letter, written on 15 October, was published in the *Public Ledger* on 17 October, and thence reprinted. It helped to make Pitt's position more controversial, inspiring a press and pamphlet war during the winter of 1761–2. The letter also helped to revive Pitt's popularity in London which had suffered from his acceptance of the pension. On 22 October 1761 the Common Council of the City of London passed unanimously a vote of thanks to Pitt for arousing the 'ancient spirit' of the nation and extending the sphere of British trade. The City's

---

[3] Henry Liddell to Richard Middleton, 10 October 1761, Aberystwyth, National Library of Wales, Chirk Castle MSS E 6132; K. W. Schweizer, 'Lord Bute and William Pitt's Resignation in 1761', *Canadian Journal of History*, 8 (1973), pp. 111–22; Schweizer, 'Lord Bute and the Press: The Origins of the Press War of 1762 Reconsidered', in K. Schweizer (ed.), *Lord Bute* (Leicester, 1988) pp. 83–98; Newcastle to Bedford, 10 October 1761, Bedford vol. 44.

MP's were instructed to press for the continuance of Pitt's firmly anti-French policies. On 9 November when George III attended the Lord Mayor's banquet he received less applause than Pitt. London's voice was echoed elsewhere. On 23 November 1761 *Aris's Birmingham Gazette* reported that the Mayor, Aldermen and Common Council of Chester had resolved to thank Pitt

for his eminent and effectual services to his King and Country; and that he be assured, that this ancient and loyal city does most heartily concur in the opinion and recent resolution of the Common Council of the very respectable metropolis.

As also, that we deeply share in the general anxiety, and concern, that Great Britain, by a rational resignation, is, at this time, deprived of a Minister, whose salutary counsels, steady conduct, and truly patriot spirit had retrieved the honour of these nations, rendered us happily unanimous at home, and gloriously formidable to our adversaries abroad.

Pitt did not seek to create an opposition to the new ministry and its policies. During the winter of 1761–2 he fulfilled the promise he had made to George III on his resignation. A proud man, and aware that his political weight depended on his reputation, Pitt was nevertheless determined to defend his policies and views as minister, a course that was politically controversial. Unlike Walpole in 1742, he was not obliged to fear parliamentary prosecution, and he was able to defend his position in person, rather than taking shelter behind an Old Corps majority. The Commons met on 13 November 1761. The Bavarian envoy wrote of the popular joy when Pitt got out of his carriage, 'It was really one of the ancient Roman scenes . . . he is always one of the chosen of the people and if he had not accepted the pension I really think that they would have made him a dictator.' A German visitor recorded, 'There can be no denying that he is one of the most powerful speakers of our time . . . when he speaks, a look of

fixed attention is promptly visible upon the features of all
present, and absolute silence reigns in the whole House.'[4]
The newly elected James Harris made it clear that Pitt spoke at
the end of the debate in response to attacks on his position.
He was impressed by Pitt's measured tone, a point noted by
other commentators,

Mr Pitt arose, and spoke with great dignity and temper – giving an
account of that dissension with the Cabinet, which drove him to
resign – avowed the sincerity of his own sentiments, yet did not
deny but that others were as sincere, who were of contrary opinion
– defended the German war with great force of eloquence on the
same principles with Beckford, of its being a diversion to the
French with respect to the operations in America – dwelt with some
feeling on a phrase dropped (as I remember) by Harvey, of his
courting a Spanish war – solemnly denied it, and said that if in
anything he had been to blame, 'twas in his backwardness to break
with Spain – explained or endeavoured to explain the individious
term of guidance – vindicated it on his use of the word responsible. He
had not said, he could not agree to measures, but be responsible for
measures he could not guide – said he should not seek to come into
place again – professed to concur as far as he could with the
measures of government and particularly, as he knew the difficulty
in the manner of raising the supplies, that he should not, when the
Budget came to be opened, obstruct matters with any fastidious
criticisms – dwelt much on having the Spanish Papers laid before the
house – spoke as to the Fishery, owned that he had always opposed
any concessions, but that in the Cabinet he had been supported by
almost as few, as in the Spanish affair. He was well heard, and
deservedly.

On 9 December Pitt defended himself again, refuting
criticism of his subsidy treaties,

[4] Haslang's report, 13 November 1761, Munich Bayr. Ges. London 238; Count
Frederick Kielmansegge, Diary of a Journey to England in the Years 1761–1762 (1902) p.
163.

he too entered into a long detail in deducing the war, of which he showed himself not to be the author, but that he found it, when he came in – prefaced with strong professions of temper in his debate – justified the German war, both as Hanover had been invaded on our account, and as a diversion – spoke of the burden it was to France . . . justified his phrase about Hanover's being a millstone round our necks, that it was now so round that of the French – gave the highest encomiums of the King of Prussia and Duke Ferdinand . . .

Pitt also advanced the thesis of the importance of the ends rather than the means, as argument that could serve to justify past alterations in his views,

the whole inference that can be drawn from the arguments of those who differ from me is that we have done our business effectually the wrong way. As long as we are right as to the matter of fact, I shall not dispute much with them about the means. Politics is a conjectural science, and its greatest strokes are only justified by the success of the event.

The hostile Richard Rigby wrote that night to the Duke of Bedford,

Stanley made a very fine set speech in praise, Pitt brought down with his feet in flannels spoke after him, but by no means replied to him, though he spoke sometimes sitting and sometimes standing for three hours and a half. He took a draught of brandy or something out of a phial in the middle of his speech, in short his whole appearance and performance was as affected and absurd as possible. He was huzzaed to the very door of the House in the lobby by a mob prepared on purpose, who attended also his going out and paid him the like compliment. I never heard Pitt so dull in my life.

Pitt's political honesty and consistency were at issue in the debate. One of the critics of the German war, Francis Delaval, accused Pitt of having lately received a subsidy himself.

Another critic of the German war, Thomas Bunbury, making his maiden speech on 10 December, 'talked of Mr Pitt's violent oppositions, and then coming in, and chameleon like changing colour to the ground, on which he was got'.[5]

On 11 December 1761 the Commons debated a motion for communicating papers on negotiations with Spain, an issue that could serve to vindicate Pitt. Lord John Cavendish noted Pitt's defence 'of his resignation, said he could not do otherwise when refused to do what he thought right in his own department, said he never interfered in the department of others'.[6] Pitt was savaged by the newly elected Isaac Barré, who presented Pitt's motion as tending to bring 'the power of making peace and war into this House, to lower the King's prerogative' and Pitt

as inconsistent, as having gone into every measure that he himself had condemned, and now engaged us in a ruinous war, which would prove the destruction of his country; that he had no regard (this and the following motion Mr Pitt had just used) to eyes lifted to heaven, to a hand laid on the table, or striking the breast or heart; these and the flowers of rhetoric had no weight with him; that the person, who had engaged us in our ruinous measures was not now ashamed to desert his sovereign's service when assistance was most wanted.[7]

Pitt's resignation, the bitter controversy over national goals and policies that the failure of peace negotiations with France and the developing crisis with Spain gave rise to, and the impact of a new generation of politicians, thus helped to ensure that, however much Pitt might have hoped to be an universally honoured elder statesman whose views were sought by the ministry, his reputation had instead been

[5] HP Harris memoranda, 13 November, 9, 10 December 1761, Bedford vol. 46.
[6] Cavendish to Devonshire, 12 December 1761, HP Chatsworth.
[7] HP Harris, 11 December 1761.

affected by the newly divided political world. The sense of a new political agenda and of new players helped to allow Pitt's opponents to see him as redundant. Both Henry Fox and George Selwyn saw him as 'dying', a 'dying gladiator' according to the latter.[8] On the other hand the outbreak of war with Spain helped to vindicate Pitt, in the eyes of many, and led to calls for his return to office in January 1762.

Bute's growing determination to break with Frederick II and reopen negotiations with France helped to ensure that the vindications of Pitt's past policies produced by the former minister and by his supporters were unwelcome. In addition, what had been initially a rift that was ostensibly only over the question of how best to confront the Bourbon alliance became a more wide ranging difference of opinion over the entire direction of government policy. George III was closely identified with a specific 'patriotic' agenda, the rejection of his grandfather's tradition of intervention in German affairs. Pitt's trumpeting of the values of such intervention in recent years compromised his reputation and helped to anger the government, Bute writing to Andrew Mitchell on 9 April 1762 that 'without some total change of every idea; hitherto cherished; these gentlemen never can return into office again'.[9]

Given the accusations of his critics that Pitt was like a chameleon, it is worth stressing that he did not seek to accommodate himself to the views of George III, nor to explain how he would satisfy the widespread desire for peace. On 12 May 1762, when the vote of credit for the war was debated, Pitt, who 'said he would avoid altercation', insisted that Britain could afford to continue financing her German war at the same time as she paid for the expedition-

---

[8] Fox to Devonshire, 17 December 1761, HP Chatsworth.
[9] Bute to Mitchell, 9 April 1762, MS 6/143.

ary force sent by the new ministry to defend Portugal from Spain, a proposition that was doubted, with considerable reason, within the government,

The continental plan is the only plan, otherwise all Europe will be interdicted by these haughty oppressors of the House of Bourbon from receiving you whom they affect to treat as an overgrown pirate from their ports. Increase of power must be continued with increase of commerce or both will dwindle . . . I am convinced this country can raise 12, 13, 14 or even 15 million the next year. I know it without seeking information from bundles of papers and accounts . . . the only question is whether grievous and permanent as that tax must be, it is not to be preferred to the perpetual dishonour of the nation, the aggrandisement of the enemy and the desertion of your allies, all which tend to an inglorious and precarious peace . . . I rejoice at the extinction of parties.

Pitt pressed for the maintenance of good relations with Prussia and claimed that 'Continental measures had been practised by all our great princes, by Queen Elizabeth, by King William and were the reverse of those, which dishonoured this country for four reigns [meaning the Stuarts].'[10] He thus demonstrated the flexibility of historical examples, for the reign of Elizabeth was generally cited by the proponents of maritime war with Spain. However, Pitt's linkage of the national tradition to Continental interventionism would have surprised many.

Harris commented on Pitt's impracticability,

Mr Pitt I call an Inigo Jones in politics, a man of great ideas, a projector of noble and magnificent plans – but architects, though they find the plan, never consider themselves as concerned to find the means.

Gilbert Elliot similarly thought Pitt unrealistic,

[10] HP Harris, 12 May 1762; BL Add. 32938 ff. 187–8.

It is supposed that this summer must either produce peace, or contract our plans of war, as the possibility of finding 14 millions for next year is scarce conceivable. Mr Pitt indeed asserted roundly yesterday that it might be done with ease, but his assertion is not sufficient, unless it could be supplied with facts.

The lack of realism in financial matters was not a new development. During the Seven Years War Newcastle, who directed the Treasury and was responsible for raising the vast loans the government required, had complained of the same feature. In 1766 Lady Mary Coke recorded an attack on Pitt by Lady Blandford,

she said all she knew of him was that it had been his measures that had involved the nation in debt . . . he had always declared himself above thinking of accounts or studying economy; I rejoiced he was above such trifles, hoped his schemes were great and extensive, not bounded by the dirty economy of a shilling.[11]

Pitt's disregard of such constraints was politically inopportune in 1762 because of growing concern about the size of the National Debt, the war having been largely fought on credit, and because taxation helped to bring home to individual politicians and voters the consequences of an aggressive foreign policy. In 1762 Pitt reverted to his attitude of 1738–9: criticising a ministry trying to follow a prudential foreign policy and to maintain or obtain peace, on the grounds that it was betraying national interests, while at the same time failing to discuss the implications of his policy, especially in financial terms. This was an obvious contrast to his prudential defence of foreign policy after the War of the Austrian Succession.

Pitt's attitude towards the peace terms helps to explain

---

[11] HP Harris, 12 May 1762; Elliot to Lord Minto, 13 May 1762, NLS MS 11001 ff. 82–3; *The Letters and Journals of Lady Mary Coke* (4 vols., 1889–96) I, 46.

why so many political figures of the period thought him unrealistic, and yet there was a widely held opinion that Pitt's presence was somehow necessary to the stability and strength of a ministry. Having fallen out with Bute over the latter's determination to obtain peace and his conduct of the government, Newcastle resigned in May 1762 and made a major effort to obtain Pitt's support against Bute and, in particular, against the preliminary peace terms that he had negotiated with France. However, Pitt was unwilling to commit himself to Newcastle. He was angry with the Duke's failure to join with him in resisting the rise of Bute, distrusted Newcastle and did not wish to anger the Tories by joining with the Old Whigs, although he had no love of what he termed 'Tory government'. In July 1762 Newcastle informed Devonshire that he was not surprised by Pitt's hostility, 'I have long known his inveteracy to me . . . I have a great deal to complain of him, for his ingratitude, for many years. In this reign, I own, I did, in concert with your Grace and my friends, prefer my Lord Bute to him.' By November 1762 Pitt, increasingly concerned about Bute's attitude towards peace terms, had allowed himself to be brought round to promise 'to concur in measures with the Duke of Newcastle', but the relationship was acrimonious on Pitt's part and he refused to discuss how the opposition to the preliminaries should be conducted.[12] Newcastle's conduct was vacillating, if not feeble. He had failed to make any tactical alliance with Pitt, while on the other hand Hardwicke had several times warned him that the peace terms were not unpopular outside of London and that opposition to them would appear to be based merely on personal dislike of Bute. It was very much as a loner that Pitt came to the Commons of 9 December 1762 in order to attack the terms.

---

[12] Newcastle to Devonshire, 23 July, conversation between Mr Pitt and Mr Nuthall, 5 November 1762, BL Add. 32941 f. 277, 32944 f. 277.

The Bute ministry had a number of spectacular triumphs in 1762, taking Havana and Manila from Spain and Martinique from France. The failure of Spanish efforts to live up to French expectations led to a revival in French interest in peace that coincided with the wishes of George III and Bute; although the consent of the entire Cabinet was only obtained with some difficulty, Pitt not being alone in thinking that Bute was insufficiently firm towards the Bourbons. The terms finally negotiated were better than those that had been in prospect in 1761 because Pitt had been proved correct in his prediction that Spain could be defeated speedily. Martinique, Guadeloupe, Goree and Belle Isle were returned to France and Havana and Manila to Spain, but, among her gains from France, Britain kept Canada, Senegal and several West Indian islands, while Spain ceded Florida, acknowledged the British right to cut logwood on the Honduran coast and abandoned her claims to the Newfoundland fishery. France returned Minorca, evacuated her German gains, returned Dunkirk to its former state and accepted an Indian settlement that left Britain in an obviously superior position. France retained her right to a share in the Newfoundland fishery, although her drying stations, the islands of St Pierre and Miquelon, were to be unfortified.

These were the best terms that Britain was ever to obtain in a peace treaty until in 1815 at the Congress of Vienna she was able to play a major role in rearranging Europe as well as cementing her position as the leading European colonial power. And yet to Pitt they were unsatisfactory, both because the ministry could have obtained better terms and because they did not end the danger of a Bourbon *revanche*, although it is not clear how fears on that head could have been assuaged. 'Posterity will read the articles of that Treaty, and with astonishment contrast them, with the writings against it, and the opposition that was made to it in both houses of

Parliament', was the reasonable verdict of one informed commentator. Pitt's opposition to the terms of what was to be the Peace of Paris of 1763 was to play a major role in fostering the image of defender of national interest, but it is clear from accounts of the reception of his speech on 9 December 1762 that he made little impact in the Commons. Harris recorded that Pitt,

Spoke with great digressions upon the prerogative of the Crown, upon revolution principles, upon his own resignation, upon the Duke of Cumberland and by way of panegyric, the declaring himself withal to be united with no party (in this he alluded to the party formed by the Dukes of Cumberland, Devonshire and Newcastle) allowed the North American part of the peace to be good – excepted strongly to the fishery, to the cessions in the West Indies, to that of Goree, to the East India article, and last of all ended with the stale story of our magnanimous ally and ever cordial friend the King of Prussia – he spoke three hours and twenty five minutes, partly standing and leaning on a crutch, partly (with leave of the House) sitting. All people I spoke to, of all sides, confessed a languor and tediousness in this speech, to which they had not been accustomed . . . spoke of the Spanish debility, and all along considered it as a postulation that another year's war in its full extent (that is to say, another 18 millions, and sure success) was a thing practicable.

John Campbell, a supporter of Bute's, informed his wife, H.S.E. [presumably a facetious His Serene Excellency]

spoke without intermission, three hours and a half; he came into the House with his legs covered with a great deal of somewhat under large white woollen or flannel stockings, and some black things that came up half his legs over that like half boots and with a crutch under one arm. On account of his infirmity, the House indulged him to speak when he pleased sitting, so he was enabled to hold out the time I mention. Some short pieces of his speech were good and spirited, but the greatest part verbose, tedious, round about, and back again, over and over. Indeed what man in the most perfect health could speak to the purpose, and without useless, disagreeable repetitions $3\frac{1}{2}$ hours.

Herbert Mackworth noted that Pitt, 'had not his usual spirit, the speech was thought to be tedious and languid', while Elizabeth Montagu commented 'none wept at the sweet notes of the dying swan'. Pitt was especially scathing about the provisions for the Newfoundland fishery and argued that they and the return of Guadeloupe and Martinique gave France the means to recover from her losses and to threaten Britain's maritime and commercial position again.[13]

To Pitt, therefore, the Peace of Paris contained the seeds of a future war and indeed Britain and France were to go to war again in 1778 and 1793, Britain and Spain in 1779. In 1779 a Bourbon invasion fleet challenged British control of the Channel. Two years later the French fleet played a major role in forcing Cornwallis to surrender at Yorktown. Pitt might therefore appear to have been vindicated and indeed this view was advanced during the War of American Independence. However, his limited impact in December 1762 was not due simply to his poor health nor to the overrated effects of ministerial bribery. The government carried the address of thanks by 319 to 65, a decisive majority. As in 1713, when the Treaty of Utrecht was attacked on the grounds that Britain had deserted her allies and that the terms favoured the Bourbons, peace was popular and support for Britain's allies was limited. Pitt had earlier in his career stressed that he would advocate policies he believed necessary whether they were popular or not, but he had either backed popular

[13] Thomas Robinson to Bute, 8 April 1763, MS 11/78; HP Harris, 9 December 1762; Campbell to his wife, 11 December 1762, Cawdor, Box 138; Mackworth to his father, 14 December 1762, Swansea, University Library, Mackworth papers no. 860; Montagu to Elizabeth Carter, [December 1762], HL MO 3089; K. Hotblack, *Chatham's Colonial Policy* (1917); Z. E. Rashed, *The Peace of Paris* (Liverpool, 1951).

positions, such as criticism of Hanoverian subsidies in 1742–3, or defended less widely favoured moves, such as the commercial settlement with Spain in 1750 or the dispatch of troops to Germany in 1758, when opposition to them had become attenuated and they could appear necessary. In 1762 Pitt advocated a cause, the continuance of war, that appeared both unnecessary and dangerous. His comments on the likely future policy of the Bourbons appeared of limited relevance in light of Britain's gains from the treaty. Pitt's detailed criticisms of the terms were weakened by his stress on the need to preserve a Prussian alliance and by his clear hostility to the peace.

A strong desire to vindicate his past conduct clearly played a major role. Indeed Pitt's tendency to self-justification, which had led to repeated charges of hypocrisy and egoism, was to become after his resignation a dominant theme in his personality. This may have owed something to the relative subordination of his desire for office that was to become another characteristic. Pitt found it impossible to give up politics and episodically continued to seek office, in part in order to exonerate his reputation. At the same time a weariness of spirit can be discerned in his attitude, one that probably owed something to his poor health, but that can also be traced to disillusionment with the collapse of the ministerial system of George II's last years. In December 1762 and January 1763 Pitt suffered from a 'succession of severe fits of gout',[14] and was pessimistic about the nation's prospects. In his eyes the wishes of Providence had been thwarted and Pitt feared the rapid descent of the country into decadence.[15] His attitude was to colour his political conduct and to help to make Pitt a difficult, at times maddening, figure to deal with. Ill for protracted periods and without

---

[14] Chatham Corresp. II, 203, 208.   [15] Chatham Corresp. II, 209.

much apparent drive for power, Pitt was less willing to compromise his views than he had been during his earlier rise to office. He distrusted George III and most other political figures and feared that engagements with them might lead him into dishonourable commitments.

Given these attitudes it might appear surprising that Pitt had any political consequence. During the early months of 1763 he had little, Bute appeared reasonably secure and the opposition was divided. John Campbell wrote of Pitt and Temple, 'There certainly is not the least inclination towards them at present.' After 9 December 1762 Pitt did not attend the Commons again until 4 March 1763 when he supported the proposed army establishment on the grounds that 'the peace was inadequate, was hollow, was no better than an armed truce'. He was also reported as arguing that a larger force in America would not threaten local liberties, 'This peace an armed truce only. Therefore for a greater number of men . . . Thinks that the American force is hardly sufficient for so large an extent of country. The crown can acquire no influence by means of that force . . . 10,000 men hardly enough to speak to one another if a communication is needed.'

Pitt's criticism of the proposed use of the Sinking Fund to repay part of the navy debt was countered by James Oswald pointing out that the same had been done when Pitt held office under Pelham, the sort of remark that could hardly encourage him to enter a ministry whose policies he did not direct. The French envoy suggested that Pitt's opposition to cutting the army would not help his popularity, while on 7 March 1763 he advocated raising taxes as a means to pay off debt. Pitt's revived energy was focused on the ministry's proposal for a cider excise and, in opposition to that, he moved closer to the Old Whig aristocracy, Devonshire, Newcastle and the latter's protégé the Marquis of Rockingham, a step encouraged by Tory adherence to Bute. Pitt attacked the excise and savaged his brother-in-law George Grenville, who was a member of the ministry. His revived prominence helps to explain why Bute, seeking to weaken the opposition, sought his support, but Pitt refused.[16]

THE QUEST TO BE A STATESMAN ABOVE PARTY
1763–1766

By the spring of 1763 Bute, whose enthusiasm for high office had never been total, was disillusioned with government. Although the ministry enjoyed solid majorities in both Houses of Parliament, Bute found the stress of politics unbearable. The intention seems to have been that he should retreat to being 'the minister behind the curtain', George III writing to him that April, 'thank God I have a friend . . . that comforts me and makes me look on my Ministers as my tools solely in my public capacity'. Bute's failure of nerve was very different to that of Newcastle in 1756, as were its consequences. Opposition politicians were not to gain office immediately as a result of Bute's resignation on 8 April 1763. Earl Gower commented,

Lord Bute has at last tired with abuse, ingratitude and business, but pleading ill health resolved to retire from employment entirely; but the King is resolved not to be taken by storm, and be hereafter a prisoner for life, and is therefore forming an administration out of those who have at least not opposed since his accession . . . if something is not formed to stem the present intrusion upon the court, the King must submit to Mr Pitt, Lord Temple, Mr Legge and Lord Hardwicke.[17]

[16] HP Harris 4, 7, 21 March 1763; Duke of Nivernais to Duke of Praslin, French foreign minister, 7 March 1763, AE CP Ang. 450 f. 41; Campbell to his wife, 7 April 1763, Cawdor, Box 138. Aside from Schweizer (ed.) Bute, J. D. Nicholas, 'The Ministry of Lord Bute, 1762–3' (unpublished Ph.D. University of Wales, Aberystwyth, 1988) is very useful.
[17] R. R. Sedgwick (ed.), Letters from George III to Lord Bute 1756–1766 (1939) p. 233; Gower to Bedford, no date, PRO 30/29/1/116.

The sense that a ministry had to be created in order to protect George III from Pitt was one that Pitt was to seek to overcome, because he appreciated that were he to return to power, that could only be lasting if he enjoyed royal favour. However, he faced the same problem that other politicians outside government had faced: should he attack the ministry he might anger the King. Nevertheless, within several months, Pitt was to be asked by George III to return to office, a measure that stemmed from the King's poor relations with the new First Lord of the Treasury, the aggressive George Grenville, and the argument that Pitt's inclusion in the ministry would make it more stable. The King was persuaded to open negotiations with Pitt in late August 1763 by Bute, not the least kaleidoscopic of the shifts that were to mark the politics of the decade. The negotiations were abortive, because George III was not prepared to accept Pitt's demands. Grenville reported,

The King offered to dispose of the two great offices of Secretary of State and President of the Council in any manner that might best contribute to the general satisfaction and to take such farther arrangements as could be made agreeable to the parties concerned in them, but declared that he would upon no account consent to any proposal that was inconsistent with his honour in regard to the measures which he had followed or to the protection of all those whose conduct towards him he had reason to approve. Mr Pitt on the contrary proposed to exclude all who had any hand in the peace which he represented as dangerous, dishonourable and criminal, although he did not intend to break it but to ameliorate it in the execution. To make an universal change by turning out every civil officer in the King's service, and by introducing all those who had engaged in the opposition in their stead. He urged that this was a Tory government not founded upon revolution principles but adopting the opinions of prerogative and of the power of the Crown and therefore it was necessary to make an alteration of it.

Unacceptable to George III, Pitt's demands also appeared excessive, his language unwarranted, to others. The Earl of Oxford argued that

The terms insisted upon were not only incompatible with the dignity, and inconsistent with the honour of His Majesty, but of such a nature and extent, as must have rendered him dependent upon the power, and left his subjects to the mercy of one set of men, the most dangerous event, which could possibly befall this country.

As so often in Pitt's career, however, the response among well-informed 'insiders' was not that of the public. The fact that the negotiations took place was well known and they attracted considerable interest. Elizabeth Countess Cornwallis wrote to her son William on 29 August,

Mr Pitt was alone with the King from twelve o'clock till three yesterday noon at Buckingham House, numbers of people waiting at the gate with anxious countenances the whole time to observe him when he came out . . . It is a very remarkable proceeding their choosing this conference should be made so public, as such things are usually kept quite private till they are settled.

On 17 September she noted the general response to the failure of the negotiations, namely that by declining office Pitt had 'gained great credit by his behaviour'.[18]

Having failed to take over the government by the invitation of the King, Pitt displayed no interest in doing so by joining with the opposition and in September 1763 he rejected Newcastle's proposal for co-operation in the forth-

[18] Grenville to Fourth Earl of Oxford, 1 September 1763, HL st7 vol. 1; Earl of Sandwich to Henry Fox, Lord Holland, 6, 26 September 1763, Earl of Ilchester (ed.), Letters to Henry Fox, (Roxburghe Club, 1915), p. 176, 180; Oxford to Grenville, 10 September 1763, Bod. MS Eng. Letters d. 109 f. 71; Lyttelton to Elizabeth Montagu, 25 September 1763, HL MO 1312; Viry to Charles Emmanuel, 2, 6 September 1763, AST LM Ing. 68; HP Harris, 30 August 1763; G. Cornwallis-West, The Life and Letters of Admiral Cornwallis (1927) pp. 30–1; P. Lawson, George Grenville (Oxford, 1984) pp. 159–63.

coming session, declaring that he would oppose what he thought wrong, but not seek to force his way into office,

Mr Pitt, in his usual way desired to be excused; that his case was singular; that his health would not permit him to attend . . . that he never liked a plan of general opposition; that he should, as he did, the last year, come to the House, when his health permitted him; and oppose, what, he thought, was wrong . . . that nothing could be done in the House of Commons . . . Mr Pitt has, at present, the gout; and will not be able to stir in some days.[19]

Pitt's hesitation about co-operating with opposition politicians, other than on his own terms, influenced his response to the controversy over John Wilkes. Wilkes, a Rabelaisian MP who had supported Pitt, had founded a weekly newspaper, the North Briton, to attack Bute. His denunciation in number 45 of the Peace of Paris led to the charge of seditious libel. The government issued a general warrant for the arrest of all those involved in the publication of number 45, sought to arrest Wilkes, despite his parliamentary privilege, and charged him with blasphemy because he attributed his indecent Essay on Woman to a cleric. Though Pitt criticised Wilkes as an individual, he saw parliamentary privilege as a crucial bar to royal despotism. However, he found Newcastle unwilling to condemn the Attorney General, Charles Yorke, one of Hardwicke's sons. This proved to be a bar to co-operation, Pitt complaining to Newcastle in October 1763,

I could wish I had been told the full state of the thing sooner, that I might not have proceeded in the vain dream that some solid union upon real Revolution Principles and an assertion in earnest of the freedom of the constitution, in so sacred an article as privilege of Parliament, was indeed practicable; under the various byasses, managements, and intanglements which draw various ways.

[19] Substance of conversation with Pitt on 27 September 1763, BL Add. 32951 ff. 201–2.

This drew a retort from Hardwicke that focused both on Pitt's intransigence and on the ambiguous nature of the Whig legacy, an issue that was to recur in the debate over the response to the French Revolution. Hardwicke claimed that Pitt had initially treated the Wilkes affair

slightly, and as what would little affect public affairs, makes it now his principal point; and this is all he has meant whan he has talked of . . . constitution points – Magna Carta, – and Revolution-doctrines; as if the differing in opinion upon a question of privilege of the House of Commons, never yet determined by that House itself . . . was of the essence of Magna Carta, and of the liberty established at the Revolution . . . Is it the rule that, because people differ from one another in politics, therefore all civil intercourse must be cut off? Upon my word, great and able as he is, if he goes on in this way, he will be thought to give too much countenance to what the king was once reported to have flung out – *What do They mean? Do they mean to put a Tyrant over me and themselves too?*

Newcastle criticised Pitt, 'he . . . will on no account enter into an active part, in support of a proper opposition. His resentment to, and suspicions of the Yorkes is beyond anyone's imagination . . . men of honour and conscience cannot form their opinion upon points of law, just as Mr Pitt would have them.'[20]

When the Wilkes issue was raised in the Commons on 15 November 1763, Pitt spoke in what appeared to be a self-consciously classical manner. For a social order brought up on classical authors there was something very Roman about Pitt. Just as his hostility towards France during the Seven Years War echoed the theme of Rome versus Carthage, so Harris recorded of the Wilkes debate that Pitt,

[20] Pitt to Newcastle, 14 October, Hardwicke to Newcastle, 15 October, Newcastle to Rockingham, 16, 26 October 1763, BL Add. 32951 ff. 413, 429–30; WW R146–7, 9.

seemed to plan his eloquence upon the model of Caesar's in the Catilinarian conspiracy, as recorded by Sallust; openly to blame the criminal, tacitly to favour him; to seem in all his words to have no regard to anything but the preservation of forms, of rights, of shunning acts of violence, not constitutional etc. but secretly to turn all this . . . talk to the benefit of the accused – his words, his phrases, his tone of voice, his humour, his sublimity and tone were in their turn most excellent and striking, nothing wanting but a plan or order, of which there not being the least trace, it is impossible to record anything but glowing scraps or splendid morsels.

Pitt spoke fifteen times, though Harris thought his effort wasted on Wilkes. Harris' comments did, however, provide some guide as to why Pitt, whom he described as 'impatient to bear either a superior or an equal' and unwilling to 'spare nor friend nor foe', was so difficult to work with. Those were apt descriptions of a masterful political outsider without a connection. The following day, in the debate on the Address, Pitt's criticism of the ministry was muted, and he offered scant comfort to its opponents, while stressing his distance from politics, 'that no man had so much done with the political world, as he had, saving his duty in Parliament'. His poor health was certainly debilitating, although it did not prevent him from speaking on behalf of parliamentary privilege on 24 November 1763 for 'two hours, leaning on two crutches with both his legs and both his arms in flannel'.[21] However, the following month he retired to 'quiet and country air', and was still away from Parliament in January 1764.[22] Pitt returned to attack the government over the legality of general warrants the following month, only to have those he had issued as Secretary brought up. Asserting

[21] HP Harris, 15, 16, 24 November 1763.
[22] Chatham Corresp. II, 268–9.

that he had never granted one in the case of a libel, Pitt offered on 14 February a histrionic account that revealed his historical perspective and his pride in his role during the war, 'said he thought liberty at her last stand . . . compared the times of Pym and Hampden with these . . . that he was regarding his fleets and armies whom he considered as his children and that had raised this kingdom to a power unknown again'. Three days later he claimed he had been 'called into Administration to *invigorate* the war'.[23]

This self-justification was Pitt's last appearance that session. Critical of the ministry, especially George Grenville who should have been a central figure in any connection that Pitt might have created, he was also disparaging of the former governmental colleagues whom he would need to co-operate with should he wish to force his way into office. Regretting the strength of the ministry, Charles Townshend observed in April 1764, 'Mr Pitt seems withdrawn into himself, and retired to his family and amusements.'[24] Poor health kept Pitt a recluse at Hayes, but his isolation was due to inclination as much as gout. He seems to have been suffering from acute depression and to have more or less withdrawn from politics, but he certainly wasn't mad, nor was he alone in having his conduct affected by poor health. George III may have had physical symptoms of porphyria in 1762 and again in 1765. His acute irritability helped to sour his relations with Grenville and bring on the changes of ministry which eventually brought Pitt back to office.

Pitt's public reputation continued to suffer as a result of his acceptance of the pension. In 1769 Pitt's selling of the people was compared, probably by Wilkes, to Pulteney's a generation earlier, and Pitt was depicted as a hypocritical opportunist,

---

[23] HP Harris, 14, 17 February 1764.
[24] Townshend to Newcastle, 30 April 1764, Beinecke, Osborn Papers, Townshend Box 1.

He declared for and against continental connections, for and against foreign wars, for and against Hanoverian subsidies, etc., etc., still preserving an unblushing, *unembarrassed* countenance, and was the most perfect contradiction of a man to himself which the world ever saw.

The attack ended with the single throwaway line, 'He is said to be still living, at Hayes in Kent.'

Given his concern with his reputation, it is not surprising that Pitt replied in late 1764 to an approach from Newcastle that he join in opposition planning, by offering a declaration of independence from connections that looked back to the anti-party Patriot rhetoric of his early days in politics,

I purpose to continue acting through life upon the best convictions I am able to form, and under the obligation of principles, not by the force of any particular bargains . . . whatsoever I think it my duty to oppose, or to promote, I shall do it independent of the sentiments of others . . . I have no disposition to quit the free condition of a man standing single, and daring to appeal to his country at large upon the soundness of his principles and the rectitude of his conduct.

Pitt linked this declaration to his anger over the failure of other politicians to defend the conduct of the Seven Years War, 'having seen . . . the system of that great war in which my share of ministry was so largely arraigned given up in silence in a full House, I have little thoughts of beginning the world again upon any new center of union'.[25]

As so often in Pitt's career, self-justification was linked to recrimination, a declaration of independence to a specific political position. The ministry's opponents felt that they had to humour him. Rockingham commented on Pitt's letter by arguing that 'he knows his own popularity and that if

[25] *Letters between the Duke of Grafton . . . Chatham . . . and John Wilkes* (1769) I, 166–8; Pitt to Newcastle, no date, WW R1–440.

opposition prevails, it would be in a degree obliged to call upon him for his sanction, and to take part in any future arrangement'. As Rockingham felt that Pitt was correct, he argued that the opposition had to try to win his approval 'ever availing ourselves of the idea of his connection with us'.[26] Thus, Pitt was of value because of what he symbolised, rather than thanks to any particular abilities or connections that he might have. Pitt's political importance arose from his capacity to make an ordinary factional combination appear popular and significant, and this was despite the unpopularity of some of his individual views and his own poor health. Fortunately for Pitt's public reputation, the Seven Years War appeared increasingly heroic in retrospect, while his bellicose attitudes appeared vindicated by a number of colonial confrontations with the Bourbons in 1764–5. Pitt was increasingly favourably contrasted with his successors. A correspondent in the St James's Chronicle of 16 October 1764, who argued that the country should have fought on in 1763 and retained its gains, and claimed that the French could not be trusted, defended Pitt's conduct in office and called for the maintenance of 'the dignity of the British flag'. The association between Pitt and the defence of national interests was asserted elsewhere.[27] It led contemporaries to give his supposed views and intentions an extraordinary weight.

Pitt was seen in 1765 as the likely head of the new ministry with which George III hoped to replace that of Grenville. In May Pitt was approached by Cumberland. On the 16th the Duke's friend the Earl of Albemarle visited Pitt at Hayes to be told that support for a new government would depend on the reappointment of office-holders, especially officers, dismissed on account of their parliamentary opinion, on the negotiation of a counter-alliance to the Bourbons, on the

---

[26] Rockingham to Newcastle, no date, after 14 November 1764, WW R1–441.
[27] Anon., The Contrast (1765) p. 12.

repeal of the cider tax and the abandonment of general warrants. Three days later Cumberland himself visited Hayes with his escort of guards, but Pitt refused to take part in the projected ministry because he suspected correctly that George III had no intention of giving him his confidence. George Sackville reported,

the King had determined upon a total change of his Ministry, and that the whole power of negotiation was placed in the hands of the Duke of Cumberland who condescended to go to Hayes and offer Mr Pitt every condition which a subject could expect, but all to no purpose for he did not choose to accept of the government of this country, some say on account of his health, others that he dreaded the secret influence of Lord Bute.

The King, who did not accept Pitt's policy agenda, felt obliged to turn back to the bullying Grenville, but George III's loathing of him led to a direct approach to Pitt in June. In audiences on the 19th and 22nd the King agreed to the return of many to office, with Temple to get the Treasury while Newcastle would be Privy Seal, and he appears to have accepted Pitt's views on policy, although they differed considerably about foreign policy, George III not sharing Pitt's desire for a Prussian alliance.

However, Temple, never an easy man and increasingly resentful of being expected to follow Pitt's lead, refused to accept office. Without him, Pitt was unwilling to form a ministry in which he might be overborne by Newcastle and dependent on Cumberland. Harris recorded, 'Pitt's reasons against accepting, were said to be that he was too far advanced in life to form new connections, and therefore could not act, when Lord Temple had declined.' The role of poor health is unclear, although it may have sapped Pitt's wish for office. On 22 June he wrote of his 'despair' that his 'wretched health' would never improve. Pitt was characteristically also both despondent and melodramatic, 'I am disposed to believe that if the country were not, from past fatal errors, too far gone, that all might be well.'[28]

The Grenville ministry was replaced in July 1765 by a new government that was not much to George III's wishes. While the new ministry, with Rockingham at the Treasury and Newcastle as Privy Seal, was accustoming itself to office, Pitt remained aloof and concerned about his health, and able to polish further his self-image of man above faction, virtuous exile from an evil world, an image that looked back to the rejection of city vice and Walpolean corruption that had played such a major role in opposition, especially Tory, writing earlier in the century. Planning to go to Bath at the beginning of November 1765, he wrote of how he had been frustrated in his 'views for the public good . . . I move in the sphere only of measures. Quarrels at court, or family reconciliations, shall never vary my fixed judgment of things. Those who, with me, have stood by the cause of liberty and the national honour, upon true Revolution-principles, will never find me against them',[29] fine sentiments but not much of a detailed guide for government. The new ministry sought his support, Newcastle writing of following 'Mr Pitt's plan' in foreign policy, and urging Rockingham that 'the plan of administration should, in general, be made as palatable to Mr Pitt; and as agreeable, as possible, to his notions, and ideas'. Newcastle therefore pressed for the maintenance of links through the Duke of Grafton, the Secretary of State for the Northern Department who admired Pitt, in order to prevent any opposition from Pitt. He further suggested that as a mark of favour to Pitt, his ally Charles Pratt, Lord Chief Justice of the Common Pleas, be raised to the peerage and appointed to the Cabinet. It was characteristic of Newcastle to think of such

---

[28] Beinecke Library, Osborn Files 34.13; HP Harris, 2 July 1765; Pitt to Temple, 22 June 1765, *Grenville Papers* III, 61. [29] *Chatham Corresp.* II, 329.

matters. Six days later the Duke returned to the theme of a peerage for Pratt, 'I see the world is running mad again about Mr Pitt. Pray, My Dear Lord, for your own sake, as well as for the sake of the whole, don't despise it; and show the King the necessity of it.'[30]

Pratt was created Lord Camden on 17 July 1765. As during the Newcastle–Pitt ministry, the Duke was trying to placate Pitt by persuading his colleagues and the King to make concessions to him. Pitt, however, was unwilling to give assistance to the Rockingham ministry and instead spent his time at Bath. He was not well, and on 1 August he wrote to his sister Ann from his new seat at Burton Pynsent of

my health, which I found mend on the journey and by change of air. I still continue lame but have left off one crutch, which is no small advance, though with only one wing, my flights, you will imagine, are as yet very short. The county of Somersetshire is beautiful and tempts much to extend them.[31]

Pitt's letters home to his wife from Bath suggest that his morale was relatively good, that he was concerned about his health and missing his family. They offer a picture of a family-minded private man, 'I have no pain worth mentioning, but that of being separated from my kind love, and not seeing five little faces, which form round her a group, which sums all delight – all which my heart can taste.'[32] His eldest child, Hester, had been born in 1755, a year after his marriage. John, Harriot, William and James Charles followed in 1756, 1758, 1759 and 1761. Pitt took a close interest in his family and was clearly delighted by his children. As so often in his life, the impression created is of a private and intense man.

---

[30] Newcastle to Rockingham, 6, 12 July 1765, WW R1–456, 465.
[31] BL Add. 69289 no. 65.   [32] *Chatham Corresp.* II, 332.

Politically Pitt was hardening his heart against the new ministry which he saw as dominated by the baneful influence of Newcastle. His inability ever to reach a reconciliation with Newcastle, meant that despite the King's efforts, the wartime coalition was never reconstructed. As at the start of his career Pitt had attacked what he saw as the corrupt purposes and intentions of Walpole and Old Corps Whiggery, so at what seemed likely to be his close he was again attacking the same evils, clearly both resigned to and comfortable in the role of Cassandra. He wrote to the Earl of Shelburne in December 1765, 'The evils are, I fear, incurable. Faction shakes and corruption saps the country to its foundations.' Pitt wanted an alteration in the methods of government: a change in the ministry would not suffice. This was a measure of his alienation from Hanoverian politics, and this unwillingness to be included in the political calculations of the period posed a serious problem for his contemporaries. Pitt was willing to abandon his role of political outsider only if he was given a free hand to new-mould government. This can be seen as egoism but it was also a response to Pitt's increasingly marked hostility towards the practice of politics, the world of compromise and connections that he saw himself as little suited for. For Pitt this world was personified by Newcastle, but removing him would serve more than a psychological purpose. It would also demonstrate that royal confidence had been given to Pitt and thus both bring ministerial stability and apparently banish the need to deal with connections. Pitt made his wishes clear to Shelburne,

until the King is pleased to signify his pleasure to me, that I should again submit my thoughts upon the formation of such a system, both as to the measures and as to the instruments which are to constitute that system, and that in so ample and full an extent as shall leave nothing to the eyes of men equivocal in the outside if it, nor any dark creeping factions, scattering doubts and sowing discords within . . . I can never have confidence in a system, where the Duke of Newcastle has influence.[33]

Pitt left Bath not in order to be present at the beginning of the sessions or to take part in political manoeuvres, but because he was determined to give his opinion in the growing crisis over America. The strains of paying for the Seven Years War, never appreciated sufficiently by Pitt, had forced the ministers of the early 1760s to think of retrenchment and new taxation. Both had led to political difficulties, the first in the debate surrounding the ending of the conflict, the second initially with the cider tax of 1763[34] and then with the Stamp Act of 1765. The crisis over the Grenville ministry's Stamp Act, which imposed a series of duties in the North American colonies, was greater than that over the cider tax, which was repealed in 1766, because it raised the question of parliamentary authority in America. Concerned about the violent response in America and influenced by pressure from British merchants, worried about an American commercial blockade, the Rockingham ministry favoured reform, although George III was unenthusiastic.[35] Speaking on 14 January 1766, Pitt made a determined plea for repeal, Harris recording,

Pitt, whom the House had not seen for more than a year, rose and with a torrent of eloquence flowed like a spring-tide, and almost as

[33] Chatham Corresp. II, 359–60.
[34] P. Woodland, 'Extra-Parliamentary Political Organization in the Making: Benjamin Heath and the Opposition to the 1763 Cider Excise', Parliamentary History, 4 (1985), and 'Political Atomization and Regional Interests in the 1761 Parliament: The Impact of the Cider Debates, 1763–66', Parliamentary History, 8 (1989).
[35] P. Langford, The First Rockingham Administration, 1765–1766 (Oxford, 1973) pp. 109–98; P. D. G. Thomas, British Politics and the Stamp Act Crisis. The First Phase of the American Revolution, 1763–1767 (Oxford, 1975) pp. 154–252; K. Perry, British Politics and the American Revolution (1990) pp. 40–2.

long – his first part was on the dignity and authority of Parliament, which could not be held too sacred, nor too strongly maintained – so far, so good – but then came . . . taxes could be legally imposed *only on those, whom the imposers represented* – the Commons of Great Britain were *no* representatives of the people of America – ergo could impose *no* tax on them – many kind and affectionate things were said of America, great harangues upon the 2 or 3 millions that she annually paid us, and how pitiful it was to lose that sum for a paultry 50 or 60,000 pounds per annum.

He also declared that he feared the potential might of a united House of Bourbon. John Pringle MP saw the quest for popularity as the explanation of Pitt's conduct, a reflection of what was widely believed to be the central feature of Pitt's career. Pringle wrote of the pains Pitt 'took to embroil affairs by becoming the advocate for the colonies and to make himself as popular there as he was here . . . he had kept his sentiments on this great affair entirely to himself that should the Act be repealed he might have all the popularity of it to himself'. In fact Pitt appears to have been motivated by his 'belief in the principle of representative government.'[36] This display of Pitt's vitality led Rockingham to seek and receive George III's permission for another approach to Pitt, but at their meeting on 18 January 1766 Pitt demanded too much. He insisted on forming a new ministry in which Temple would be included and Newcastle and Grenville excluded. These terms were rejected, but Pitt's revived role in politics continued to be important.[37]

Though he was still bothered by gout, Pitt was fired by enthusiasm and spoke in Parliament on a number of occasions in the debates linked to the repeal of the Stamp Act.

[36] HP Harris, 14 January 1766; R. C. Simmons and P. D. G. Thomas (eds.), *Proceedings and Debates of the British Parliaments respecting North America 1754–1783* (New York, 1982–) II, 90; HMC Polwarth V p. 362; Thomas, *Stamp Act* pp. 172, 175.

[37] WW RI–553–7, 559; W. R. Anson (ed.), *Autobiography and Political Correspondence of Augustus Henry, Third Duke of Grafton* (1896) pp. 63–8; Thomas, *Stamp Act* pp. 175–6.

He strongly asserted the right of the Americans not to have internal taxes laid on them by Parliament, but also claimed that it was reasonable to control American trade and levy external taxation, and that Britain could not subsist without America. Pringle noted, 'Mr Pitt would not give up his idea of our having only the right to lay external and not internal taxes, though he was argued out of every position he advanced. He was very mild and though he spoke long was very moderate.' Pitt was therefore caught up in an extremely illogical situation of his own making, condemning acts of internal taxation as unconstitutional, but not acts of external taxation. This view did not commend itself to the Commons. When the Stamp Act was repealed that spring, a Declaratory Act was also passed, stating that Parliament 'had, hath and of right ought to have full power and authority to make laws and statutes of sufficient form and validity to bind the colonies and people of America in all cases whatsoever'.[38]

Pitt's energetic interventions were not restricted to American topics. He seconded the bill for the repeal of the cider tax, providing a classic example of his ability to amplify traditional opposition themes,

'twas for the cause of liberty – that mens houses should not be violated . . . revenue matters not his province or passion . . . the loss might be 20,000 pounds a year – what that to a blemish upon liberty – every man's house his castle . . . the poor man's walls of mud and covering of thatch were his castle, where though the rains might enter, the king could not.[39]

If the theme of excise as a threat to liberty looked back to the opposition to Walpole, Pitt also brought up another echo of

[38] HMC *Polwarth V* p. 363; HP Harris, 21 February, 4 March 1766; I. R. Christie, 'William Pitt and American Taxation. A Problem of Parliamentary Reporting', *Studies in Burke and his Times*, 17 (1976), pp. 167–79; Christie, 'The Changing Nature of Parliamentary Politics, 1742–1789', in J. Black (ed.), *British Politics and Society from Walpole to Pitt 1742–1789* (1990) p. 114; Thomas, *Stamp Act* pp. 189–90, 198–9, 202–4, 207, 232.   [39] HP Harris, 7 March 1766.

the past with a sharp defence of the militia that revealed his self-righteousness and his paranoia, Harris recording, 'he then told us, what pains he had taken to establish it in the beginning – that the late King had become a convert to . . . its utility, but that some of the ministers were then its latent enemies, and that he feared some of the same connection were still in power', a pointed criticism of Newcastle.[40] These parliamentary attacks on the ministry indicated its vulnerability in the Commons and Pitt's determination to destroy it. William Rouet, who had described Pitt in January as 'King William the Fourth, for he holds in the greatest contempt a law enacted by all the powers of the legislature' suggested in March that,

The great Quinbus has kicked up some, soothed others, but given pretty severe wipes [sic] to all, in order to demonstrate, both at home and abroad, that *he* and *he alone*, is fit to be grand Minister of this country, for he has forced Ministers to espouse or even defend, as their own measures, what they secretly disapproved.

In a fashion reminiscent of his change of mind over Walpole, once the minister had fallen and could serve as a basis for comparison with the present ministry, Pitt praised Bute, as 'a friend to his King and his country', on 4 March because he had rejected an approach from Grenville and Bedford. This led Pringle to suggest that a new ministry, including Bute's supporters, would be formed after the end of the session and that Pitt might head it. Pringle added 'He wants it but is very coy and requires much wooing, and a vixen he'll be to whatever party weds him.'[41] On 21 April 1766 General Conway, the Secretary of State for the Southern Department, wrote to Rockingham,

---

[40] HP Harris, 14 April 1766. He also defended the militia on 22 April.
[41] Rouet to William Mure, 10 January, 11 March 1766, *Caldwell Papers* II ii 61, 81.

I feel and think much as you do in many parts of what relates to Mr
P.'s behaviour etc. but yet I think I differ still as to the point of some
farther treaty with him: unless his behaviour should make it
impracticable. I think there are many reasons respecting ourselves
which may make it advisable.[42]

Rockingham, however, stated his refusal to serve with Pitt on
the latter's terms, and on 21 April he told the Duke of Grafton
that he would never again advise George III to send for Pitt, a
move that led Grafton to desert the ministry. On 24 April
1766 Pitt outlined his views on British politics and her
colonies in a debate over sugar duties,

fears his health will call him to Bath . . . values the colonys, as they
were the great mart of consumption for our commoditys – but that
this [Britain] was the conducting head, the animating heart, the
inspiring soul, which gave life to all the rest . . . the government was
a free limited monarchy – wishes for such a ministry as the king
himself should choose, the people approve, and who should be
eminent above others for their ability and integrity – that the
people would grow weary of our divisions – that the public was
tottering to its foundations – that he probably should never return
to the House – yet disclaimed all connections . . . Though the
Chancellor of the Exchequer and other friends of government were
against the petition's going to the committee, yet, Pitt having
approved it, it went without division.[43]

Pitt's apparent dominance of the Commons' debates
contrasted with Rockingham's weakness as head of a divided
ministry and both led George III to make a new approach to
Pitt. He, for his health, had gone to Bath, whence he wrote to
his wife that 'all the waters of these copious springs, will not
wash away for a moment the memory of parting, nor the
wish of meeting'. Pitt was also anxious about the health of his

[42] Conway to Rockingham, 21 April 1766, WW R1–660.
[43] HP Harris, 24 April 1766.

son William and keen to receive letters from all his children. Characteristically he wrote 'it will do them good, and give papa pleasure'. The *Gloucester Journal* of 16 June reported, 'A gentleman just arrived from Bath informs us that such crowds of people fill the Pump Room when Mr Pitt goes there, that he is obliged to vary his hour of drinking the waters every day, to avoid this inconvenience of popularity.' By then Pitt was 'buried deep in Somersetshire', enjoying the air of his new seat of Burton Pynsent and recovering from a 'troublesome cough' arising from 'an incautious use of the [Bath] waters'. As in the early 1750s, he found exercise and a rural lifestyle therapeutic, observing on 1 June, 'the air of this hill and my horse have quite set me up again'.[44]

He was soon to be faced with different problems. The Rockingham ministry had been weakened by the session and by Grafton's resignation. On 7 July 1766 George III wrote seeking his views on, 'how an able and dignified ministry may be formed' and noting how completely his 'ideas concerning the basis on which a new administration should be erected, are consonant to the opinion' Pitt gave on the subject in Parliament on 24 April 1766.[45] The Earl of Thomond reported,

the day before yesterday the K. sent to Mr P. with Carte Blanche to form a Ministry: having given to the present ministers the reason for so doing, that they had not formed any plan, for acquisition of strength to carry on his Government.[46]

THE CHATHAM MINISTRY

The King, hoping 'to extricate this country out of faction', saw Pitt on 12 July. They agreed to form an administration on

44 *Chatham Corresp.* II, 416–17, 423–4.
45 *Chatham Corresp.* II, 436; Thomas, *Stamp Act* p. 281.
46 HL STG Box 23 (44); *St James's Chronicle* 19 July 1766.

as broad a basis as possible, but both were determined to exclude those they felt unable to co-operate with. George III wanted Grenville kept from office and indeed his decision to turn to Pitt had owed much to his being persuaded that the latter had decisively broken with Grenville. Pitt had Newcastle and Rockingham dismissed as he would have no one in the Cabinet who had previously served as head of administration and because he distrusted Newcastle and his chosen heir, not least as exponents of the methods and purposes of connection, or, as it could be termed, faction or party. Sir George Savile, an ally of Rockingham's, wrote to the Marquess on 13 July 1766 comparing Pitt to a then painfully formidable and necessarily brutal figure,

If anybody is a long while before they can consent to send for the toothdrawer, sending for him then can have but one sense; and he may probably give the jaw a great shake, for he has no light hand. Sending for him therefore is I suppose to clean and file and pull out and put in and wire and set even etc.[47]

However, Pitt's return to power, like earlier discussions to the same end, seemed to some to be based on the worst kind of backstairs deals, so that by 1766 the new generation of 'Patriots' were portraying him as no more than a puppet of Bute, still supposedly influential with George III.

The new ministry was not without talent, but there was no unity of purpose to hold it together while several of its members were inexperienced. It is known as the Chatham ministry but this identification of minister and government was weakened by Pitt's decision not to take one of the leading offices of business and by his abandonment of the task of leading the Commons when he was created Earl of Chatham on 29 July 1766. Grafton became First Lord of the Treasury, while Conway and Shelburne were the Secretaries of State.

---

[47] *Chatham Corresp.* II, 440–69; WW R1–647.

Pitt accepted the post of Privy Seal, one that had been lately an office of prestige rather than power, though Bedford had held it in 1761–3 and Newcastle was his immediate predecessor. It was suggested that 'Pitt, having by this arrangement a cabinet place void of business, interferes in measures just so far as he pleases, while both the responsibility of office and the drudgery of it fall totally upon others',[48] but that ensured that one less minister of experience was available for the offices of business.

Pitt's acceptance of a peerage was widely criticised. *A Letter to Will Chat-em of Turn-about-Hall* presented it inaccurately as a consequence of Bute's influence, although in fact the formation of the Chatham ministry was accompanied by the final break between King and favourite. George III had promised Grenville in May 1765 that he would not consult Bute again. He sent Bute details of the negotiations with Pitt in a letter of January 1766; and in July 1766 told him of the formation of the Chatham ministry, explaining that he had not consulted him because of the promise to Grenville. It was the King's last letter to Bute. Nevertheless, the pamphlet claimed that,

every body who had for a few years past heard of the private negotiations carried on between Will Chat-em and the northern lord, who has now got his wanton will of him . . . but must have been prepared for some scandalous defection, some act of vile apostacy on the part of turn-about Will . . . after your strenuous exertion against the American stamp-act, you were whirled up anew to the pinnacle of popularity, and did you soar the higher, but to plunge the lower into the sink of titled infamy! . . . Lord Chat-em is now the object of universal detestation.

Among the numerous other printed attacks was a facetious inscription designed for the statues of Pitt being sent to America to commemorate his opposition to the Stamp Act,

---

[48] HP Harris, 'Account of the Political Storm in July 1766'.

In Memory of W. P. Who with an inflexible constancy and inimitable uniformity of life persisted, in spite of many bodily infirmities, in the practice of every human artifice, to raise himself and family, from an obscure obscurity, or larger possessions, and a most respectable title and place in the state . . . He was the only person of his time, who with specious pretences and harangues, could persuade the people their service only was the intended fruit of his labours, when they had before their eyes numberless instances of his actions, which indicated the contrary: in fine, after a life of near sixty years, spent in pretended patriotic actions, the cloven foot appeared from under the robe of an Earl of G. B. and with the weight of a pension, place, and coronet, he sunk into a general discharge and contempt, on the 30th of July 1766.[49]

The impact of Pitt's translation to the Lords on the effectiveness of the Chatham government was more important than the effect on his popularity. Lord North, who accepted a post in the new ministry, described Pitt's move as foolish, writing, 'I should have thought administration more steady with him in the House of Commons.'[50] 'Foresight', writing in the *Court Miscellany* of August 1766, suggested that had Pitt 'remained a commoner, he might harangue people out of their senses, or terrify them out of their own opinions'. Pitt had been motivated by his health, which had been poor after his return to London in July 1766 as the result of a fever. Debates in the Commons were seen as dangerous by others. In 1770 the Irish peer Viscount Downe (1728–80), who suffered from violent gout in the stomach and bowels and was told by his doctor that late nights would be fatal, decided to resign, 'as now all the material business of the House of Commons occasions such very long debates, that it is seldom finished before the morning, I am quite incapable of the

[49] Sedgwick (ed.), *Letters from George III* pp. 241–54; *Letter to Will Chatem* pp. 41–3; *A Genuine Collection of the Several Pieces of Political Intelligence . . .* (1766) pp. 59–60.
[50] North to his father, the Earl of Guildford, 31 July 1766, Bod. MS North adds. c 4/1 f. 59.

fatique, which the duty of a member of Parliament obliges him to undergo'.[51] For Pitt the experience of the past few years suggested that his health would not permit him the regular attendance in Parliament that was necessary if he was to be a successful Leader of the Commons, but it had also revealed that he could be a powerful and effective speaker in that crucial chamber on major occasions. That opportunity was abandoned by the move to the Lords, as was the possibility of supervising the management of the House. The importance of this should not be exaggerated – the ministry was not to collapse through defeat in the Commons – but Pitt's presence there might have helped to make the government more coherent. Before the time of Lord Liverpool there was not to be a single Lords-led Hanoverian ministry that endured any time. On the other hand, the only ministry led by someone sitting in the Commons not to have a substantial period in office was that of George Grenville. Circumstances were different in the various cases, but it seems clear that dividing the key functions of the Treasury and the leadership of the Commons made for weak and unstable government. In Chatham's case, the focus of power was even more confused, since he did not hold either position. The dearth of Commons leadership is an important aspect of 1760s instability, that was related closely to the ending of Old Corps Whig cohesion. It is difficult to imagine Walpole, or even Pelham, losing power as their successors in the 1760s were to do.

The chances of Chatham creating a more stable ministry to any long-term extent were lessened by his age and poor health, and in the spring of 1767 he succumbed to what may have been a serious attack of manic depression. However,

---

[51] Downe to Rockingham, 16 October 1770, WW R1–1317.

even before that the ministry was in serious difficulties and in some respect his collapsing health was a release from an increasingly sterile political situation. In October 1757 Charles Townshend had claimed that Pitt was unsuited to government, his 'talents which were so irresistable in opposition . . . so ineffectual in Administration'. Pitt was certainly unsuited to management, but in 1757–61 he had Newcastle to do that for him. In 1766–7, however, the Duke was no longer at his side, there was nobody to take his place and issues and circumstances were more divisive than had been the case during the earlier ministry.

Problems had been anticipated by some commentators when the ministry was formed in 1766. Though the Earl of Thomond referred to 'the idol which the King and People have set up', Viscount Hampden was convinced that Pitt's acceptance of a peerage would cause political problems, 'If the new peer has not gained as much ground in the Closet, as he has lost in the public; he must soon have but a very narrow and tottering basis left to stand upon: – I wish he may not be driven to some new act of Quixotism, in order to repurchase popularity.' The Sardinian envoy suggested that there would be a major distinction between Pitt's entry into the direction of government in war and peacetime, and this was to be the case. Amidst the complexities of peacetime politics, the sense of national unity that Pitt had been able to benefit from and to foster during the Seven Years War was absent, and these problems helped to place the already poorly united ministry under strain. Irrespective of the chamber he sat in, Chatham was not skilled in political management, and his strong will had become increasingly imperious as a consequence of his successful role in the Seven Years War, while his subsequent political isolation had made him more aloof. Pringle wrote in December 1766, nothing can prevent the system being effectual but the risk there is of the ministers disagreeing amongst themselves, which may very possibly happen as it is said Lord Chatham is very absolute and [has] little communication with the best of them. I will have this done, is the language used; no reply, not one iota shall be altered. These are the answers said to be made to some of the ministers on their remonstrating against some measures proposed, and, mortifying to tell, they were obliged to support them in the House though some of them did it very awkwardly.[52]

Chatham devoted most of his attention to attempting to reverse the breach with Prussia that he blamed on Bute. In holding an evil adviser responsible Chatham reflected a strong tradition of political thinking that had for example been seen in attacks on Walpole, a tradition that attributed much to sinister intentions and that combined naturally with Chatham's paranoia. This, however, led both to a failure to probe causes sufficiently and to a misguided belief that a change in leadership would right the situation. Although it was attractive to blame the breach with Frederick II in 1762 on Bute, in fact it was substantially due to an absence of shared interests that had been disguised by the consequences of the fortuitous diplomatic changes of 1756. Frederick was essentially interested in a Russian alliance. Once he had achieved that in 1764, he was not interested in diluting his influence by including Britain, a move that would also raise the danger of involvement in British confrontations with the Bourbons.[53]

Chatham on the other hand had hoped that Britain would

[52] Namier and Brooke, *Charles Townshend* (1964) p. 56; Thomond to George Grenville, 10 July, Hampden to Grenville, 17 August 1766, HL STG Box 23 (44), (35); Perriere to Charles Emmanuel, 1 August 1766, AST LM Ing. 72; HMC Polwarth V p. 365.
[53] P. F. Doran, *Andrew Mitchell and Anglo-Prussian Relations during the Seven Years War* (New York, 1986) p. 383.

benefit from the Prusso-Russian realignment of 1762 that had followed the death of the Tsarina Elizabeth. The failure to do so had led him to feel that Bute's abandonment of the Prussian alliance was as much evidence of his failure to defend national interests as the peace terms with the Bourbons. Out of office Chatham had pressed for the formation of a 'triple alliance' with Prussia and Russia and once he had returned to power that became his first priority, and a sphere in which he interfered in the departmental responsibility of another minister. Chatham's enthusiasm for the scheme took no note of the actual state of relations with Prussia and Russia: there was a naive sense that in office he could 'invigorate' the government and thus obtain success as if only will-power was required. The veteran envoy in Berlin, Sir Andrew Mitchell, was much better informed of the actual state of relations and his accurate prediction that Frederick would reject the approach was proved correct. Frederick told Mitchell that British governmental instability made negotiations with her pointless.

Rebuffed in September 1766, Mitchell found Chatham unwilling to accept Frederick's refusal, and he was ordered in November to make another approach, which had a predictable fate on 1 December. Grafton observed, 'Mr Pitt's plan was Utopian . . . he lived too much out of the world to have a right knowledge of mankind.'[54] As Chatham had intended to approach Russian via her Prussian ally, the failure of this approach spelled the end of his system. The chances of a Russian alliance were slight anyway because George III was opposed to granting Russian demands for a peacetime subsidy and a commitment to assist Catherine the Great in any war with Turkey. Chatham's policy was as unrealistic as

---

[54] Michell, Prussian envoy in London, to Frederick II, 8 November 1763, Williams, *Chatham* II, 225; *Chatham Corresp.* III, 31; *Grafton* p. 91.

Newcastle's complaint the following July of 'the total neglect of foreign affairs, even by My Lord Chatham, who raised himself, and his reputation, by a contrary conduct'.[55]

These failures depressed Chatham, for it was on the international stage that he really wished to feature, a tendency strengthened possibly by his departure from the Commons, the parliamentary arena he felt most at home in. Other aspects of government policy had appeared more intractable and they were less interesting to Chatham. Charles Townshend, the Chancellor of the Exchequer, played a large role in government policy towards America and India. Chatham's proposals for redefinition of the relationship between the government and the East India Company on the basis of a parliamentary inquiry into the Company and a declaration that it had no right to revenues from conquered territories, were rejected in favour of Townshend's policy of an amicable agreement involving a grant. By allocating revenues to these territories to public purposes, fleecing the Company in Pringle's eyes, Chatham hoped to ensure a reliable financial basis for the defence of India, thus avoiding the difficulties that the British government faced in protecting America. Townshend's success was ensured by Chatham's breakdown in early 1767. The Company was a monopolistic trading concern whose financial viability was seen as crucial to British government finances and the reduction of the national debt. The Revenue Act that Townshend drew up imposed American customs duties on a variety of goods including tea, which was brought from India by the East India Company. It led to a serious deterioration in relations between the British government and its American

---

[55] M. Roberts, *Splendid Isolation* (Reading, 1970); J. Black, 'Anglo-Russian Relations after the Seven Years War', *Scottish Slavonic Review*, 9 (1987), pp. 27–37; H. M. Scott, *British Foreign Policy in the Age of the American Revolution* (Oxford, 1990) pp. 97–101; Newcastle to Rockingham, 8 July 1767, WW R1–812.

critics. The Americans responded with a trade boycott and action against customs officials, leading the British ministry to send troops to Boston in 1768.[56]

Other issues caused controversy during the early months of the Chatham ministry, including the management of Irish politics and an embargo on the export of grain, arising from the grain shortage of the summer of 1766, that was criticised as unconstitutional. However, these were overshadowed by two increasingly related questions, Chatham's health and political rivalries. He failed on both counts. The leading study of the ministry argues that 'all other questions – the American problem, relations with the East India Company, or foreign affairs – were subordinate to party conflict'.[57] Chatham's poor physical and mental health eventually incapacitated him, and good health was essential for a leading politician. It had been one of the keys to Walpole's ministerial longevity.

Suffering from gout, Chatham spent October 1766 in Bath, although he took an active interest in government policy while he was away. Returning to London in November for the opening of the parliamentary session, Chatham went back to Bath in January 1767, remaining there until March. This was not conducive to the fostering of a stable ministry and was especially serious because of the absence of any 'party' basis around which it could cohere. Chatham's expectation that all good men would come forward to further national interests was shown to be naive, while he was, as ever in the post-war period, deficient in 'man-management' skills, a weakness that may have owed something to his inexperience, as a politician without connection. The possible tendencies of Chatham's anti-party ideology were

[56] L. Sutherland, The East India Company in Eighteenth-Century Politics (Oxford, 1952) pp. 147–76; L. B. Namier and J. Brooke, Charles Townshend (1964) pp. 158–72; Thomas, The Townshend Duties Crisis. The Second Phase of the American Revolution 1767–1773 (Oxford, 1987) pp. 18–36; HMC Polwarth V pp. 365–7.
[57] Brooke, The Chatham Administration 1766–1768 (1956) xiv.

displayed in the Lords' discussion of the embargo on grain exports, which had been criticised because unaccompanied by an act of indemnity.

He addressed this point in his maiden speech to the Lords on 11 November 1766, and again on 10 December 1766, the only two occasions that he appeared as a minister in the Lords. Chatham quoted Locke in arguing that if there was a clash between the executive power and the people over a right claimed as prerogative, the good of the people must settle the matter, but he implied that the Crown must be the sole judge of necessity, a view that clashed with much of what he had stood for. Pressed on the point, Chatham agreed to a bill of indemnity to cover those who had advised and executed the illegal order but his attitude was controversial. The Earl of Dartmouth wrote of the debate on 11 November,

Lord Chatham's fluency was agreeable, but his tautology a little tiresome. His first speech was in a low, soft voice of bashfulness and humility, which entertained me and made amends for the loss of the matter, of which I could hear very little. He recovered himself in the second speech and I dare say will never be troubled with the same complaints again . . . You will without doubt hear it observed that men change their opinions with their situation . . . [that] Lord Camden and Lord Chatham [were] the patrons of prerogative, but I think without reason . . . [They] did not assert the legality of an act of the Crown against law, but in the case of inevitable necessity and upon that maxim which is fundamental to all government of every kind, *salus populi suprema lex*. In explaining themselves they did (as men in the eagerness of debate almost always do) drop expressions which taken by themselves, without regard to the scope of the argument, might admit of a construction very foreign to their intentions and sentiments.

Another peer commented,

our great Governor and his Viceroys, from not being contented with having an extraordinary act justified by necessity, and applauded from that emergency which sanctified it, have exposed themselves to very disagreeable and nearly general animadversions. The doctrine of a latent power in the crown of dispensing with laws justified by necessity of which the crown was to be judge, could not be brooked . . . Lord Chatham, drove to the wall, reasoned for the doctrine, and declared against it.

Wilkes was also critical of Chatham's attitude towards the constitution. After his arrest for libel and release on habeas corpus in 1763, Wilkes had compromised his case by going to France, and this led to his expulsion from the Commons in January 1764. His expulsion and the general question of general warrants were exploited by opposition politicians keen to throw doubt on the legality of ministerial actions, but Wilkes himself remained an embarrassment. His extravagant demands for a full pardon and financial compensation were unacceptable to the Rockingham ministry, not least because of George III's hostility to the blaspheming Wilkes. When Wilkes returned to Britain during the Chatham ministry and approached the King for clemency via Grafton, the Duke recorded that

Chatham . . . remarked on the awkwardness of the business, with which it was so difficult to meddle; and on my pressing to know what was to be done, he answered: 'the better way, I believe at present, is to take no notice of it'. And his advice I followed. The session opened in a week after; and from the hurry of weighty business, the concerns of Mr Wilkes engaged but little the attention of Ministry, or indeed of the Court. To some of his friends, who once or twice pressed me to intercede for a pardon, I constantly replied, that I thought my shoulders were not yet equal to the business, and that I conceived the weight of Lord Chatham's name could alone effect it.

Grafton probably exaggerated what Chatham could have done, but such comments and the general association of Chatham with liberty and the constitution helps to account for the fury of Wilkes' response to the failure to act on his behalf. He accused Chatham in print of self-interest, claimed that he was now 'the abject, crouching deputy of the proud Scot', in other words Bute, whose sinister intentions and influence were taken for granted, and complained that Chatham had let him down. Wilkes continued with a savage indictment of the minister's conduct, both at the time and during the Seven Years War,

He has served the public in all those points, where the good of the nation coincided with his own private views; and in no other . . . The invincible bravery of the British troops gave success even to the most rash, the most extravagant, the most desperate of his projects . . . The constitution of our country has no obligations to him. He has left it with all its beauties, and all its blemishes. He never once appeared in earnest about any question of liberty. He was the cause that in 1764 no point was gained for the public in the two great questions of General Warrants and the seizure of papers. The cursed remains of the court of Star-chamber, the enormous power of the attorney general . . . continued during his administration the same as before. Every grievance, which was not rooted out by the glorious revolution, and the later struggles of our patriots, still subsists in full force, notwithstanding the absolute power he exercised for several years over every department of the state.[58]

Thus, Chatham's reputation was under fire, while the entanglements of office when the heroic aura of war was absent were by the end of 1766 pressing home on him. The ministry was divided over policy towards America and India, the ministers unsuited to their tasks: Conway a poor leader of the Commons, Charles Townshend determined to follow his own views, Grafton without purpose and confidence. Chatham also found that many would not support the

---

[58] Earl of Dartmouth to Earl of Guildford, 13 November 1766, Bod. North MSS d 10; Earl of Buckinghamshire to Colonel Hotham, 13 December 1766, Hull University Library, Hotham papers 4/15; *Grafton* p. 193; Wilkes, *A Letter to His Grace the Duke of Grafton* (1767) pp. 12–15; HMC Polwarth V p. 365.

ministry. The groups led by Bedford and Grenville had not been comprehended at the outset, but the Rockingham faction was not then in opposition. However, Chatham's unwillingness to extend sufficient patronage to his supporters led Rockingham to go into opposition. Newcastle agreed with the Marquess, 'that Mr Pitt's total silence as to the party . . . not even . . . to show the least mark of attention to them, by wishing or desiring to have their countenance is such a mark of indifference at least, as, I am not surprised, should much offend them'.[59] By the start of 1767 the ministry faced a strong, though disunited, opposition.

The Chatham ministry had failed its creator. Chatham had hoped to demonstrate that government in the national interest and without faction was possible, but instead he had found the first difficult to further, the second impossible to achieve and had compromised his reputation and popularity in the process. Chatham's complaint of December 1766 with reference to the East India Company question, 'all marred, and thrown away by fatal weaknesses, cooperating with the most glaring factions', could be extended to his view of affairs in general. Edward Sedgwick wrote to another former Under-Secretary in March 1767, 'What is to become of this country, Heaven only knows. It is, as you very justly observe, but too evidently at present in the high road to destruction, and from whose hands are we to expect relief? The People seem no longer to expect any from our present ministers.'[60]

Chatham's health collapsed, probably as a consequence of the combination of stress and depression. From the spring of 1767 he became an invalid, neither handling the business of government nor being willing to see more than a few people. He was able to leave the house in order to take the air, but not

---

[59] Newcastle to Rockingham, 26 July 1766, WW R1–661.
[60] Chatham to Grafton, 7 December 1766, *Grafton* p. 110; Sedgwick to Weston, 28 March 1767, BL Add. 57928 f. 211.

to discuss business, excusing himself in June 1767 from seeing George III on the grounds of 'extreme weakness of nerves'. Chatham had refused to allow Grafton to call on him the previous month and only agreed to do so when pressed by the King. The Duke found Chatham able to discuss politics but recorded 'his nerves and spirits were affected to a dreadful degree . . . his great mind bowed down, and thus weakened by disorder'.[61] Although politicians continued to talk about the likelihood of his resumption of activity, Chatham's health did not improve. In August 1767 he made over legally the care of his private affairs to his wife, and the following year she wrote, 'Lord Chatham has the gout . . . wishes she could add it was a fixed regular fit, but though the pain has been considerable, and the soreness and lameness so much as to oblige him to keep his bed, yet hitherto it is too much of a flying gout to be perfectly a regular salutary fit, but Doctor Addington gives great hopes that this beginning will be productive of it, sooner or later, and give Lord Chatham's health that relief which it so much wants at present.'[62]

Others looked for more serious problems than gout; Harris recorded being told by Lord Lyttelton in July 1767, 'Pitt disabled by dejection of spirits almost approaching to insane melancholy . . . Beckford offered him a Letter of Business, which threw him into an agitation on the sight of it, and he would not open it . . . scarce any one sees him, but Lady Chatham . . . criminal to ask how he does – servants turned off for inquiring.' Anthony Addington had a special reputation for the treatment of mental disease. He believed that gout was best treated by inducing fits of the condition and accordingly prescribed alcohol, plenty of meat and little exercise. This was not the best way to deal with Pitt's ill-health, although that would not surprise those accustomed to reading of

[61] *Chatham Corresp.* III, 252–6, 259–66, 271–5, 277–8; *Grafton* pp. 132–7, quote p. 137.   [62] Lady Chatham to Earl of Lincoln, undated, NeC 4251/2.

eighteenth-century medical ingenuity. Convinced that William Pitt the Younger had inherited his father's gout, Addington prescribed, probably in 1773, the drinking of a bottle of port a day.

Unwilling to have Chatham resign, George III was confident that he would recover and in the meantime he assured that minister in January 1768 that 'your name has been sufficient to enable my administration to proceed'. Others were also convinced that Chatham would emerge from his delphic seclusion, the former diplomat Sir George Macartney writing to his patron Lord Holland the same month,

Lord Chatham is still in statu quo at Hayes, i.e. he sees nobody, does no business, and has no communication with the King's servants. I do believe notwithstanding, and I believe it upon good grounds, that he has mens sana in corpore sano as much as ever he had, but perhaps that is not saying much. I cannot help thinking that he will emerge again, and add one more surprise to the many he has so often given us.

Chatham's health and intentions remained a topic for speculation. Beckford, for example, told Harris on 1 July 1768 'that Lord Chatham constantly rode out, but declined all business'.[63] However, the political world increasingly continued with little reference to him. In February 1768 the office of Privy Seal was placed into commission, although it was not until October 1768 that, in his wife's words, 'the very weak and broken state' of Chatham's health 'reduced him to the necessity' of asking the King for permission to resign.[64] However, the government had long ceased to be one that could be described accurately as the Chatham ministry. Grafton had succeeded to his position as first minister,

---

[63] *Chatham Corresp.* III, 318; Ilchester (ed.), *Letters to Henry Fox* p. 283; HP Harris, 1 July 1768.
[64] Lady Chatham to Anne Pitt, 21 October 1768, BL Add. 69289 no. 66.

politicians no longer felt a pressing need to beat a path to Chatham's door.

IN THE SHADOWS 1769–1773

Chatham is perfectly well, and must have been for some time, since, though in general he seems to be very weak in his legs, yet, when playing at skittles, which is his favourite amusement, he now and then neglects his crutch stick for a quarter of an hour, and does not seem to have any great need of it then. He is very lively and good humoured, as a man ought to be in pursuit of power and popularity, and at the same time so brisk and boyish that he seems rather indifferent whether he catches them or not. (John Campbell, September 1769)[65]

Although he returned to politics in the autumn of 1769, Chatham was no longer a politician who could make or break ministries. The political agenda had changed and a new generation of politicians dominated the scene. Dodington had died in 1762, Granville in 1763, Hardwicke and Bath (Pulteney) in 1764, Cumberland in 1765, Newcastle in 1768. Chatham was not without his admirers and supporters among the new generation, such as the Earl of Shelburne,[66] but he was a largely isolated figure. The contrast with Newcastle in opposition was instructive. Although many former supporters had preferred staying in office to following the Duke in 1762, Newcastle had still enjoyed widespread support in opposition and he was able to see his protégé Rockingham take over his connection. Chatham suffered from his failure to make friends and cultivate a connection. Robert Wood, an MP who had been Chatham's Under-Secretary, told Harris in 1767 that 'no man had less feelings of friendship, or less desire to make or serve friends', while the

---

[65] Ilchester (ed.), *Letters to Henry Fox* p. 287.
[66] P. Brown, *The Chathamites* (1967).

same year Wilkes claimed that Chatham's 'flinty heart' did not know 'the sweets of private friendship . . . A proud, insolent, overbearing ambitious man is always full of the ideas of his own importance, and vainly imagines himself superior to the equality necessary among real friends, in all the moments of true enjoyment.' In 1768 Chatham stressed his constant refusal to intervene in elections,[67] which would have been an obvious way to win support.

Chatham's return to politics was aimed against the Grafton ministry in which supporters of the Duke of Bedford, who had joined the government in December 1767, were playing a greater role. Chatham was dissatisfied with this, especially with the removal of Shelburne in October 1768, a move that had precipitated his resignation, and angry with the domestic, colonial and foreign policies of the ministry. At the end of April 1769 Chatham's health recovered and, 'though still extremely lame', he was able to take the air in a carriage. On 7 July he returned to Court. Seeing the King for the last time, Chatham, characteristically insensitive and self-righteous, criticised the government's policy towards America, the East India Company and Wilkes, who had been expelled from Parliament, after being elected for Middlesex. Chatham added

that he doubted, whether his health would ever again allow him to attend Parliament: but, if it did, and if he should give his dissent to any measure, that His Majesty would be indulgent enough to believe that it would not arise from any personal consideration . . . that it could not arise from ambition, as he felt so strongly the weak state from which he was recovering, and which might daily threaten him, that office, therefore, of any sort, could no longer be desireable to him.

Despite this, rumours persisted that Chatham would return to the ministry. Harris noted the report that when

[67] HP Harris, 13 May 1767; Wilkes, *Letter to Grafton* p. 10; *Chatham Corresp.* III, 332.

Chatham had seen the Marquis of Granby, the Commander-in-Chief, who had remained in the Cabinet after his ally Chatham had left the ministry,

Chatham did not refuse to act with them; agreed that all that was past of any sort should be forgotten except that he could never agree to what had past with regard to Wilkes's expulsion . . . this he would by no means recede from. He added, that if he proposed a plan, he expected it should be followed by the Ministers – that he was now for cultivating peace, since we had one, as much as he had formerly been for war.

George Pitt (whom we saw this day at the Blandford race ordinary) says that Lord Chatham has been thrice at Court lately, at two levees, and a drawing room – says he appeared pleased at coming out, and that it was the opinion of people there that he had no objection to coming in.

George Pitt, a member of the Strathfieldsaye branch of the family and thus a kinsman of Chatham, was mistaken. Chatham felt betrayed by Grafton and spent the summer plotting to divide and attack the ministry. To that end, and accompanied by his wife, four children and twenty servants, he visited Temple at Stowe and Grenville at Wotton, a return, albeit in more style, to his old habits of peripatetic enjoyment and intrigue.

When the new session of Parliament began on 9 January 1770 Chatham asserted the importance of liberty and attacked the government's handling of American affairs and the Middlesex election. 'This did not make much impression; this is no longer Mr Pitt', observed the Bavarian envoy,[68] and Chatham himself was reported as disappointed by his speech, but his declaration of opposition led the Chathamites in the ministry, Camden and Granby, to desert Grafton. In order to

---

[68] *Chatham Corresp.* III, 355; *Grafton* p. 237; HP Harris, 18 July 1769; D. A. Winstanley, *Lord Chatham and the Whig Opposition* (Cambridge, 1912) p. 285; Haslang report, 12 January 1770, Munich, Bayr. Ges. London 248.

put pressure on Grafton, Chatham sought to co-operate with Rockingham. Grafton resigned on 27 January 1770, but George III turned to Lord North and at last found a first minister able to lead the Commons, manage government business and maintain a united government.[69] North was helped by the disunited nature of the opposition and by a rallying of support to the Crown, the natural focus of most politicians' loyalty, in response to the extremism of some of the Wilkesites.

Chatham was to attack the new ministry in the sessions of 1770 and 1771 but the nature of his political intentions was and is far from clear, a problem exacerbated by the lack of much real confidential correspondence. Whereas Newcastle had been a politician who committed himself readily to paper and had an extensive confidential correspondence with, among others, Hardwicke, and George III was an active correspondent, Chatham was not. This owed much to his gout, but was also a consequence of his Olympian style of politics, his reluctance to trust others and his distaste for what he called factions. Pitt usually wrote in order to persuade rather than to explain. The extent to which he sought office in 1770–1 can be questioned. The experience of 1766–8 was scarcely encouraging. More probable is a desire on Chatham's part to restore a reputation for disinterested patriotism, the beacon of national interest, which had been compromised when he was in office. In addition, Chatham might hope to act as an elder, albeit partisan, statesman, as he had clearly hinted he would like to do when resigning in 1761, could he help to ensure that a favourable ministry was in office. He was not alone in displaying an indifference to office. Harris recorded that when he saw Grenville on 18 February 1770, the latter 'held the same doctrine of his

[69] Thomas, Lord North (1976); F. O'Gorman, The Rise of Party in England. The Rockingham Whigs 1760–82 (1975) pp. 244–57, 272–93.

indifference to taking up public affairs – said that neither Lord Temple, Chatham, Rockingham, Dowdeswell or himself (these he enumerated) has formed any scheme to themselves of power or office – said he should never thrust himself in against the King's consent, nor come unless called'. This was also Chatham's position, but such a call was unlikely to come given his attacks on government policy and there is little sign that he expected one. In the debate on the sensitive subject of the Civil List debt on 14 March 1770, Chatham questioned George III's veracity and declared that Camden had been dismissed for his opinion in favour of the right of election in the people. Such wild claims led one listener, the Earl of Marchmont, to tell Harris that 'Chatham acted like a mad man.'

Chatham's behaviour in 1770–1 would not have surprised readers of Tobias Smollett's *The Adventures of an Atom*, published in 1769, in which his distinctive features were described as 'a loud voice, an unabashed countenance, a fluency of abuse, and an intrepidity of opposition'. However, his conduct raised the question of whether he could judge any ministry favourable. Chatham was unhappy in the political world in 1767 after his effective withdrawal from his own ministry. But he seems to have settled down relatively happily to the world of opposition politics, and especially the Petitioning Movement of late 1769 which demanded a dissolution and elections, on the grounds that Parliament was no longer truly representative. This interesting switch of political role models suggests that Chatham preferred active opposition to inactivity. The 'Chathamites' were too few to constitute a ministry and, had they come to direct a government, might well have been found wanting as a result of close scrutiny by Chatham. Grafton had proved a broken reed. The range of options available to any politician manoeuvring against the ministry had narrowed. The Bedford connection had joined the government, as, after his death in November 1770, did most of the supporters of George Grenville, and, in June 1771, Grafton. Grenville had been younger than Pitt, as was Bedford, who died in January 1771, and Townshend, Beckford and Granby who had died in 1767, 1770 and 1770 respectively. Their deaths were a reminder that longevity was denied many eighteenth-century politicians and an indication of Chatham's growing isolation in a changing political scene. Rockingham was to die in 1782 at the age of fifty-two, William Pitt the Younger in 1806 at forty-seven. Aside from his poor health, Chatham, already in his sixties, appeared to be living on borrowed time. He had become a celebrity that foreigners wanted to see, rather than a politician of consequence. A sense of the corruption of the times and of passing time led Chatham to concentrate anew on his reputation for integrity. In November 1770 he stated his determination 'to be found in my post when destruction falls upon us. The times are pollution, in the very quintessence.'[70]

This attitude did not make co-operating with the leading opposition group, the Rockinghams, easy. The Rockinghams could not forget Chatham's role in the fall of their ministry. Chatham could not dispense with his suspicions of connections, especially aristocratic connections, even though Newcastle was dead. The two were divided over America. Chatham had never accepted the Declaratory Act of 1766, by which the Rockinghams had stated Parliament's right to legislate for the colonies 'in all cases whatsoever', asserting comprehensive legislative supremacy at the same time as they repealed the Stamp Act. By claiming as his bedrock 'Revolution Principles', the Whig legacy of 1688, Chatham asserted both his willingness to support major reforms and his belief that national union should flow from backing for principles

[70] Smollett, *Adventures of an Atom* (1769) p. 271; *Chatham Corresp.* IV, 32.

of liberty, rather than what he termed 'the narrow genius of old-corps' connection'[71] which he felt had weakened Whiggism.

Whiggism had to be constantly renewed in the furnace of liberty; the process of such constant renewal was true Whiggism, and by that standard the Rockinghams were deficient. In 1770 they dissented from Chatham's pressure for a dissolution to a supposedly corrupt Commons and new elections, and lent little support to his advocacy of increased parliamentary representation for the counties by adding two MPs for each county, as a means of redressing the corruptibility of 'rotten boroughs' and thus reforming the state.[72] This proposal, which Chatham advanced in the Lords on 22 January 1770, looked back to a theme of opposition criticism of the Walpole ministry, as did Chatham's consideration in 1770–1 of the revival of triennial elections. As an MP Chatham had, thanks to the strength of connections, sat for pocket boroughs, and he had not attacked them when in office, evidence possibly for Wilkes' claim in 1767, based essentially on the issue of general warrants, that Chatham's support for liberty was hypocritical. Once out of office Chatham, at least in his own eyes, saw the true nature of politics more clearly, but made no allowance for his own past compromises, and possibly remembered them with mortification only too well, when he criticised the Rockinghams for failing to share his views. He did not press the idea of triennial elections because he was advised against it by Temple and convinced that it would lead to 'more frequent returns of corruption'.[73]

In the session of 1770 Chatham took a major role in discussing the Middlesex election, moving motions that the

[71] Chatham Corresp. IV, 187.
[72] Chatham to Rockingham, 12 May 1770, WW R1–1299; Cobbett, XVI, 747–55; O'Gorman, Rise of Party pp. 275–6.   [73] Chatham Corresp. IV, 156–7.

capacity of a person to be elected did not depend finally on the Commons; to reverse the Commons' decision against Wilkes; in protest against George III's answer to the aggressive City remonstrance; and for a dissolution of Parliament on the grounds of the Kingdom's dangerous state and that the Commons were 'the violators of the people's rights'. All were unsuccessful, but they saw Chatham adopting liberty as his cause and the alleged corruption of the Commons as his target, an echo of the 'patriot' themes of his first years in Parliament. He criticised the King's answer to the City remonstrance on the grounds that 'a more unconstitutional piece never came from the throne, nor any more dangerous, if less unnoticed', although, as ever, Chatham failed to note the ambiguous nature of the constitution. He wrote to Rockingham of reviving the clouded spirit of opposition to slavery by action. It is not surprising that North told Harris on 8 December 1770 that George III disliked Chatham more than anyone else.[74]

Chatham also returned to another theme of those years: supineness in the face of Bourbon aggression. He called for an inquiry into the failure of the Grafton ministry to prevent the French acquisition of Corsica in 1768. The French were unimpressed, their envoy finding his attacks on the ministry absurd and claiming that Chatham sought a new war in order to gratify his ambition, while Louis XV thought that he deserved execution.[75] The Spanish expulsion of an English settlement from the Falkland Islands during the recess provoked eight speeches from Chatham between November 1770 and February 1771, although their reception was mixed, Richmond claiming of one, he 'spoke an hour and 50 minutes so dull and heavily that nobody could follow him or would attend to him. He meant to be very argumentative in

[74] Chatham to Rockingham, 10 May, 27 April 1770, WW R1–1297, 1294.
[75] AE CP Ang. 491 ff. 168–9.

which he always fails.' Lord Lyttelton complained 'that Lord Chatham in his speeches always refuted himself, declaring for war, and at the same time insisting on our defenceless state, and our inability to make war'. In a pamphlet supporting the ministry, Dr Johnson attacked 'the feudal gabble of a man who is every day lessening that splendour of character which once illuminated the kingdom, then daz-zled, and afterwards inflamed it; and for whom it will be happy if the nation shall at last dismiss him to nameless obscurity'.[76] Chatham pressed for a strong navy, a popular administration and the vigorous pursuit of national interests. Refused French support and influenced by a major British naval armament, Spain backed down, denying Chatham the opportunity to attempt a campaign similar to that directed against Walpole in 1738–9. In his speech on 22 November 1770 Chatham cited the Convention of the Pardo of 1739 and his advice for war with Spain in 1761 and justified his German policy during the Seven Years War. However, the opposition vote was poor. Over the Falklands Chatham felt at ease, asserting national interests and criticising the ministry.

In contrast, the complexities of domestic issues and political co-operation were revealed in 1771 in the contro-versy surrounding the bill of the Rockinghamite William Dowdeswell, which would have given juries the sole right to determine guilt in libel cases; as opposed only to finding the fact of authorship, which Lord Mansfield, the Lord Chief Justice, had recently ruled was the law. Chatham loathed Mansfield, the former William Murray, and, asserting that the legal principles were crucial, insisted on a 'declaratory' bill, stating what the law had been in the past, as well as its future shape. Chatham told the Duke of Richmond, an ally of

[76] Richmond to Rockingham, 16 February 1771, WW RI–1363; HP Harris, 13 December 1770, 14 February 1771, Johnson, *Thoughts on the Late Transactions respecting Falkland's Islands* (1771) p. 37.

Rockingham's, that something had to be done, otherwise 'said it was betraying the rights of jurors and the people', but he refused to back their bill, and demanded instead that Dowdeswell drop his bill and that the Rockinghamites support one based on Chatham's ideas. In consequence the Chathamites helped to defeat the bill in the Commons, and thus to sustain the enmity of the Rockinghamites. Chatham's language was, as so often, extreme, and he was especially animated against what he saw as the work of 'connection', a word that focused his hostility to aristocratic power and presumption, and the methods and objectives of factions, the alienation of a man who saw himself as an outsider to both, and who certainly no longer understood how to work with them in order to further his goals. Chatham's extravagant and self-righteous language can be seen in his letter to John Calcraft, his parliamentary factotum,

Dowdeswell's inflexibility, on a point manifestly absurd, is a melancholy proof of the spirit of connection. I trust this compound of tyranny and folly will meet with the reception from the public which such a task-master deserves. However, I will keep down rising sensations, so justly founded, and rather give way to laughter than animosity, during the reign of dulness in Opposition; the constitution, however, I will not sacrifice, even to union.

This talk of tyranny and sacrifice cannot be ascribed to bad weather or a ferocious attack of gout. Chatham noted he had 'just got off my horse, after riding about two hours in sunshine'. Dowdeswell complained, 'The ascendancy of Lord Chatham and Lord Camden over the minds of many, after so many tricks played us is amazing.'[77] Chatham's attitude ensured that when the bill came to be debated ministerial supporters had to do little bar watch the

---

[77] Richmond to Rockingham, 12 February 1771, WW R1–1358; *Chatham Corresp.* IV, 97–100, 103–5, 108–12; Dowdeswell to Rockingham, 8 February 1771, WW R1–1356; O'Gorman, *Rise of Party* pp. 281–3.

contention among their opponents. Talk of a united opposition had scant resonance in Chatham's personal experience
of divided oppositions in the 1740s, 1750s and 1760s. He had
succeeded when opposition had been disunited. However, in
1754–6 the ministry had lacked perseverance and in 1766
George III had turned to Chatham to save him from
Rockingham and Grenville, whereas in the early 1770s North
was determined, seemed able to overcome problems, and
enjoyed royal support.

Chatham also revealed somewhat mixed views on politics
in general, stressing the value of independence and Whiggery, the right of the King to choose his ministers and making
obvious his reluctance to accept the consequences of party.
He told Richmond 'that there were many eccentric men who
would not belong to a party, that they were the real strength
of opposition . . . that he was the oldest Whig in England and
could not now submit to be called only an ally of the Whigs.
He was a Whig . . . that the Whigs alone could and ought to
make the basis of an administration'; in opposition to 'the
fatal system of disunion so much practised by the court'.
Chatham, however, made it clear that he opposed George III
being forced to accept Rockingham as First Lord of the
Treasury, leading Richmond to reply that 'if it was really
meant to take in the Whigs as the basis of an administration it
was natural to let them choose the minister, or to choose their
leader to such' and that 'Lord Chatham had never turned his
mind towards finance and therefore I supposed he would
rather prefer foreign affairs.' Chatham agreed that he did not
want to take the Treasury.[78]

By the end of the session of 1771 Chatham was essentially
isolated politically. With Beckford dead and the rise of
Wilkes, Chatham's influence in the City was diminished,

---

[78] Richmond to Rockingham, 12 February 1771, WW R1–1358.

although his reputation there remained strong. The Commons was responding well to North's leadership and George III was satisfied with his government, no longer helping to destabilise politics by intriguing against his ministers. Co-operation with the Rockinghams could not be sustained, while Chatham had fallen out with Camden. Arguing on 1 May 1771 that no remedy for poor government could be expected from a corrupt Commons, Chatham pressed again for a dissolution and fresh elections, but he was defeated. That December he wrote from Burton Pynsent to Calcraft of 'how little satisfaction the political world affords – The state of things is indeed most pityable; strange and contradictory is our situation! Government has lost its *essential powers*, and the country has lost its liberty!'[79] In the meantime Chatham had had a pleasant trip to Boconnoc, the seat of his nephew Thomas, and had admired the Cornish countryside, before spending the autumn at Burton Pynsent, enjoying the delights of landownership, farming, hunting, and planting. He also found that ale agreed with his health and devoted much time to his children's upbringing.

He only spoke once in Parliament in 1772, travelling, in response to an appeal from the Dissenter Richard Price, from Burton Pynsent, where he had spent most of the session, to speak on 19 May in support of more rights for Dissenters. This was a cause that was grounded on 'Revolution Principles' and integral to traditional Whiggery. Chatham criticised the bishops and declared his support for toleration, but the bill was rejected. He then returned to family and estate in Somerset, depressed by the political situation and saddened in August by the death of Calcraft, yet another younger man.

Chatham did not attend the Lords during the 1773 session,

---

[79] Pitt to Calcraft, 18 December 1771, PRO 30/8/6.

and instead returned to the theme of the superiority of rural life, writing in January to Shelburne from Burton Pynsent, 'how much more tranquil and full of hope a farmer's chimney-corner is, than the Royal Exchange, the Bank of England, or the palace of a nabob!'[80] In fact Chatham had both bad gout, and serious financial problems, but he was able to take his oldest sons to Lyme Regis that summer and take great pleasure in the company of his boys and in 'nature in her free and wild compositions'. In bemoaning 'the last symptoms of a decaying state', he was writing of the country, not his own health, which was 'considerably strengthened by frequent riding'.[81]

AMERICAN EPILOGUE 1773–1778

In late 1773 Chatham became very concerned about the increasingly volatile American situation. Rising hostility reflected increasing democratisation in American society, which was related to the emergence of new political groups in the 1770s; a millenarian rejection of British authority; the borrowing of British conspiracy theories about the supposed autocratic intentions of George III; specific constitutional, ideological and commercial concerns about relations with Britain that arose from the disputes and economic difficulties of the 1760s; and British policies whose firmness could be interpreted as tyranny and whose changes of policy as sinister. The British ministry decided in 1769 to abandon all the Townshend duties save that on tea, whose retention was seen as a necessary demonstration that they would not yield to colonial views. However, relations remained poor, with serious constitutional disputes of varied cause in a number of colonies, particular tension in Massachusetts and a growing

[80] *Chatham Corresp.* IV, 242.   [81] *Chatham Corresp.* IV, 265–75.

hostility towards parliamentary claims to authority over American affairs.

Chatham was alarmed by the rise in tension, and observed, 'I hope government will have wisdom and humanity enough to choose the happy alternative; and give to America a constitutional representative, rather than hazard an unjust and impracticable war.'[82] Chatham's constant theme until he died in May 1778 was the need for conciliation because he saw the American crisis as a tragedy. The danger in his mind was obvious. If America was driven to rebellion she would turn to the Bourbons for assistance, as indeed was to be the case. There was also a deep personal anger that the achievements of the Seven Years War were being squandered. The Boston Tea Party of 16 December 1773 forced the British government to confront the growing problems of law and order and the maintenance of authority. They believed these arose from the actions of a small number in America, rather than from widespread disaffection, and thus mistakenly hoped that tough action against Massachusetts, the so-called Coercive or Intolerable Acts of early 1774, would lead to the restoration of order. The Boston Port Act was designed to protect trade and customs officials from harassment, the Massachusetts Charter Act to strengthen the executive, the Administration of Justice and Quartering Acts to make it easier to enforce order. These measures were criticised by the opposition in Britain as oppressive, but passed by overwhelming majorities. More troops were sent to Massachusetts.

Chatham's desire for conciliation and his criticism of specific acts of governmental policy in the worsening American crisis combined with genuine admiration for those colonists who in defending their liberties seemed to be

---

[82] *Chatham Corresp.* IV, 301. The best guide to the background is B. Donoughue, *British Politics and the American Revolution 1773–1775* (1984).

asserting the cause of liberty and affirming the Whig tradition. Benjamin Franklin who visited Chatham at Hayes in August 1774, recorded,

That truly great man received me with abundance of civility, inquired particularly into the situation of affairs in America, spoke feelingly of the severity of the late laws against Massachusetts . . . and expressed great regard and esteem for the people of that country, who he hopes would continue firm and united in defending by all peaceable and legal means their constitutional rights. I assured him, that I made no doubt they would do so.

Franklin appealed to Chatham's sense of imperial mission, arguing that but for wrong policies,

we might have gone on extending our western empire, adding province to province as far as the South Sea [Pacific] . . . He replied . . . that my idea of extending our empire in that manner was a sound one, worthy of a great, benevolent and comprehensive mind. He wished with me for a good understanding among the different parts of the opposition here, as a means of restoring the ancient harmony of the two countries, which he most earnestly desired; but he spoke of the coalition of our domestic parties, as attended with difficulty, and rather to be desired than expected . . . he expressed much satisfaction . . . in the assurances I had given him that America did not aim at independence.

When he saw Franklin at Hayes on 26 December 1774, Chatham praised the Continental Congress, which had been formed in order to co-ordinate resistance to the coercive legislation passed in 1774, and which met in Philadelphia in September 1774. He said

they had acted with so much temper, moderation and wisdom, that he thought it the most honorable assembly of statesmen since those of the ancient Greeks and Romans in the most virtuous times. That there were not in their whole proceedings above one or two things he could have wished otherwise; perhaps but one, and that was their assertion that the keeping up a standing army in the colonies in time of peace, without consent of their legislatures was against the law . . . He expressed a great regard and warm affection for that country, with hearty wishes for their prosperity, and that government here might soon come to see its mistakes and rectify them.[83]

Colonists opposed to the policy of the North ministry were certainly encouraged by Chatham's speeches. In May 1774 he praised the Americans and urged conciliatory measures. In June he denounced the Quebec Bill, an attempt to establish a system of government for the province of Quebec that alarmed opinion in the Thirteen Colonies, because of the extension of the province's boundaries to include the country between the Great Lakes and the Ohio and Mississippi rivers, and because the system was seen to prefigure possible changes in America. The establishment of the French civil law without a jury, the recognition of the Catholic establishment in Quebec and the granting of the right to collect tithes, and the absence of any element of popular government acting through an elected assembly aroused concern and were attacked by Chatham. On 20 January 1775 Chatham pressed for the withdrawal of the troops sent to intimidate Boston, warned the Lords about the danger that France would exploit the situation and, quoting Virgil, again pressed the need for conciliation. Having discussed the situation with Franklin, Chatham on 1 February 1775 introduced a bill designed to pacify America, by giving the newly formed Continental Congress a role in devising a new constitutional and financial settlement. He proposed that the colonies accept parliamentary sovereignty and the Crown's right to keep an army in America, but, in return, recent coercive British legislation was to be repealed, Parliament

---

[83] *The Diplomatic Correspondence of the United States* II (Washington, 1889) pp. 11–13, 31–2.

was to agree that taxes should not be raised other than with the approval of a provincial assembly, and the representative role of the Continental Congress was to be recognised. The bill was defeated, as Chatham's motion the previous month had been. There was little sympathy in the British political establishment for the Americans who were seen as ungrateful for the efforts made on their behalf during the Seven Years War and as acting in an illegal manner.[84]

Given Chatham's speeches and his contacts with Franklin and other Americans, it is easy to appreciate both why he was seen as a champion of the colonists and why after his death it was claimed that had his advice been followed there would have been no war of independence. However, Chatham's position was more complex. Although he pressed for conciliation and was prepared to envisage an abolition of parliamentary taxation of America, Chatham was fixedly against American independence. The integrity of the British empire, the political, strategic and economic interdependency of different parts that he saw so clearly and that had led him to oppose concessions to France over the Newfoundland fishery 1761, would be destroyed by American independence. Chatham felt that economic and political strength were related, that the monopoly of American trade supported British power and that without political links it would be impossible to maintain economic relationships. Chatham's views differed from those of the colonists in that they regarded immunity from parliamentary taxation as an inherent right, while he argued that it would have to be granted as a concession by a sovereign Parliament, in return for which Chatham envisaged a financial contribution from the colonies. Although in 1766 he had distinguished between

---

[84] Ibid. pp. 38, 41; Donoughue, British Politics pp. 231–8.

internal taxation and the external duties decreed by Parliament, such a distinction had been abolished by the Declaratory Act of 1766 and therefore in February 1775 he pressed for the emendation of that act in order to leave domestic taxation under the control of the colonists. In 1775 he described his 'whole system for America – which is, to secure to the colonies property and liberty, and to insure to the mother-country a due acknowledgement, on the part of the colonies, of their subordination to the supreme legislative authority, and superintending power of the Parliament of Great Britain'.[85]

As so often in Chatham's career, his own position was somewhat different to that generally attributed to him, in this case as a friend of America, but whereas this led to charges of opportunism and hypocrisy when he accepted or acted in office, by 1775 his position was less controversial because of less consequence. Eventually the British government was to adopt the path of conciliation, unsuccessfully in the case of America in 1778 when the Carlisle Commission was sent to try to negotiate a settlement, successfully in that of Ireland in 1782–3 when British legislative authority was renounced in favour of the Dublin Parliament. Chatham's proposal for a permanent American legislature to exercise the powers of taxation renounced by the Westminster Parliament might therefore appear prescient, but it was not politically viable in 1774–5. It would not have been easy to win widespread support for the proposal in America, still less for the preservation of parliamentary sovereignty and for the maintenance of a British army there, but, more seriously, there was no consensus in favour of compromise in Britain.

---

[85] Chatham Corresp. IV, 407; Diplomatic Correspondence II, 355; I. R. Christie, 'The Earl of Chatham and American Taxation, 1774–5', The Eighteenth Century, 20 (1979), pp. 258–9.

Nor could Chatham create one. The British government viewed the claims of Congress as an unacceptable challenge to parliamentary authority. Well supported in Parliament, but keenly aware that a show of weakness towards the colonies might well alienate decisive elements of that support, it decided to use force, although at the same time it hoped to assuage grievances, as indicated by the conciliatory propositions North put before Parliament in February 1775. However, the government was determined to retain control of the constitutional position for Parliament and to reimpose order in America. The outbreak of fighting at Lexington and Concord on 19 April 1775 should have come as no surprise, although the ministry was to be startled by the scale and extent of American resistance.

The problem facing Chatham was commented on in an apocryphal story of 1775 that also indicates that some contemporaries believed wrongly that Chatham's gout was an imaginary illness, but correctly that it could be convenient in its timing. On 30 January Pringle recounted

the following droll anecdote of that charlatan in politics, Lord Chatham. It seems Dr Franklin and some other of the agents waited upon him and told him they were instructed by the Congress to wait upon his Lordship to know if he approved of what they had done and in everything to be directed by him. They have done extremely right and just what they ought, answered his Lordship. But, my Lord, What steps shall we next take should neither the King or Parliament attend to their petition but proceed to coercive measures as is suspected? At this instant my Lord was seized with a violent gouty pain. Oh! Oh! that cruel tormenting disease that seizes me almost always when I apply my mind intensely to business. My dear Friends! Oh! You must excuse me, I cannot bear it. I cannot speak, I am in such agony. Come some other day. O no, I shall send to let you know when I am able to confer with you; and so dismissed them without any answer to that very important question, and as yet has not sent for them. And yet this imposture continues to cheat a whole people. You see how convenient a disease gout is to a politician.[86]

The beginning of conflict made Chatham's position very difficult. He was out of line with dominant British opinion in favouring a limitation of the sovereignty of Parliament. Vice-Admiral Augustus Keppel, a Rockinghamite MP who refused command in American waters, reported in January 1776 on a recent meeting with Shelburne,

I said it could hardly be hoped that Lord Chatham would ever be able to come forth again, and that if even he did, the practice of his coming to the House of Lords with his propositions, without previous communication, rendered it very difficult for my friends to do what they would by a more confidential treatment. I don't think Lord Shelburne expressed much expectation of Lord Chatham ever again being able to go into great business; but he seemed to have such a high opinion of him, that attention was due to opinions, so far as they were known; but told me, in very explicit terms, that he was a single person – that he meant to say no more in Parliament, seeing no probability of being of service in the present disunited opposition.[87]

Chatham's reputation improved somewhat as the attempt to crush the American revolution foundered. Having been in poor health and absent from Parliament for two years, Chatham was 'enough recovered . . . to crawl to the House of Lords' on 30 May 1777.[88] He warned his audience that it was impossible to conquer America and proposed that the government seek to end the revolution by redressing all the American grievances and accepting their right to dispose of their money. His motion for an address to the King

---

[86] HMC Polwarth V pp. 370–1.
[87] Keppel to Rockingham, 5 January 1776, WW R1–1651.
[88] Chatham Corresp. IV, 432.

advocating peace was easily rejected, 28 to 99,[89] but Chatham's prophecies of danger and doom seemed increasingly apposite. He sent his nephew Thomas on 25 September 'a sight of the handwriting, which has so long lain in inaction', and, referring to '*useful pain*', wrote

I am recovered beyond expectation, and can say, I am all but well. The last fit of gout has proved more salutory than all the preceding and has almost removed all complaints but grey hair . . . I tremble for news from America. Till the event, (which in every alternative, must be ruin), is known, the date of England's greatness seems protracted for a few days. Sad tenure, of more public happiness and prosperity than Providence has ever given to a nation and infatuated counsels have ever thrown away.[90]

Chatham spoke next on 20 November 1777, in the debate on the Address, and aimed 'to save America'.[91] He pressed for peace with America, which he declared could not be conquered, the recall of British troops from thence, and preparations against the Bourbons. His speech included bitter criticism of the use of Red Indians, whom he accused of atrocities, and of German mercenaries. Chatham claimed that his suggested policy would lead the Americans to a 'happy and constitutional reconcilement' with Britain. However, he was still opposed to independence, the course that the Rockinghams were increasingly urging. Chatham pressed for Americans to enjoy the same rights as the inhabitants of Britain, but argued that Parliament must still regulate the trade of the empire in order to preserve its prosperity.[92]

In December 1777 Chatham castigated the ministry for failing to take adequate preparations against the Bourbons, criticised the use of Indians, stressed his Whig credentials, and opposed a Christmas adjournment on the grounds of the

---

[89] Cobbett, XIX, 317–20.   [90] BL Add. 69288 no. 35.
[91] Chatham to Rockingham, 18 November 1777, WW R151–6.
[92] Cobbett, XIX, 354–80.

seriousness of the situation. Chatham's opposition to independence separated him, however, from the Rockinghams,
so that yet again the opposition was divided. His policy of
reconciliation but no independence was unrealistic, reveal-
ing him to be 'a stranger to American politicks', although the
initial successes of British operations in 1777 suggested that it
was indeed time to think about a possible settlement.[93]
Convinced of the prescience of his views and despite
continued ministerial majorities, Chatham remained, as he
characteristically put it with unequivocal conviction, 'persuaded that the constitution, strenuously asserted within
doors, and backed by the sense of the people without, must at
length prevail'.[94] His language was still as histrionic as ever,
British policy in America being described after Burgoyne's
surrender at Saratoga in October 1777 had made success
unlikely as 'this combined labyrinth of imbecility, cruelty
and horror'.[95]

This loss of one of Britain's two field armies in America led
to a political crisis in Britain. North suffered a failure of nerve
and sought both to strengthen the ministry and to reach a
new settlement with the rebelling Americans. The latter led
to the dispatch of the Carlisle Peace Commission, the former
to an attempt to persuade George III to send for Chatham.
North suggested for 'Lord Chatham Honours, and Emolu-
ments, and perhaps of the Cabinet without any Office', and
wrote to the King on 15 March 1778,

there is nothing which seems so likely to stem the first violence of
the torrent as sending to Lord Chatham . . . Lord Chatham would
certainly be more reasonable than Lord Rockingham's party; He

[93] Chatham to Rockingham, 27 November 1777, 22, 27 January 1778, WW R151–
10, 11, 15; O'Gorman, Rise of Party, pp. 363–4; L. H. Butterfield (ed.), Adams Family
Correspondence II (Cambridge Mass., 1963) pp. 405–10.
[94] Chatham to Rockingham, undated, WW R151–20.
[95] Chatham to Rockingham, undated, WW R151–22; J. Black, War for America
(Stroud, 1991).

would alter the Cabinet, but he would not proceed to remove persons from inferior departments and he would bring into government but a few followers; add to this, that, in the manner of doing the business, he would be more attentive to the appearance of the dignity of the Crown, than the others.

George III was unenthusiastic,

no advantage to this country nor personal danger can ever make me address myself for assistance either to Lord Chatham or any other branch of the Opposition honestly I would rather lose the Crown I now wear than bear the ignominy of possessing it under their shackles.

The King was informed Chatham was only willing to join the government under certain conditions, which reflected his experience of politics in the 1760s, 'that he expects to be a confidential Minister, that he must have the appearance of forming the Ministry, that the most important offices being filled with efficient men', but the King was unprepared to see him 'as Dictator . . . planning a new Administration'. Encouraged by the government's strength in Parliament, George III in late March firmly resisted repeated pressure from North to turn to Chatham.[96]

Chatham himself was ill in early 1778 and unable to attend the Lords, but on 7 April he made his last parliamentary appearance. The Earl of Denbigh had found the debate on 20 November 1777 'very dull', but there was nothing dull about the occasion five months later. The occasion was a motion by Richmond for an address to George III calling for the withdrawal of troops from America and the resignation of the ministry. The Duke argued that Britain had to recognise American independence in order to free herself for the imminent war with France. Chatham, obviously ill, wrapped

---

[96] Sir John Fortescue, The Correspondence of King George the Third (6 vols., 1928) IV, 54–88; Lord John Russell (ed.), Memorials and Correspondence of Charles James Fox (4 vols., 1853–7) I, 186–7; Lord E. Fitzmaurice, Life of William, Earl of Shelburne (3 vols., 1875) III, 25.

in flannel and supported on crutches, replied that Britain could wage both struggles simultaneously, claimed that the abandonment of the colonies would be a national humiliation and would lead to national ruin and stated that the King could not consent to the loss of part of the empire. Richmond in turn argued, correctly as it was to turn out, that the country could not fight France and the Americans successfully. After Richmond had replied, Chatham rose to speak, but collapsed. 'He fell back upon his seat and was to all appearance in the agonies of death.'[97] Chatham was carried from the chamber and taken two days later to Hayes where he died on 11 May 1778, at the age of sixty-nine. There was a definitely heroic note to his collapse in the Lords and it struck many contemporaries in that light. The heroic image was to be propagated visually, most obviously in Copley's picture The Death of Chatham, which was reproduced in engravings. The dying Chatham had William read to him from the Iliad on the death of Hector. Harris recorded,

Lord Nugent said in the House of Commons and repeated it after to me in private, that Lord Chatham's last words were to his son, who was going to join his regiment – 'Leave your dying father, and go to the defence of your country.' The same told me his last words in the House of Lords were, 'If the Americans defend independence, they shall find me in their way.' He then fainted, fell and was carried away, in appearance dead.

He and Lord Granville appear as heroes, a superior species to the frisking, bowing, false, insincere crew, whom we foolishly admire more from the names of their great offices, than their intrinsic abilities.

Neither of the two above scraped up money. Pitt (like Saladin) died without a penny. Both were classical men . . . Granville seems to have resembled Demosthenes; Chatham, Cicero.[98]

---

[97] Camden to Grafton, April 1778, Grafton p. 300; Fortescue, George the Third IV, 100.
[98] HP Harris, 13 May 1778.

On the day of Chatham's death the Commons voted unanimously an address for a public funeral and a monument in Westminster Abbey, a measure that surprised George III who informed North that he would find it offensive if intended as a compliment to Chatham's 'general conduct', rather than 'as a testimony of gratitude for his rousing the Nation at the beginning of the last War, and his conduct whilst at that period he held the Seals of Secretary of State'.[99] The Commons voted to pay his debts, although the Lords defeated by one vote Shelburne's motion that they attend the funeral.

After Chatham's body had laid in state for two days, the funeral took place on 9 June 1778. On his monument in Westminster Abbey are inscribed the words

> Erected by the King and Parliament
> As a Testimony to
> The Virtues and Ability
> of
> WILLIAM PITT EARL OF CHATHAM
> During whose Administration
> In the Reigns of George II and George III
> Divine Providence
> Exalted Great Britain
> To an Height of Prosperity and Glory
> Unknown to any Former Age
> Born November 15, 1708; Died May 11, 1778

[99] Fortescue, *George the Third* IV, 139–40.

Chapter 5

Chatham as Hanoverian Patriot

> War . . . certain. I sincerely hope Lord Chatham will be minister.
>
> (Admiral Sir George Rodney, 11 April 1778)[1]

> No statesman ever exhibited greater inconsistencies during his political career.
>
> Dictionary of National Biography

Elusive because reclusive, Chatham was an individual who is difficult to fathom. Lord Rosebery, possibly the most prominent example of a species that is extinct, the scholarly and literary Prime Minister, stressed Chatham's secret personality: 'he revealed himself neither by word nor on paper, he deliberately enveloped himself in an opaque fog of mystery . . . seems to have cut off all vestiges of his real self as completely as a successful fugitive from justice. And so posterity sees nothing but the stern effigy . . . made himself a prebiographical figure.'[2] Written in 1910, this judgement is still essentially true. The intervening years have thrown up more material, but it is almost all comments on, rather than by, Chatham. In consequence the views of past biographers

[1] G. B. Mundy (ed.), Life and Correspondence of Admiral Lord Rodney (2 vols., 1830) I, 180.
[2] Lord Rosebery, Chatham. His Early Life and Connections (1910), xi–xii.

are of considerable value. They wrote in an age when the central achievement of Chatham's career, the defence and expansion of empire, was still a living reality, although his other major preoccupation, the nature of British politics, with specific reference to the influence of the Crown and the existence of party, had changed substantially by the Victorian and Edwardian period, years when so much more of the map was coloured red and when it was natural to search out and admire the founders of empire.

Today these values appear remote. In his scholarly attempt to present an unheroic account of Chatham's achievement during the Seven Years War, that would stress the limited nature of his role, abilities and success, Richard Middleton cited the influence of his own environment, specifically the trend towards an egalitarian society, the questioning of the ability of governments to control affairs, the support of 'opinion' for European unity and international co-operation and the corresponding hostility towards imperialism and war.[3] These may indeed be the values of many, although the popularity of the attempt by so many of the governing class to bury national identity in the quicksands of European co-operation can be questioned, as can the extent to which egalitarianism has struck deep roots. Instead, one of the central features of Britain in the last century has been the ambiguous response towards the democratisation of society, while the renown, if not always popularity, enjoyed by Mrs Thatcher for so many years and the outburst of national feeling at the time of the Falklands War suggests that hostility to the notion of great individuals and the strength of anti-heroic views should not be exaggerated. The dominant theme of much popular culture is the brave hero battling complacency on his own side and sinister foes elsewhere in

[3] R. Middleton, *The Bells of Victory. The Pitt–Newcastle Ministry and the Conduct of the Seven Years War* (Cambridge, 1985) p. 228.

order to triumph in the defence of true national or group interests. Middleton's analysis of the *Zeitgeist* can be queried.

Chatham could be described, and thus implicitly or explicitly criticised, by the standards of many intellectuals today, as imperialistic, paternalist and patriarchal. It could be suggested that empire was a poisoned chalice for Britain from the late eighteenth to the twentieth centuries. Even if his values are not condemned by anachronistic and partial modern standards, his achievements can be queried. It can be argued that far from wrenching the country from the course of peace and retrenchment on which Britain had been set by Walpole and Pelham (and which Newcastle might have pursued if he had been able after 1754), Chatham merely accelerated a drive towards world domination that was inherent in eighteenth-century Britain. However, this view fails to place sufficient weight on Chatham's determination to confront France in the maritime and colonial sphere and his conviction that Britain must make substantial territorial gains. To a certain extent he was the prophet of an idea whose time had come, however much of an accommodator he may have been in domestic politics in the late 1750s.

British success in the Seven Years War can be attributed in part to his actions, political as much as strategic, but the beneficial consequences of the conflict can be queried. Did it make the American Revolution inevitable by removing the threat to America from French proximity in Canada and was 1776 therefore ultimately Chatham's responsibility? Can the French intervention that led in 1781 to the humiliating British surrender at Yorktown be attributed to the desire to take revenge for the Seven Years War and the terms the British government had imposed? There is a measure of truth in both claims, but the American Revolution had many causes and precipitants, and French intervention can be ascribed in large part to the understandable desire to weaken a rival, the changing nature of European international relations, and, more specifically, to the British failure to defeat the Americans in 1775–7.

Leaving aside these questions of achievement, Chatham's methods can be challenged. Was he anything more than a hypocrite, an opportunist, an egoist determined to over-throw any ministry that he could not dominate? In addition, was he made truly dangerous by his inability to accept the views and compromises of others, so that all had to bend before his will, even though this will was unrealistic in aspiration as well as megalomaniacal in demands? Chatham can be condemned both for his unscrupulous tergiversations and for his maddening constancy.

There is truth in many of these charges, but these different bases for criticism do not take us very far. To challenge the reputation of someone because he did not hold values that were those of the commentator is at the very least unhelpful, evidence not of Olympian detachment but of foolish conceit. There were pacifists in the eighteenth century but Quakers excluded themselves from politics because of their objections to oaths. War and the seizure of the territory of foreign rivals might have been held to be inopportune at a given moment, but few rejected them and those who did were also not in politics.

As quotations from contemporaries illustrate, it was possible to criticise Chatham in terms that made sense (as well as political point) in Hanoverian Britain, especially so in light of the values he claimed to represent and the constituency of national and 'patriotic' beliefs that he sought to foster and speak for. This is scarcely surprising. Chatham was a politician in a world that was far from constant. In 1745 'Revolution Principles' appeared challenged by a Highland army under the Jacobite heir at Derby, sixteen years later by a

Scottish favourite supported by a new monarch who gloried in the name of Britain, but refused to be patronised by a minister who saw himself as representing and furthering British interests and who had, after much difficulty, been accepted by the previous monarch in that light. In the late 1730s Britain was overshadowed by the Bourbons, apparently betrayed by a corrupt first minister and a venal political system. Two decades later she was seemingly rescued from disaster and carried to imperial triumph, only another two decades later to succumb to civil war within the empire. Chatham saw political combinations come and go. Apparently secure interests collapsed: those who looked to Prince Frederick in 1751, the seemingly stable Pelham ministry in 1754, the victorious Newcastle–Pitt government in 1761, the Chatham ministry in 1766–8. The extraordinarily rapid changes of 1742–6, 1754–7 and 1761–70 suggested a frenetic and kaleidoscopic political world, one of instability in which it was well nigh impossible to chart a straight path.

It was easy in these contexts of changing international situations and an uncertain domestic political sphere to bring charges of opportunism and hypocrisy against politicians, especially when they made the transition to office. Chatham faced especial problems. Although he began his political life as a member of a political connection, the Cobham cubs, he was both an outsider by temperament and outside office. He could have tried to rise to power by using the power of connections more and seeking influential patrons. A fellow cub, and from 1754 his brother-in-law, George Grenville did so. Although four years younger than Chatham and entering Parliament only in 1741, Grenville held office from 1744 until 1765 with only brief intervals from November 1755 until November 1756 and April to June 1757. By 1754 he had been a Lord, first of the Admiralty and then of the Treasury, for a decade. However, Chatham found it difficult to employ the customary political arts. This was probably due to his personality. He did not find it easy to co-operate with others, still less to win or hold friends. For Chatham politics was a matter of absolutes and, although he was willing to compromise, as he did after accepting office in 1746 and 1757, his demonstrative attitude did not inspire confidence. Although he sat for a Newcastle pocket borough, he was unhappy about accepting patronage and in following the leadership of others.

Given this situation it is not surprising that Chatham sought to impose himself by cultivating the political world 'out-of-doors'. This was not an easy process, not least in terms of the suppositions of the period, including those held by Chatham. He might believe that the Commons was corrupt, but he stressed the sovereignty of Parliament, against both royal favourites and American colonists. Chatham was unhappy in the political world of Wilkes.[4] In the 1730s hostility to Walpole had been organised from within the political elite, but that was less true of opposition to the government three decades later and Chatham appeared increasingly dated then, unsurprisingly so in light of his age, his determination to defend his reputation and his fixed hostility to the politics of connection. In February 1780 when the Lord Lieutenant of the county, the Duke of Chandos, was criticised in the Commons for intervening in the recent by-election in Southampton, Robert Nugent cited the dead Chatham's election for Seaford in 1747, 'through the interest of the late Duke of Newcastle'. Nugent, who stated that 'God never made . . . an abler statesman and sounder patriot than Mr Pitt', noted that a complaint was made to the Commons, but that it

---

[4] J. Brewer, *Party Ideology and Popular Politics at the Accession of George III* (Cambridge, 1976) p. 197.

was rejected. He urged that the example be followed in the current case. Wilkes, in reply, denied the similarity of the interference, but added that 'however great or able Lord Chatham might be, he was far from thinking him infallible'.[5]

Chatham was a name to conjure with, cited frequently in parliamentary debates during the American War of Independence.[6] He did appreciate the dangers of not conciliating America. He was one of the few politicians of the age who made much of an impact outside the political world and who penetrated the public consciousness. Chatham's reputation had its shadows as far as contemporaries were concerned. Aside from his apparent acts of hypocritical opportunism, he defended a number of unpopular causes, especially continued war in 1762–3, Dissenters in 1772 and conciliation of America from 1773 until his death, although he was fortunate that in the light of hindsight he was apparently proved correct in each case or at least that his stand on them was to accord with a triumphal conception of British history. His acceptance of a peerage was singularly unfortunate, not least in translating him to a chamber where he had little influence. Nevertheless, whatever his failings in contemporary eyes, Chatham struck a resonance that other politicians failed to emulate and that most did not even seek to do. His understanding of the political world and of 'Revolution Principles' was one in which opinion 'out-of-doors' was not simply a device with which to inconvenience the ministry and seek to force one's way into office, although there is no doubt that they were also both for Chatham. To many contemporaries Chatham was a hero. Rodney wrote in December 1779 of

[5] Cobbett, xx, 1316–17. Nugent misdated the election.
[6] e.g. Cobbett, xx, 161–3, 391.

the memory of that great and glorious minister, who, to all succeeding ages, will be quoted as an illustrious example, how one great man, by his superior ability, could raise his drooping country from the abyss of despair to the highest pinnacle of glory, and render her honoured, respected, revered, and dreaded by the whole universe.[7]

Chatham was definitely a hero to the Victorians and the Edwardians, who also approved of his apparent religious liberalism. When his reputation was challenged in 1907 by his German biographer von Ruville, who queried Chatham's motives and sincerity, von Ruville was castigated in an address published in the *Transactions of the Royal Historical Society*.[8] The values and judgements of the later age can be rejected, but it is impossible to ignore the views of Chatham's contemporaries. They wanted to hear the bells of victory. They had been scared by the French and they wanted to beat them. If these triumphs owed much to a man who could be accused of betraying his past views, that was not a surprise in a political world that seemed singularly inconstant. There were no other politicians who could appear as heroic, and that judgement should not be ignored today.

Under the scholarly microscope the entrails of the past rarely appear laudatory. Modern academics rarely praise men of action and tend to be suspicious of politicians. Instead it is the intellectuals and bureaucrats of the past, if not the women, peasants, criminals, and rioters, that attract favourable attention. And yet Chatham's achievement was considerable for a politician who was distrusted by so many, a man who was dogged for much of his life by poor physical health and considerable mental stress. His position as political outsider

[7] Mundy (ed.), *Rodney* I, 204–5.
[8] A. von Ruville, *William Pitt, Earl of Chatham* (3 vols., 1907), II, 77–9; *Transactions of the Royal Historical Society*, 3rd series III (1909), pp. 34–49.

was crucial. It helped to make his reputation and to make him an unsettling figure. It caused particular problems when he gained office. But it also ensured that Chatham was and seemed different. He was a man whom the national interest could be associated with, not simply because he made the claim, but also because he seemed apart from the world of court and connection. Chatham was a Hanoverian hero, tarnished no doubt by the exigencies, complexities and compromises of politics, but a hero for a country that gave that description to no other politician.

Bibliographical note

All books published in London unless otherwise stated.

There are a large number of biographies of Chatham. The Whig classic is by Basil Williams, *The Life of William Pitt, Earl of Chatham* (1913), both scholarly and very prejudiced, especially at the expense of George III. A generally overlooked near-contemporary biography by the German A. von Ruville (1907) is more judicious. Studies by W. C. B Tunstall, *William Pitt, Earl of Chatham* (1938), and O. A. Sherrard, *Lord Chatham* (1952–8) are readable, but offer little new. Of the modern biographies, that by Stanley Ayling, *The Elder Pitt, Earl of Chatham* (1976) is less laudatory than that of Peter Brown *William Pitt Earl of Chatham. The Great Commoner* (1978). Valuable recent introductions to the period include J. B. Owen, *The Eighteenth Century* (1974); W. A. Speck, *Stability and Strife. England 1714–1760* (1977); I. R. Christie, *Wars and Revolutions. Britain 1760–1815* (1982); B. W. Hill, *British Parliamentary Parties 1742–1832* (1985); P. Langford, *A Polite and Commerical People. England 1727–1783* (Oxford, 1989); and J. Black (ed.), *British Politics and Society from Walpole to Pitt, 1742–1789* (1990).

On the Walpole period, J. Black (ed.), *Britain in the Age of Walpole* (1984); and J. Black, *Robert Walpole and the Nature of Politics in Early Eighteenth Century Britain* (1990). On 1742–54, J. B. Owen, *The Rise of the Pelhams* (1957); R. Browning, *The Duke of Newcastle* (New Haven, 1975). On 1754–7, J. C. D. Clark, *The Dynamics of Change* (Cambridge, 1982). On the Seven Years War, M. Peters, *Pitt and Popularity. The Patriot*

Minister and London Opinion during the Seven Years War (Oxford, 1980); R. Middleton, The Bells of Victory. The Pitt–Newcastle Ministry and the Conduct of the Seven Years War (Cambridge, 1985). On the reign of George III, J. Brooke, The Chatham Administration (1956); J. Brooke, George III (1972); P. Langford, The First Rockingham Administration (Oxford, 1973); J. Brewer, Party Ideology and Popular Politics at the Accession of George III (Cambridge, 1976); P. D. G. Thomas, Lord North (1976); P. Lawson, George Grenville (Oxford, 1984); K. Schweizer (ed.); Lord Bute (Leicester, 1988).

It may be as valuable to read some of the printed sources from the period. The Correspondence of William Pitt, Earl of Chatham, edited by W. S. Taylor and J. H. Pringle (1838–40); The Political Journal of George Bubb Dodington, edited by J. Carswell and L. A. Dralle (Oxford, 1965); The Devonshire Diary. William Cavendish, Fourth Duke of Devonshire. Memoranda on State of Affairs 1759–1762 (1982), edited by P. D. Brown and K. W. Schweizer (1982); Horace Walpole, Memoirs of King George II, edited by J. Brooke (New Haven, 1983); The Memoirs and Speeches of James, 2nd Earl Waldegrave, 1742–1763, edited by J. C. D. Clark (Cambridge, 1988) are but a selection of the many sources available that range from the Correspondence of George III, edited by J. Fortescue (new impression, 1973); to the Political Writings of Dr Johnson, edited by D. J. Greene (New Haven, 1977); and from Junius to Smollett.

Index

Index

Index

Index

53, 57–9, 61–4, 67, 69, 72–5,
79, 82, 90–1, 96–7, 99–100,
102, 106–10, 123–7, 130, 133,
138–46, 150, 154, 157, 159,
161, 174, 177–8, 180–1, 193–5,
201, 204, 209, 258
George III, 13, 23, 26, 28–30, 62, 90,
107–8, 121, 138, 140, 145, 150,
179, 199–202, 204–6, 210, 221,
227, 229, 233, 237, 242–4, 248,
251, 253, 258, 260–2, 267, 271,
274–5, 277, 279–80, 283,
286–8, 297–8, 300, 305
Gibraltar, 89, 169–70, 191, 219
Goree, 179, 191, 210, 213, 237–8
Gout, 92, 263
Gower, Granville, Second Earl, 63–4,
66, 77, 84, 127, 176, 214, 242
Grafton, Augustus, Third Duke of,
252, 258, 260–1, 267, 271–2,
274–5, 277–81, 283
Grafton, Charles, Second Duke of, 24
Granby, John, Marquis of, 278, 281
Grand Tour, 9–10
Grandison, Katherine, Viscountess, 2
Granville, Earl, see Carteret, Lord
Grenville, George (1712–70), xiv, 11,
14, 36, 54, 56, 58, 65, 100, 109,
119–20, 130, 134, 226, 242–3,
248, 250–2, 256, 258, 261–2,
264, 273, 278–9, 281, 286, 305
Grenville, George, First Marquis of
Buckingham (1753–1813), 14
Grenville, Henry, 11
Grenville, Lady Hester, see Pitt, Lady
Hester
Grenville, James, 11
Grenville, Richard, see Temple, Second
Earl
Grenville, William, 14
Guadeloupe, 164, 191, 210, 213, 237,
239

Habeas Corpus Bill, 152–3, 161–2, 177
Hagley, 19–20, 92, 94
Halifax, 173
Halifax, George, Second Earl of, 97,
144
Hampden, John, 112

Hampden, Robert, First Viscount, 265
Hanover, 43–5, 47–55, 68, 71, 74,
106, 109–10, 112, 117, 124, 126,
132–6, 138–42, 144, 149, 152,
154, 168–9, 174, 176, 193,
195–6, 209–10, 212, 231, 240,
249
Hardwicke, Philip, First Earl of, 28,
64, 69, 77, 99, 102, 106, 108,
123, 153, 160, 176, 202, 206,
216–17, 236, 242, 246, 276, 279
Harrington, William, First Earl of, 64,
91
Harris, Henry, 83, 97, 103, 114
Harris, James, 115, 230, 234, 238,
246, 255, 258, 274–7, 279–80,
283, 299
Harrison, Thomas, 10
Hartington, Lord, see Devonshire,
William, Fourth Duke of
Haslang, Baron, 181, 229, 278
Hastenbeck, battle of, 167
Havana, 185, 237
Hawke, Admiral Sir Edward, 138, 187
Hayes Place, Kent, 20, 22, 120,
128, 157, 198, 248–51, 275,
290, 299
Hervey, John, Lord, 37
Hesse-Cassel, Hessians, 17, 65–6, 75,
106, 117, 132
Hillsborough, Wills, Second Viscount,
96–7
history, 104–5
Hodgson, General Studholme, 207–8
Holdernesse, Robert, Fourth Earl of,
91, 97, 100, 107, 118, 124, 129,
133, 146, 159–60, 162, 175,
194, 200–1, 206
Honduras 218, 237
Hume Campbell, Alexander, 33, 63,
67–8, 79, 111

Imperial Election Scheme, 85
Indemnity Bill, 270
India, 165, 193–4, 237, 268, 272
Indians in America, 296
invasion of Britain, 56–7, 76, 118,
186–8, 190, 239
Ireland, 293

315

Index

Index

Index

Quebec, 76, 172–3, 185, 187, 191, 195
Quebec Bill, 291
Quiberon Bay, 187, 189

Radway, 19
raids, coastal, 169–71, 178–9, 181
Reading, 103–4
reform, parliamentary, 42, 47, 61, 282
Regency Bill, 89
Richmond, Charles, Third Duke of, 133, 146, 283–4, 286, 298–9
Rigby, Richard, 134, 208, 215, 231
Robinson, Luke, 79
Robinson, Sir Thomas (First Lord Grantham), 99–100, 103–4, 109
Robinson, Thomas (Second Lord Grantham), 238
Rochefort, 169–71
Rockingham, Charles, Second Marquess of, 156, 188, 241, 249–50, 252, 255, 258, 261, 271, 273, 280–7, 297
Rodney, Admiral George, 301, 307
Rosebery, Archibald, Fifth Earl of, 6, 101, 301
Rossbach, battle of, 176
Rouet, William 258
Russia, 89, 106, 109, 115, 121, 154, 266–7
Ruville, Albert von, 308

Sackville, Lord George, 117, 123, 127, 194, 251
St Malo, 178–9
St Pierre, 237
Salisbury, 1
Sandwich, John, Fourth Earl of, 58, 77, 84, 89, 91
Saratoga, battle of, 165, 297
Savile, Sir George, 261
Saxe, Marshal Maurice de, 77
Saxony, 86–7, 121
Seaford, 11, 78, 306
Secretary at War, 27–8, 58–9, 69–73
Secretary of State, 77–8, 91, 99–100, 106–7, 123, 126, 150, 216
Sedgwick, Edward, 273

Selwyn, George, 233
Senegal, 179, 237
Septennial Act, 36, 42
Seven Years War, xii–xiii, 165–97, 237
Shebbeare, John, 148
Shelburne, William, Second Earl of, xii, 2, 254, 261, 276–7, 288, 295
Shenstone, 20
Silesia, 43
Smollett, Tobias, 280
Southwell, Edward, 68
Spain, 32, 39–40, 43–4, 63, 68, 83–5, 165, 167, 169–70, 186, 212, 214, 218–22, 227, 230, 232, 237, 240, 284
Spencer, John, 16
Spencer, John, First Earl, 16, 22–3
Stair, John, Second Earl of, 44
Stamp Act, 255–7, 262, 281
Stanhope, James, First Earl, 2, 63, 82, 98, 224
Stanhope, Philip, Second Earl, 69
Stanley, Hans, 213, 216
Stone, Andrew, 86
Stowe House, 15, 19–20, 92, 120, 218, 278
Strasburg, 9
Strathfieldsaye, branch of Pitts, 1, 19, 204, 278
Sturt, Humphry, 204
subsidies, foreign, 44–5, 48, 60–1, 75, 86–7, 89, 106, 109, 111, 115, 133, 230, 249
Sunderland, Charles, Third Earl of, 63, 82
Sunderland, Robert, Second Earl of, 27
Sunninghill, 107
Sweden, 121

Temple, Richard, Second Earl, 11, 14, 21, 24, 110, 126, 184, 220–1, 241–2, 251, 256, 178, 280, 282
Test, The, 131–2, 136, 160
Thatcher, Margaret, 302
Thirsk, 1
Thomond, Percy, Earl of, 260, 265
Ticonderoga, 178

Index

Tories, 2, 18, 34–5, 41–2, 44–5, 47, 49, 53–60, 66–8, 112, 117, 130, 143, 145–6, 152, 164, 167, 184–5, 196, 202–3, 205, 241, 243, 252

Toulon, 187

Townshend, Charles, Second Viscount, 91

Townshend, Charles, 125, 149, 163–4, 223, 248, 265, 268, 272, 281

Townshend, George, 141, 177

Townshend, Thomas, 18

Triennial parliaments, 282

Tucker, John, 47, 49, 56, 59, 70

Tunbridge Wells, 91, 93

Tweeddale, John, Fourth Marquess of, 61

United Provinces, 5, 44, 60, 64, 68, 70, 77, 106, 165, 180

Utrecht, 5, 9

Utrecht, Peace of, 211, 218, 239

Vernon, Admiral Edward, 40

Versailles, Treaty of, 121

Virgil, 291

Viry, Count Francesco, 134, 140, 145, 171, 205, 220

Vyner, Robert 164

Waldegrave, Lady Betty, 214

Waldegrave, James, First Earl, 9

Waldegrave, James, Second Earl, 24, 97, 103, 138, 143, 147

Wall, Richard, 208, 215, 222

Walpole, Horace, (Fourth Earl of Orford), 20, 58, 65, 84, 86, 88, 90, 92, 110, 113–14, 148, 171

Walpole, Horatio (First Lord Walpole of Wolterton), 15, 72, 78, 81, 87

Walpole, Sir Robert (First Earl of Orford), xiv–xv, 2, 10, 12–13, 25–7, 31–2, 35–43, 49–50, 59, 63, 67, 81–6, 97, 116, 126, 140, 158, 164, 192, 202, 229, 252, 254, 264, 266, 282, 284, 303, 306

Wandewash, battle of, 193

Warburg, battle of, 196

West, Gilbert, 102

West, James, 162

West Wickham, 20, 102, 120

Westminster Abbey, 300

Westminster, Convention of, 115

Whigs, 34–5, 49, 55, 110, 146, 154, 219, 282, 286, 290

Wilkes, John, 17, 103, 227, 245–7, 271–2, 277–9, 282–3, 286, 306–7

William III, 15, 27, 44, 49, 234

Williams, Basil, 38–9, 310

Williams, Sir Charles Hanbury, 74

Williams Wynn, Watkin, 67

Wilton, 2

Winchelsea, Daniel, Eighth Earl of, 144

Winnington, Thomas, 72–3

Wolfe, General James, 179, 182, 186, 195

Wood, John, 21

Wood, Robert, 194, 276

Wotton, 19–20, 101, 278

Wyndham, Charles, see Egremont, Charles, Second Earl of

Yarmouth, Amalie, Countess of, 124, 153, 194

Yonge, Sir William, 58, 72–3

Yorke, Charles, 245

Yorke, Joseph, 69

Yorke, Philip, Second Earl of Hardwicke, 78

Yorktown, battle of, 188, 239, 303